Government
Financial
Management
Theory

PUBLIC ADMINISTRATION AND PUBLIC POLICY

A Comprehensive Publication Program

Executive Editor

JACK RABIN
Professor of Public Administration and Public Policy
Division of Public Affairs
The Capital College
The Pennsylvania State University–Harrisburg
Middletown, Pennsylvania

Other volumes in preparation

Public Productivity Handbook, *edited by Marc Holzer*

Government Financial Management Theory

Gerald J. Miller

Department of Public Administration
Rutgers, The State University of New Jersey
Newark, New Jersey

Marcel Dekker, Inc.   **New York • Basel • Hong Kong**

350.72
M64g

Library of Congress Cataloging-in-Publication Data

Miller, Gerald.
  Government financial management theory / Gerald J. Miller.
      p.   cm. -- (Public administration and public policy ; 43)
  Includes bibliographical references and index.
  ISBN 0-8247-7910-X
  1. Finance, Public.   2. Budget.   I. Title.   II. Series.
HJ131.M55   1991
350.72--dc20   90-28409
                                                                    CIP

This book is printed on acid-free paper.

MARCEL DEKKER, INC.
270 Madison Avenue, New York, New York 10016

Current printing (last digit):
10 9 8 7 6 5 4 3 2 1

PRINTED IN THE UNITED STATES OF AMERICA

To my father
Cecil Miller
and to
Milan W. Nelson II

Preface

In deciding that governmental financial management lacks a sustained research program, I was struck by how many different fields of study and schools of thought battle to determine what is done. This fact was brought home to me by a recent attempt the senior researchers in the field of public budgeting made to determine what conceptual agreement actually existed (Rubin, 1988). Answering the question of where the critical assumptions come from to drive public budgeting, they concluded that many people from varied fields have tried and failed to excite agreement in a way that would lead to cumulative research.

The notion emerged that perhaps financial management is involved in a battle to determine whether economics, public administration or political science will dominate the way we do research and how we practice the craft. So far there are no clear winners, the researchers surmised; the field is multidisciplinary, not yet interdisciplinary.

The idea that a research tradition will define government financial management as a profession may be naive. However, there does seem to be some agreement between research and practice, agreement that forms the starting point of this book. Let me suggest three orienting ideas.

First, a substantial research tradition has followed Simon's start in *Administration Behavior* (1976). Roughly and simplistically, Simon argued that people, having defined the situation in a certain way, readily choose the one best way in which to act. The problem lies basically in the definition of the situation, in a sense, a value premise. Therefore, if one can control the value premise—the definition of the situation—one can control the decision (March and Simon, 1958). It is clear from the normative approaches espoused by practitioners that battling for the value premise is what they spend their time doing (Miller, Rabin, and Hildreth, 1987).

Second, much of financial management derives from a primary concern with process. Weick (1969), for one, has argued that process stands prior to substantive end. Harmon and Mayer (1986:351; Weick, 1969:79) quote him approvingly: "The basic property of interdependence [in organizations] is that patterns and relations among variables are the realities that you have to deal with, substances are trivial."

Third, traditional and not-so-traditional financial management research dwells not on technique but indirection. That is, the idea that much of what organization members know is known through symbols, metaphors, and language. Much of this is conveyed through post-event construction of meaning or story-telling.

The glue that holds these concepts together, giving action to what goes on in financial management, is the idea of interpretation. By interpretation, I mean "the immediate apprehension . . . of an objective event as expressing meaning . . ." (Berger and Luckman, 1966:129). With interpretation, one acts in social structures in ways that modify, but eventually enable internalization, of the apprehensions. Internalization takes place in a social setting, one in which "plausibility structures" emerge for its maintenance.

The battle waged in financial management, and in organizations that have an important concern with financial matters, is one over the interpretation of complex events. Financial managers find themselves engaged in interpreting, and finally gaining the upper hand in determining critical assumptions. The value of values is clearly the determination to be made in valuing budgets and parts of budgets, in short. Derived processes—interpretation through symbol and metaphor, for example—are means of indirection in determining and gaining consensus over the value of values.

In financial management terms, consider an application in public budgeting (Schick, 1988:64–65). The process by which resource claimants and allocators meet brings together interpretations of adequacy and conservation in specific areas in which indirect communication of subject matter, participation, and appropriate models of discourse and choice are conveyed. Ultimately, the process influences and is modified by a value premise: efficiency, sometimes equity, and parsimony.

This book embeds the question: where do the critical assumptions come from to drive financial management? The book takes the organization of the field on its own terms: budgeting, cash management, debt management, information systems, and revenue administration have grown professionally into distinct specialties. The critical assumptions guiding them, I argue, are different.

Because this book emerges from organization theory, it is easy to see who has exerted influence. First and foremost, Bob Golembiewski gave persuasive testimony to the centrality of organizations to individuals' lives and to the importance of understanding this centrality for allowing people to control their own destinies. Second, Bart Hildreth is a major force for steadiness, for care, and for productivity in research. And finally, Jack Rabin has persisted in getting this project completed for many reasons, all of which I shared. I appreciate their help.

Gerald J. Miller

Contents

Government
Financial
Management
Theory

1

Financial Management:
A Function of Organization Theory

What does a government financial manager do? For the first three-fourths of the twentieth century, the role of governmental financial officers has centered around raising and spending dollar resources in accord with government policy. In the last twenty-five years, fiscal stress has introduced resource variability, and financial managers have confronted their new organization boundary roles: exploiting opportunities to relieve stress and *managing* organizations to ease the adjustment to volatile periods of feast and famine.

In past and present, organization theory and management theory have played some role in helping design procedures that "rationalized" various individual and group contributions to finance. Beginning with Golembiewski (1964), however, students of financial management began to see a more central role for organization and management theory that described and evaluated what financial managers in government do, since the activities were as much *management* as financial in nature. By incorporating values, Golembiewski forced theorists to recognize the headwaters of financial theory in organization behavior.

Financial managers act much the same as all other managers: both try to reduce the ambiguity that comes with uncertain sources and amounts of resources; both act by "aligning" the demands of critical outside interests or contingencies with the capabilities and interests of organization members. Financial managers, like all managers, hope to achieve the same ultimate goal, and to "the extent that any truly overall objective might be identified [across organizations], that objective is probably organization survival" (Caplan, 166, p. 418).

However, by handling ambiguity, financial managers have strategic importance, if not always centrality, to organizations. Although the ultimate goal in all government agencies, except revenue services, is not a *financial* one, goal achievement does require financial resources. The centrality of resource acquisition and allocation makes the financial manager a critical, even pivotal, actor in organization life. This strategic and pivotal importance is permanent, diminishing only when there is no scarcity among resources and no perceived uncertainty about their availability. The greater the impression of unpredictability, however, the greater the likelihood of unforeseen dependencies, and the greater the importance given to the finance function. Ultimately, in some cases, resource sensitivity may lead to finance goals that replace existing organization goals.

FINANCIAL MANAGEMENT: A SOCIALLY NEGOTIATED PROCESS

Given the looming importance of finance in public organizations, knowing the "meaning" of procedures and the position financial managers take in the processes, an observer should be able to predict the future of organizations in government. But such is not the case, for the same reasons that an observer cannot predict the course of events in private organizations. The unpredictability in both sectors derives from administrative theories that are contextual, negotiated, and socially constructed (Astley, 1985). Financial management, no more or no less than any other management process, is not an ordered process deduced from some normative first principle, but a negotiated reality constructed by the people involved.

Consider the budget process in a government. To a New Jersey county freeholder,[1] the budget is not the same exercise or game as it is for an elected county executive, a politically appointed county administrator, or a civil service budget director.[2] A freeholder sees the budget-making process as a drama, a chance to be on stage briefly but vividly and memorably. A county executive sees the budget as a strategic use of symbols on behalf of important constituencies inside and outside of government. The county administrator sees the budget as a surrogate bottom line: what tax rate underwrites a portfolio of programs and activities supporting a given dominant coalition in office? The budget director sees the budget as a collection of forms to complete and "get by" a state budget oversight process without a too-detailed scrutiny by state officials.

The budget is a political struggle, not only in terms of what amounts are allocated, but also in what the budget process itself will be. In the Essex County case (Sinding, 1986), the dramatic spectacle by freeholders, just before their opponent, the County Executive, faced reelection, alerted state officials as to what a freeholder characterized as illegalities. The executive had used litigation to oppose a state ruling on whether state or county government should provide financial support for the local hospital. The executive had not included the cost of support in the budget, even as a contingent liability should the county lose the case. The county lost the case and afterward, the freeholders called the executive's hand on the budget delinquency. The state's oversight panel investigated and then forced a tax increase to cover the liability. The County Executive, whose litigation had signaled to his constituency that greater state support for the hospital would mean tax relief, was forced by the freeholder spectacle to raise taxes. The Administrator, from a budget vantage point, saw the portfolio of programs and activities fall apart because the dominant coalition fell apart. The budget director took part of the political heat by being the person the state oversight panel found responsible for not including the liability in the budget in the first place.

In all, the budget is a formidable tool when the views of all the participants can balance or form some harmonious whole. What a budget will be is a matter in which all have a say. The budget's formulation is highly systematic in that ideas must survive an exacting process of scrutiny before they become budget items. New budgets emerge as products of a socially negotiated consensus (Astley, 1985, p. 499).

Cash investment, debt structuring, management-information systems, and revenue forecasting could be viewed in the same way: that is, there is no one best way, no objective truth on which to base management. There is only socially constructed truth formed through intense political struggle. It follows then that these socially constructed models of financial management are unique to their contexts, and that they emerge from the interplay of individuals. They tell us about the specific ways in which organizations, via financial-management technologies, make decisions, with financial-management specialists, in the lead or in tow.

THE STUDY OF FINANCIAL MANAGEMENT

Government financial management has emerged as a field of study with *few* concepts common to all organizations. Some, such as control, have greater applicability in such simple systems as financial auditing than complex ones, such as legislative auditing (Brown, 1985). Others, such as efficiency, are inapposite, as in the case of weapons procurement where the tools of war at the time of purchase may exist only in physical science theories (Enke, 1967). Still other concepts, such as maximization, lack normative appeal (Margolis, 1975).

Thus, the basic questions for research still require additional work. What are financial-management systems? That is,

1. How do they "fit" with other organization systems?
2. How do they process data for decisions that jibe with legitimate concerns of the organization and the realities of the larger politico-economic system?
3. What technologies are appropriate, and inappropriate, to the uses they are put to by this system?
4. What role does the financial-management specialist play?

My argument rests on the idea that systems, decision processes, technologies, and roles come from premises dictated by authoritative political coalitions. More specifically, political coalitions have fused from time to time to reform financial management by establishing or "vindicating" a value system as contributive to a way of life (Fischer, 1980; Taylor, 1973). Vindication allows for the validation of goals of any management system in terms of a dominant value system. And, finally, validation allows the empirical verification of any process or technology used in that management system.

In financial management, a culture or value system introduces premises following which theories of cause and effect are inferred and tested. The test verifies the phenomena which theory has isolated as being important or necessary (validation). In turn, theories isolate phenomena that are valuable to a person's culture or way of life.

What are serviceable models? Models that expand knowledge retain recognition of norms but have enough research questions and methods appropriate to them to *describe* meaningful aspects of financial management, explaining why, for example, a technique works the way it does or why people are satisfied or dissatisfied with it.

From this vantage point, models are derived from preferences of political coalitions. These preferences dictate theories that serve to suggest appropriate research methods for verification.

GOVERNMENT FINANCIAL-MANAGEMENT THEORY

My main purpose in this book is to explore new avenues down which, in theory, we might push financial management. To do so, I will introduce and explore three theories in the field, which I will call *orthodox, prevailing*, and *alternative* and use them as three different points of view throughout the book.

Points of View in Financial-Management Theory

Most of financial-management theory revolves around different approaches to explain how ambiguity is reduced and certainty is achieved. The three points of view that I outline briefly take a different direction in explaining this transformation.

Orthodox Theory

Orthodox theory is the public sector variant of business finance theory; is a design science. Its adherents argue the facility with which organizational structure and procedure create certainty by encouraging homogeneity of behavior within the organization. In fact, finance theory has become a generalized, positive theory for both sectors. It is well developed, as almost any text covering that subject will reveal. Yet, although corporate finance theory has a great deal to say to financial managers in government, it does not account for all and, possibly, even much of what government financial managers see and do, and that problem accounts for competition among theories.

For example, the question about hedging cash investments with futures contracts may be answered in one way according to finance theory, which approach assumes hedging's use as a commonplace method of insulating short-term investments from risk. However, whether to use futures or not might be answered in another way by public financial managers who find the notion of hedging somewhat slippery, hard to use, and politically or professionally dubious, if not illegal (Methe, Baesel, and Schulman, 1983; Miller, 1988).

Prevailing Theory

This theory competes with corporate finance theory to explain phenomena in public financial management that arise as the result of conflicting interests. That work exists in the broadly conceived field of organization theory, that is, in the public-budgeting theory and the politico-economic overlap known variously as the behavioral theory of the firm (Cyert and March, 1963) or strategic contingencies theory (Hickson et al., 1971).

Prevailing theory shares the maximizing assumption of orthodox theory. It achieves certainty in an organization by means of the creation of management procedures that exploit the idea that, to the extent of their facilities to do so, individuals act to achieve their own best interest. The concept of disjointed, incremental change based on the mutual adjustment of satisficing actors (Lindblom, 1965; Simon, 1976) still commands fairly broad acceptance among students of financial decision-making behavior in the public sector (Hildreth, 1989). The concept provides not only an explanation but also a satisfying metaphor, similar to the market in orthodox theory, for understanding the "intelligent" reconciliation of plural interests.

An example to apply prevailing theory lies in pension fund management. In making sure that pension funds earn a return (Hildreth and Miller, 1983) sufficient to produce the retirement benefits employees have been promised, financial strategists assess various alternative investments. Economics plays a large part in this decision, primarily by providing the rules by which financial managers calculate the principal worth of the funds (How much can be invested?). In large part, the principal worth depends on how much the government can "afford" to pay (which, in turn, is influenced by the prevailing wage rate); how much pension fund contributors earn (again the prevailing wage rate, as well as the rate of inflation); and whether the pension fund consolidates various contributors (the larger the investor, the higher the rate of return).

Political influence may then begin to play. For example, political priorities would tell the financial manager, possibly, where to invest (socially desirable projects) and where not to invest (the securities of United States industries that do business in South Africa). Finally, with economic or political considerations played, the technological calculation may hold sway: the pension fund manager may then calculate the rates of return on all remaining investment alternatives and choose the one with the highest rate. Despite their appeal, orthodox and prevailing theories follow an approach that may not be meaningful in government agency management. The approach they follow proceeds from "the premise of conscious, foresightful action guided by intent or purpose" (Pfeffer, 1982, p. 41; Cummings, 1982). Both may be inappropriate in a federalist state (White, 1989), among various political cultures (Clark and Ferguson, 1983; Wildavsky, 1975). Moreover, such an approach may not hold when basic constitutional provisions oppose unitary action and favor a governmental structure that prescribes that "ambition must be made to counteract ambition" (*Federalist* 51: p. 337).

Alternative Theory

With the alternative theory to orthodox and prevailing theory, one tries to describe public financial life without the premise of conscious, foresightful, intended action. Alternative theory argues that there is no verifiable "best interest" of an individual or group of individuals. Rather, a decision in ordinary circumstances, made by an individual, is relatively random and unpredictable. What gives an otherwise random, unpredictable decision any meaning is either post hoc rationalization or the preemption of an individual's premises through organizational superiors' definitions of problems and situations (Simon, 1976).

Ambiguity Theory. The alternative model springs from two very different fields. The first, ambiguity theory, centers on the disconnectedness of ends and means and assumes inherent ambiguity in the effort to make any choice. As March and Olsen (1975, p. 21) explained:

> Intention does not control behavior precisely. Participation is not a stable consequence of properties of the choice situation or individual preferences. Outcomes are not a direct consequence of process. Environmental response is not always attributable to organizational action. Belief is not always a result of experience.

In a situation involving unknown or contradictory goals and technologies as well as one in which individuals may differ in their levels of participation over time, choice, according to March and Olsen, comes with difficulty because the actors seldom realize their preferences until they have made choices. Or, as Weick has put it (1980, p. 19), "How can I know what I think until I see what I say."

Social Construction Theory. A second source for the alternative model comes from a field of thought that emphasizes the relativity of meaning, a field that focuses on the social construction of reality (Berger and Luckman, 1966; Goffman, 1961, 1974). This field argues that every organization, being in essence a social assemblage somewhere between evanescence and permanence, embodies a set of shared views of the world that give meaning to what organization members do. These views or "interpretations of reality" build and gain legitimacy through an interaction among individuals. Moreover, the existence of interpretations belies the notion that there exists an objective reality shared by all organizations.

Simply stated, the alternative theory I introduce here holds that interpretation forces out ambiguity; that is, the greater the number of different, constructed realities, the greater the uncertainty that exists among and within organizations. For practical problems of management, the greater the uncertainty, the less likely management prescriptions—such as program budgeting, accrual accounting, or legislative postauditing—have any real applicability. Not agreeing about what a budget, accounting, or auditing system "means" or should do, financial managers employ procedures that are "loosely coupled" to any one view of reality (Weick, 1976). As a result, the greater the compounding of differences among views in a group of individuals having some collective interest, such as an organization or a government, the greater the influence of randomness—in terms of events and specific people shaping meaning—and the larger the amount of interpretation needed by members to make sense and to act in a concerted way (Weick, 1979).

Thus, it is in the interest of a financial manager to find a role that makes for gatekeeping within this randomness. In one organization, for example, the finance officer may be an umpire among competing advocates; in another the guardian of the public purse, which is under great pressure; in still another the prime institutional memory for past decisions which were made. Moreover, the members of different organizations may develop different meanings that they attribute to instruments of financial management, such as the budget, among which we might find an analytical exercise, a pointless ritual, or the satisfaction of a mandate created somewhere else. In all cases, the set of roles and shared meanings are contextual and therefore unique, belonging as they do to the particular actors who negotiated or constructed them.

As a tool for research, the importance of the alternative way of looking at public financial management lies in the perspective it provides on the ways people think. Emerging paradigms, such as ambiguity or social construction, could describe reality or predict behavior in ways that contrast with either orthodox or prevailing approaches.

Orthodox theory and prevailing theory depend for their explanatory power on relatively large amounts of a *consensus* about organization goals and technologies. This condition may not exist in many organizations, particularly public or governmental ones, and the alternative approach seeks answers as to why and how. Alternative theory also seeks the fundamental, intersubjectively determined premises that make collective action possible.

A second difference among orthodox, prevailing, and alternative theories exists in the assumption that each holds about intention. The orthodox study of public financial management has followed a fairly simple route; public finance, political economy, and budget execution have led to the notion of a rational actor.

Prevailing theory, based on Simon's notion of bounded rationality (1976), suggests the prevalence of uncertainty and the impossibility of an entirely rational actor; that is, individuals cannot know with certainty the consequences of given courses of action. Instead, courses of action are chosen when just enough information is available to predict consequences within reasonable tolerances. The rationality of management decision-making is bounded by the costs and benefits of searches for satisfactory alternatives. Nevertheless, whether the rational effect of such decision-making is more often than not produced, *the intent purportedly exists.*

Alternative theory holds that although public financial management may operate as if all managers intended to act rationally, ends and means may relate in odd ways so that one may never know what was intended until one acts. Looking back, one can force order on the thought process, but foresight may not be so fruitful.

Moreover, "making people rational" as a basis for management is an ideology, so others have argued (Pfeffer, 1981). Some would say that ideology misuses the individual. The effect of intended rationality is to imply agreement among members of an organization about the important ways of acting. Even if it is instrumentally important to gain agreement, to assume that action depends on agreement tends to trivialize the basis for organized life—to connect too neatly the concept of organization with organized relationships among individuals, thereby effectively subjugating an individual to an abstract concept (McSwain, 1987, p. 37).

Organizations, it has been argued (Weick, 1979; White and McSwain, 1983) depend on the building blocks of relationship and the unconscious meanings and interpretations that develop out of them. Relationships may be managed in benign ways (Barnard, 1968, pp. 168–169) or in extremely harmful ways (Milgram, 1964). Not all facets of organized life mask the actual building blocks of organization; in fact, some, like "loosely coupled systems" (Weick, 1979), tend to encourage as well as sustain relationships.

Alternative theory does not assume certainty. Rather, this theory assumes a range of conditions from certainty to ambiguity. This approach searches for description and explanation of what does happen in ambiguous circumstances, especially as the guideposts in procedure or even in consensus move toward randomness. Such information may be valuable to know, and the investigation might be interesting and fruitful, especially as it influences human relationships in collective endeavors. Because ambiguity is often the result of disagreement about goals, studying life under these conditions tends to introduce, rather than ignore, preferences of values in public financial management.

ORGANIZATION OF THE BOOK

This book follows an alternative route of inquiry into financial management. The genesis of this approach came, for me, during the Carter and Reagan antigovernment eras, when the basic premises of the progressive reform era were called into question. This theory of financial reform up to the present is described in Chapter 2.

Intellectual effort and financial-management research take most, if not all, of their impetus and direction from the problems encountered in public organizations, and problem definitions depend on the "lens" through which one sees. I regard the coalitions of interests, described in Chapter 2, as assiduously influencing the research that has gone on in financial management, especially the topics chosen, the methods used, the explanations given, and the solutions to problems found. It shall come as no surprise, then, that I follow this history with a history of financial-management research, which is presented in Chapters 3 to 5.

The alternative theory described above forms the medium by which I explain important facets of financial management. Consequently, I take up alternative theory in more detail in Chapter 5. Even though I see this approach as following directly from events in public organizations and from the ideological bent of many political actors in competition, I argue that my alternative is but one of the ways to truth. I believe, like Golembiewski (1977, pp. 218–219) that, in a field where sufficient agreement about a uniform perspective does not exist to focus research and practice, scientists must recognize the value of overlapping and competing metaphors. Competition takes account of diversity and builds on the creativity existing in the early stages of the development of thought.

I illustrate the work that follows alternative theory in Chapters 6 through 10. Chapter 6 takes a semiotic view of budgets. Chapter 7 portrays the strategic financing of public projects as a product of interorganizational network that socially constructs the market for debt. Chapter 8 explains the public organization language of investment and Chapter 9 examines the intergovernmental funding process by using an organized anarchy metaphor for decision-making. Chapter 10 explains the federal government level of the economic- and revenue-forecasting apparatus as a social organization, the primary purpose of which is to construct an economic reality for budget purposes. What I do here is compare; more simply, I investigate, through my alternative approach, areas that might be used for further research and practice. These areas are (a) allocation in executive budgeting, (b) strategic project financing, (c) values guiding treasury investment, (d) management information and control, and (e) resource estimation.

I apply this framework to the subfields into which public administrators have divided government financial management; namely, choice (budgets), treasury (cash management), investment (capital finance), control (information systems), and resources (revenue management).

NOTES

1. The term *freeholder* is the title of a county legislator in New Jersey.
2. This assertion is based on research done for the Essex County, New Jersey Charter Study Commission (Miller and Klein, 1987). The research eventually defended the strong executive form of county government when the Board of Chosen Freeholders wanted to change the form to one resembling a city commission in which freeholders would actually run departments. The controversy bringing this commission into existence was based on radically different views about what a budget ought to be.

2

Historical Development

This chapter[1] identifies the radically different imperatives that have guided public financial management through modern history. These radical differences and constant change stand in stark contrast to the imperatives of nongovernmental economic organizations.

Market-driven organizations unify tasks. Their goal, which is the maximization of value to the shareholders, involves three basic decisions: (a) the *investment* decision (the allocation of capital to investment proposals whose benefits are to be realized in the future), (b) the *financing* decision (determining capital structure), and (c) the *dividend* decision (determining the amount of cash earnings to be paid to the shareholders) (Van Horne, 1986).

Ambivalence has characterized the environment and the technologies of government financial management. Those who control the fiscal affairs of government are involved in the spending and in the husbanding of wealth. Now and then, widely different interests have tried to influence one or both of these functions. Ironically, the interests that have coalesced have found common ground in forcing reform in government, often for irreconcilable reasons.

The question why this is so is quite difficult to answer. For the public sector, knowing how disparate public financial-management activities, such as budgeting, cash management, debt management, revenue administration, and accounting, developed together is easier to understand than *why* these interests have compromised thereby creating the norms that came to exist. The question remains: Normatively, what propels public financial-management activities?

In this chapter, I trace the reform episodes that have emerged, especially the periods in which coalitions materialized to create an uncontested direction in which all financial activities might head. In the first section of this chapter, I depict these episodes in various stages, from the early progressive movement to the present privatization campaign. In the second section, I distinguish the episodes as three major stages in which either efficiency, equity, or parsimony dominated. Finally, I argue that the coalition battles were bruising, profoundly affecting the formation of theories and the conduct of research in financial management.

The significance of this chapter lies in the fact that unifying normative concepts are hard to locate among the various enterprises known as public financial management. The field has grown, but the ideas that form its imperative (Do it this way!) come from different, sometimes even contradictory, points of view. For instance, in treasury operations, contradictory values guide idle cash-investment policy. Fiduciary values compel finance officers to avoid investing idle public funds for fear of risking their loss.[2] These values derive from the nature of speculative risk that has undergirded much private sector–public sector interaction over time.

Other values advise the opposite. On the other hand, the time value of the money concept[3] and the idea of opportunity costs suggest that not investing idle funds is a method of losing the money's value.

Why search for unifying ideas? Considerable concern underscores the work of public financial-management researchers and teachers. The lack of organizing concepts has become a major topic of debate (Rubin, 1988) in a field that strives for recognition (National Task Force on Curriculum Reform, 1985; MacManus, 1984; Thai, 1985; McCaffery, 1983; Golembiewski, 1980). The consequences of a lack of consensus, so the debate suggests, are insufficient farsightedness when prescribing solutions as problems are recognized. The wages of disagreement could also lead to splintered and disjointed research efforts, a lack of foresight and prescience in comprehending developing financial problems besetting government, students insufficiently equipped for programs which train for public service, and the dissipation of effort in a long tradition of inquiry into public administration.

I argue in this chapter that the normative problem is not a problem so much as a political struggle. The field has bobbed uncomfortably among different normative and ideological coalitions. Thus, the solution to the research problem lies, first, in understanding the development of the field, and, second, in adopting a unifying framework which still gives voice to competing points of view.

HISTORY OF SCIENCE IN PUBLIC FINANCIAL MANAGEMENT

First, we review the history of the study of fiscal activities, describing this development as six basic stages of thinking, from the early "reform government" movements to the current reforms sponsored by conservative economists.

The Efficient Citizenship Movement

The Progressive Movement produced, through the National Municipal League and the New York Bureau of Municipal Research, the idea of a budget and a principle with which to unify all aspects of financial management. According to Waldo (1948, pp. 32–33):

> [Progressives] were sensitive to the appeals and promises of science, and put a simple trust in discovery of facts as the way of science and as a sufficient model for solution of human problems.
>
> They accepted—they urged—the new positive conception of government, and verged upon the idea of a planned and managed society.
>
> [They] found in business organization and procedure an acceptable prototype for public business. They were ardent apostles of "the efficiency idea."
>
> [C]ivic awareness and militancy, efficiency, and "useful" education . . . together form the core of the Efficient Citizenship movement.

Involved in this movement were three basic groups: the positive government proponents who were usually called *progressives*, the government research bureau professionals or the *analysts*, and others who shared *business interests* to which openness provided a way to check large increases in tax bills. The movement[4] produced the principle that a well-informed citizenry, who were provided information through easily understood financial-management procedures (e.g., line-itemized budgets, competitively bid purchases, and audited financial statements), could check the moves of "detested politicians." Openness of government yielded a rudimentary medium through which action might follow. Efficiency stood as a "scientific" check on processes used in government, by providing a performance standard.

Openness became the great unifying principle that drew support and led to the coalition of interests supporting reform. The coalition that produced the reforms implementing Efficient Citizenship combined business interests, research-movement principles, and positive government proponents. All of these goals were complementary only when the open-government issue provided a context. At other times, business favored restrained taxation. The researchers promoted the secular notion that "proper institutions and expert personnel" could create "good" government (Waldo, 1948, p. 23). The positive government proponents sought to use government authority to provide services needed as a result of the demand for more roads and schools.

With restrained taxation, responsible procedures, and government leadership in economic and social development as the fundamental positions of the members of the original coalition, changes in size of government could continually pull the coalition apart. In fact, the later developments integrating financial management derive from variations of these three goals: parsimony, efficiency, and equity.

The upshot of the Efficient Government movement efforts to proceduralize government administration for accountability's sake led to the widespread institution of organizations for this purpose. The insistence on openness gave momentum to the institutionalizing movement. The Budget and Accounting Act of 1921, which became their major achievement, created a budget office and an auditing agency, both of which would open government to scrutiny through publication of a unified budget. Unification and openness put the spotlight on the executive; everybody could follow the decisions being made because they all took place in public view. Moreover, the implementation of these decisions could be checked by the other half of the act's purview: the expenditure audit.

The other members of the original coalition came off somewhat less well, even somewhat poorly. Researchers could look to the budget bureau and the accounting office as places where analysis might take hold. Greater faith in government decisions might come out of greater openness and might also lead to equity in vigorous government—a position of positive government proponents. Oddly enough, business interests and parsimony lost their biggest fight, that over the income tax when it was established just before the 1921 Act, and their share of the outcomes of the Efficient Citizenship movement was earned from the movement's acceptance of business operations as the standard to be observed.

The Positive Government Movement

If the muckrakers led the movement for the 1921 Act, the positive government proponents could claim to lead the movement toward the New Deal. The economic debacle of the Great Depression prompted government action as a method of ameliorating its effects. The key word was *equity*, embellished with analysis.

In fact, the Brownlow Committee's major gripe about the ineffectiveness of the Bureau of the Budget was its emphasis on preparing the budget rather than directing and controlling its execution (President's Committee on Administrative Management, 1937, pp. 15–24). In the Franklin D. Roosevelt sense of letting ideas grow even if in conflict with each other, control had become secondary to finding solutions to the pressing problems of economics and governance.

The report of the Brownlow Committee might be read as one faction of the positive government movement talking to another. This committee, by implication, saw the positive government movement splitting and thereby diminishing its effort. By devoting less attention to the ideal of comprehensive budget control and central direction, the movement had failed to capitalize on the returns of diversity. If the ideal—"the new positive conception of government [that] verged upon the idea of a planned and managed society" (Waldo, 1948, p. 32)—were to come true, a new orthodoxy must develop, especially one that integrated fiscal management under an executive with undivided powers, a clear chain of command, and sufficient planning, directing, and accountability mechanisms to bring these powers to effect. The upshot? To the positive government types, equity lay in a planned and managed society with a big but disciplined government.

The Analytical Movement

Following on President Lyndon B. Johnson's institution of Planning, Programming, Budgeting System (PPBS) in the federal government, financial systems became useful for analysis of any number of questions.

This movement was the later derivation of the efficiency emphasis in early progressive literature. The "idea," which referred more generally to the movement, was to apply rules of scientific inquiry to the solution of public problems in government.

Substantially, the PPBS reform changed the basic assumptions behind resource allocation—from equitable distribution to optimization. It also led to the analysis of programs, the establishment of goals, and the rational pursuit of goal and program achievements. Such an organization of inquiry was the basis of the "idea" in the first place: There is a principle by which all important aspects of management operate, and the discovery of that principle may come with disciplined inquiry.

Later embellishments of the original PPBS reform came with President Jimmy Carter's sponsorship of the U.S. Department of Housing and Urban Development's (HUD) Financial Management Capacity Sharing Program. Significant among the products of this program were analytical devices, especially the Financial Trend Monitoring System (Groves, Godsey, and Shulman, 1981), major initiatives in productivity measurement (Epstein, 1984), and a proposal for integrating fiscal systems (Grossman and Hayes, 1981).

The integrated fiscal system idea stemmed from the concern of state and local governments with the fiscal crises at the time in Cleveland, Ohio and in New York City. Defaults on bond interest and principal payments, near or complete, created concern that decisions made in one area of fiscal management were not immediately recognizable or the consequences foreseeable in other parts of the fiscal management system. The answer to most was the computerization of records common to budgeting, accounting, performance measurement, and auditing, which, in turn, spawned a substantial body of research (Kraemer, 1969; Kraemer, Dutton and Northrop, 1981; King and Kraemer, 1985) tracking computerization's implementation. Yet another approach sprang from the needs of investors (Price, Waterhouse & Co., 1979; Ernst & Whinney, 1979), general managers (Groves et al., 1981), and even labor unions (Berne and Schramm, 1986) for better indicators of financial condition. Finally, the movement led to a full-scale effort to integrate federal financial management procedures through leadership by officials in the federal accounting office (GAO, 1985; Joint Financial Management Improvement Program, 1988).

The Capacity Building Movement

Born in President Nixon's first administration and continuing into the Ford administration, the effort to strengthen local government came through a three-pronged effort. The first prong involved revenue sharing with local and state governments. The greater capacity of the federal government to collect revenue would be matched with the greater (and often better, some said) local capability to deliver services and implement federal domestic policy. Local problems beset the country, and state and local governments were far closer and abler in solving them, the revenue sharing partisans argued.

The second prong of the effort developed through Nixon Administration efforts to strengthen planning at the state and local government level. The HUD programs which subsidized the regional, area and city land use planning activities got new mandates to increase the management capacities of these units and the governments of which they were a part. In addition, a review and notification system for federal grants came into being to help coordinate local government planning and development efforts.[5]

Third, the capacity building effort of the later Nixon years and the Ford years directed attention to intergovernmental management and especially the relationship among policy management (leadership), resource management (organizational maintenance, adaptation, and compliance with environmental constraints), and program management (productivity and responsiveness to client needs and policy guidance). The clearest statement of the nature of capacity building ("Executive Summary," 1975) suggests that capacity building was an instrument of restraint; that is, building capacity and resources at levels of government other than the federal level would lead to federal spending and taxing restraint.

The implications of analyst dominance remain today, especially in assessing capacity building's features in common with privatization. The major plank in the election platform of Presidents Carter and Reagan was the need to put a stop to Washington administrative harmony with Congress. In other words, capacity building became a method of breaking up the positive government-bureau movement alliance that had made the Efficient Citizenship movement possible and that had produced the New Deal's infrastructure. In breaking apart analyst from progressive, the capacity building movement lead unwittingly to privatization.

The Privatization Movement

Reclaiming private goods production[6] for the private sector marks the fifth major movement and the installation of parsimony as the primary virtue in financial management. Although resting on a tradition in conservative political and economic thought (Schumpeter, 1942; Hayek, 1944; Buchanan and Tullock, 1962), privatization is perhaps best portrayed in the writing of E. S. Savas (1982). The revolt evident in privatization—government is "a horde of self-aggrandizing opportunists" (p. 1)—represents a return of the business interests to paramount influence in the ruling coalition in government financial management.

Such influence finds its source in the tax revolts of the 1970s, but privatization also represents new thinking about the production of goods and services long dominated by positive government adherents. For instance, proposals have included rethinking toll goods: Could roads and bridges be financed as private property with use and pricing like any other consumer good? Could common pool resources, such as clean air, be "regulated" by allocating its pollution among competing abuses, such as by giving manufacturers the right to continue producing pollutants if they were willing to pay higher fees for the right (Hershey, 1989)? Public goods come under special scrutiny, as managers explore ways to check expenditures by contracting the production of such services as corrections.

Finally, federal government regulators, such as the Securities and Exchange Commission and the Food and Drug Administration, have begun exploring the uses of fees to help the agencies become self-sustaining. Fees could be charged the regulated industries in such a way that industry demand for permits of one sort or another could be matched with the "supply" of administrative and regulatory effort.

Supply-side Economics

Joining the privatization of service delivery, supply side economics gained favor in explaining the need for large tax cuts coupled with genuine reform of the tax structure (Roberts, 1984). Tax cuts gained justification in the view of many that tax rates and revenue production have a curvilinear relationship—up to a point, tax rates and revenue produced increase, after which time rates increase but revenue declines.

Supply-siders argue that tax cuts and even a flat rate for income taxes would have an ameliorative effect on revenue because of two factors. First, tax rates would have a more neutral effect on economic production, leading to greater manufacturing and output of services when profits were seen as a reward rather than a penalty. Second, lower taxes would stimulate economic production in its own right as had been evident in earlier tax cuts in the Kennedy Administration.

The timing of the increase in economic production and the byproduct, greater government revenue, were never clear. The haziness became extremely consequential in marrying privatization to supply-side economics. The tax cuts in 1981 and 1986 produced large shortfalls in government revenue for the federal government without corresponding cuts in government expenditures. This deficit then produced enormous pressure to cut spending further or to privatize still other government functions.

Cutback Management

The analysts' response to tax revolts, tax reform, and budget deficits was "cutback management," the notion of managed reductions in force and program structure.[7] The hallmark of this line of thinking was the strength-of-hierarchy variable in determining orderly contraction of public organizations. Where hierarchy did not exist, it was argued, interest group resistance would rep lace orderliness, and interests groups would adapt as they vie among each other to preserve distributional patterns with policy areas they dominate (Rubin, 1985).

COALITION CONVERGENCE AND DIVERGENCE

The leaders of the successive movements that have swayed thinking in public financial management shared one important belief—that openness in government's financial dealings served their own interests, whether they were efficiency, equity, or parsimony. But those interests might be very different, for example, progressives wanted positive government, business interests favored low taxes, research bureau desired analysis, and muckrakers sought punishment for thieves. However, the coalition that was built to pursue openness believed the basic currency of financial management to be procedures and routines that were able to be observed and evaluated.[8] Observable and able to be evaluated *for what* remained to be seen.

Openness was the currency among the members of the reform coalition. It united them in opposition to what were referred to as "political forces" that were widely known as the political clubs that controlled local and often state government and that were themselves controlled by a political boss.

Openness was also the plateau to be reached before any of the beliefs of any of the reform coalition members could be realized. Positive government types had to have some measure of goodness, and the data as well, to determine equity and to counter the effects of discrimination and the less-than-ideal levels of political participation. Only openness could provide this measure and the necessary data. Analysts had to have openness to determine efficiency. Business interests had to have openness to pinpoint the threats to parsimony and the sources of inequity in their taxes. Finally, muckrakers had to have openness to root out thievery.

Openness, itself, was not accountability but rather the necessary basis on which to build accountable systems of work. Accountability was the belief, the vision to be fulfilled, whereas openness was a way of employing technology and management to achieve the vision.

Systems of Accountability as Sources of Divergence

Reform coalition members held different beliefs, advocated different management systems, and advanced the use of different technologies, all of which implied different systems of accountability. If we consider muckraking as essentially the primary position of all members of the coalition, we are left with three major, sometimes overlapping, groups and systems of accountability: positive government types—more government as service needs expanded; analytical and research types—efficient government first and foremost; and probusiness types—low taxes for greater returns on investment in private enterprise. Consider Table 1 and its portrayal of these systems.

Among the members of the group, differences existed over the *accountability premise*. Positive and probusiness interests tended to see needs outside the organization as having primary control over what the organization did; they saw responsibility in equity. This responsiveness to clients or taxpayers tended to outweigh the need for responsibility, especially that premised on efficiency calculations and held by analyticals, and that premised on parsimony arguments and held by business interests.

Technologies differed as well. Positives tended to compare programs with other programs, defining the best programs as those whose rates of return at the margin outweighed others. Efficiency as technology demanded a calculation of material inputs and outputs with effort taken to assure minimum loss in between. Typically, probusiness interests determined the worthiness of effort based on its perceived utility expressed in money terms and discounted for loss of value over time; the value of the preferred effort exceeded that of alternative ones.

Members of the coalition differed in their approach to the problems of management and in their *organization theories*. Positive government types wanted the goals and methods of organizations to be matters of cooperation reached through negotiation (Golembiewski, 1977). Analyticals from the Brownlow Committee on, tended toward hierarchy (Gulick and Urwick, 1937). The probusiness interests favored private sector provision of most services that had before been produced by government (Wolf, 1988).

Table 1 Comparison of Accountability Systems Implied by Reform Coalition Members in Government Financial Management

Group	Positives	Analyticals	Probusiness
Accountability premise	Equity	Efficiency	Parsimony
Technology	Marginality	Productivity	Monetized utility
Organization theory	Negotiated	Hierarchical	Privatization
Belief system	Government as expanding sphere	Government as fixed sphere	Government as contracting sphere

Source: Waldo, 1948; Schiesl, 1977.

Finally, the *belief system* of the three elements of the reform coalition differed. By definition, positive government types, believed in government as an expanding sphere of influence in direct proportion to the demand for public services. In contrast, probusiness interests lay in shrinking government's sphere for the sake of increasing business opportunity and decreasing taxes. Analyticals, however, tended to equivocate on the size of government issue, emphasizing the efficiency issue whatever the sphere of government.

The Long-Term, Lasting Effect of Divergences

The similarities and differences among the members of the earliest reform coalition have had a remarkably durable effect on thinking about government financial management. The three early versions of accountability, equity, efficiency, and parsimony, have competed as sources for technologies in present reforms, different points of view regarding the role financial management should play in government organizations, cognitive styles to which financial managers lay claim, and the theories of government organization to which the field subscribes.

At any point, a statement of financial-management theory, is an amalgam, or more accurately, a scorecard indicating which of the original sources of thought has the greatest current influence. Therefore, there has never been a stable belief structure—a consensus about the role of government finance in society or the role of financial management in government—on which to base theory in the field of public financial management. Political coalitions evolve, and different beliefs have influence.

Consider three basic beliefs that still compete to dominate thinking in the field, which identified and contrasted in Table 2.

Table 2 Comparison of Theories Derived from Early Reform Efforts in Government Financial Management

Theory	Cybernetics	Pluralists	Public Choice
Accountability premise	Efficiency	Equity	Parsimony
Originating from	Analyticals	Positivists	Probusiness
Technology	Productivity	Marginality	Monetized utility
Organization theory	Hierarchy	Negotiated	Privatization
Belief system	Government as fixed sphere	Government as expanding sphere	Government as contracting sphere
Culture	Hierarchical	Egalitarian	Individualistic

Source: Waldo, 1948; Schiesl, 1977, Wildavsky, 1988.

The first belief system is derived from centralized planning and control, is based in cybernetics, and is elaborated in accounting theory (Key, 1940; Simon, 1976; Beer, 1959; Smithies, 1955; Comptroller General of the United States, 1985).

The second approach and belief system, which is epitomized in budgeting theory, has a decidedly pluralistic management orientation. This approach is derived from an open-systems logic, and it achieves its highest elaboration in organization decision-making theory (Churchman, 1968; Johnson, Kast, and Rosenzweig, 1963; Lindblom, 1965; Cyert and March, 1963; Cohen, March, and Olsen, 1972).

Based in economics, the third approach influences thought as a normative device through public choice theories (Buchanan, 1987; Borcherding, 1977). Its influence extends to research methods, especially in positive methodologies (Friedman, 1953) and to such analytic technologies as cost-benefit analysis (Kaldor, 1939; Hicks, 1940).

Although the approaches compete, each, however, is strongest in different areas of analysis. Much accounting and control theory has technical application, especially in the ability to characterize and classify data. Accounting theory vaguely implies a top-down management structure and even more vaguely a hierarchical culture and belief system based on maintaining distinctions (strata or castes) among groups.

Budgeting theory has a strong managerial flavor and suggests a negotiation between bureaus and central guardian agencies—a sort of bottom-up flow of initiative and information that is subject to varying degrees of centralized discretion, control, or reconciliation. Budgeting theory implies but does not elaborate a technology based on marginal rates of substitution. Each claimant's incremental demand is compared to each other claimant's demand rather than all past demands. It also implies an egalitarian belief system because each source of initiative may be equally legitimate, even though discussions—particularly those that limit political participation—still bar total equality.

Economic analysis has very little to say about management but implies a quantification of productivity measures and their analysis. The major contribution made by this approach is the belief expressed by public choice theorists in a small or contracting sphere for government action. A probusiness culture would resemble that espoused by promarket advocates: highly decentralized decision-making that is individualistic rather than collectivist in its action.

A CONTINUING AND EPISODIC STRUGGLE

The three approaches still remain as diverging views. The struggle to dominate, to decide what public financial management will entail, is ongoing.

I characterize this struggle as an effort at political dominance. Others who have given it some attention in the budgeting literature (Schick, 1966; Hyde,

1978; Rubin, 1988) view it in different ways and suggest, instead, a gently unfolding succession of methods of analysis that build cumulatively. For instance, Schick viewed the struggle as a control emphasis that sets the stage for a management focus in budgeting, with the management focus requiring the data gathering that a control emphasis yielded. A planning gestalt succeeds control and management, adding a futuristic dimension to budgeting decision-making, but not displacing the necessary tools of control and management.

The "gently unfolding succession" idea may mask a truly titanic struggle; however, it is a struggle that befits an area of administration of such magnitude as financial management. Since knowledge acquisition here has two competing explanations, it deserves further analysis.

As a method of depicting the way specific reforms gained support, consider this model. Burchell and his colleagues (1980) and, in a more basic way, Thompson and Tuden (1959) represent different variations of consensus and disagreement as a matrix based on answers to two basic questions. First, do interests agree on what ends may be served by prevailing technologies? For example, can interests agree on what end openness would serve? Second, do interests agree on what means might be most suitable for achieving a given end? Specifically, do interests agree on what means might be most suitable to achieve equity, efficiency, and parsimony?

By answering each of these questions, we come up with the cells that are pictured in Table 3.

Table 3 may be interpreted and illustrated with specific reforms cell by cell. For example, Cell 1 suggests agreement on means and ends. The case of complete agreement is best illustrated by interpreting the original coalition's action that created modern financial management: agreement existed over means (openness in financial management) to achieve the given end (accountability).

Cell 2 portrays agreement on ends but disagreement over means. The most memorable illustration is the conflict that occurred in 1937 and 1938 between the President's Committee on Administrative Management and the Brookings Institution. Brookings (U.S. Senate Committee Investigating Executive Agencies, 1937)

Table 3 Preferences and Beliefs among Cybernetics, Pluralists, and Public-Choice Interests

		Preferences about ends	
		Agree	Disagree
Beliefs about means	Agree	1	3
	Disagree	2	4

Source: Burchell et al., 1980; Thompson and Tuden, 1959.

argued the validity of intensive analysis and classifications of activities into major functions—reorganizing for reorganizing sake. The President's Committee argued the value of solving the President's management problems, such as giving direction to budgeting through the transfer of the Bureau of the Budget to a newly created Executive Office of the President (see Leiserson and Marx, 1959, p. 30).

The same events have unfolded over the U.S. Bureau of Census model of municipal government (Fox, 1977; MacDonald, 1988). The bureau directors created functions that seemed common to city government activities. The functions became a means of reporting, in a comparable way, the data received from local governments. However, the end product was a basis not only for classifying data but also for organizing departments and for developing early professions in local government.

The mirror image of Cell 2 is reflected in Cell 3, the agreement on means and the disagreement on ends. Perhaps the best illustration is the use of PPBS during the Johnson Administration (Rabin, 1975; Schick, 1973; Wildavsky, 1966; Novick, 1968). The program had worked well in the Department of Defense as a method of maximizing choices over weapons systems (with operations research a long heralded success at the same thing). President Johnson insisted that it be adopted in other agencies, but it would have less spectacular results. Schick observed (1973, p. 416) that "analysis was to be a change agent; it would reorient budgeting by serving it." What the PPBS may actually have been was a *means* (as opposed to an end) of appearing frugal and of centralizing decision-making (Wildavsky, 1966, p. 306; Golembiewski, 1989).

In either case, the means, whether deliberately or fortuitously, determined the end. As Wildavsky (1966, p. 300) observed, "A (if not the) distinguishing characteristic of systems analysis is that the objectives are either not known or are subject to change." He quoted Hitch (1960, p. 19) to reinforce his argument. "We may, of course, begin with tentative objectives, but we must expect to modify or replace them as we learn about the systems we are studying—and the related systems."

Cell 4 represents an absence of consensus in either means or ends and also represents a method of resolving disagreement. Cell 1, for example, suggests what is to be the destination of thinking when disagreement exists over either ends or means. One expects to achieve consensus by working through disagreements whatever they may be. Cell 4 takes a different approach by suggesting the resolution of utter conflict (disagreement over ends and over means) through the redefinition or *reinterpretation* of the phenomenon entirely. In fact, Cell 4 may be a destination of thinking itself. As agreement on either means or ends becomes remote in ambiguous situations, those parties who have a stake in the outcome may interpret the events and their context, often post-hoc, in order to achieve agreement (Weick, 1979).

THE NATURE OF REFORM EPISODES

Table 3 also helps to classify all reform episodes as a whole, or the idea of how knowledge is acquired. As pointed out earlier, Schick (1966) and others (Hyde, 1978; Lyden and Miller, 1978) have depicted these efforts as a "gently unfolding succession" of developments that build on the strengths of preceding reforms. I have described them as titanic struggles that are more discontinuous than cumulative in their effects. There are still other views. What view has the greatest plausibility? What difference does it make?

Consider each cell in Table 3. Cell 1 reflects the "no change" position generally espoused by those who view the survival of a procedure or policy over a long period of reform as the survival of what was a stable state all along. Often, research has sought to interpret budgeting and tax reform legislation as failure-prone efforts to overhaul systems that require merely fine-tuning (Wildavsky, 1961; Wildavsky and Hammond, 1965). These research pieces have also related reforms to more general thinking in organization and accounting theory to show how different views of financial management can easily coexist; control, management, and planning emphases in budgeting, for example, are not successors but complements with each serving a different level of organization (Parsons, 1960; Thompson, 1967; Anthony, 1965).

Cell 2 in Table 3 portrays differences over means but agreement over ends and reflects a *linear* notion of reform. As events occur, particularly those unforeseen by the original reformers, the original reforms become "established types" and targets for new reformers who find it advantageous to attack orthodox thinking and its unpopular results.

In this instance, the struggle to dominate thought among finance professionals creates temporary solutions to a continuing problem: How to finance the aims of government adequately as well as guard the public treasury from plunder and abuse? Reforms to solve this tension gain support, are enacted, and then have foreseen and, more importantly, *unforeseen* consequences, so this interpretation argues. Those unforeseen consequences show vulnerabilities and offer opportunities for opponents to attack.

Early thinking about budgets, for example, suggested that line itemization might provide information for a public which had little idea for what and how its money was spent. Openness served the function of control. Yet large itemized lists often toppled of their own weight and actually provided more places to hide rather than less. In fact, the Hoover Commissions felt that less, rather than more, control was exerted through these types of budgets (Gross, 1969).

Cell 3 of Table 3 portrays an agreement on means but a disagreement on ends. Such a situation—a set of means searching for an end—has occurred at least three times in public financial management: in the PPBS and zero base budgeting (ZBB) episodes in budgeting and in the strategic-planning movement in debt management. Particularly evident in PPBS, the means (greater use of analysis, particularly methods of operations research) gained credence from World War II, leading to the development of a band of devoted disciples of analysis who found a succession of ends that the means could serve—bombing, strategic weapons, weapons cost analysis, and finally budgeting. ZBB, too, was a matter of taking an innovation from one context (Texas Instruments) and applying it in another (in the state government of Georgia and then in the U.S. Government), in the former to force attention on innovation and in the latter to show frugality (Pyhrr, 1977). In the strategic-planning movement, much store has been placed by early recognition of ends which the various tools of debt management—various put-and-call option variations[9]—might be employed to optimize. In either case, the means are glorified, the ends found incidental: almost any will do.

This view of reforms suggests what popular historians (Schlesinger, 1986) called the *cycles of history*; that is, issues change and opportunities appear on which one or another interest group finds easiest to capitalize. The professions have vested interests, not so much in what to gain, but in where to apply the technologies that have been developed and fine-tuned. Dominance moves from one interest group to another and back again.

Therefore, Cell 3 resembles a *nonlinear* view of reform or change in public financial management. Circumstances change and opportunities develop in which a group finds it advantageous to assert mastery over events (Kaufman, 1956, footnote 11; Ferguson and Rogers, 1986).

Cell 4 takes a different tack entirely in suggesting that differences over means *and* over ends can exist. Most closely following the logic in Wildavsky's cultural theory (1987), this position holds that preferences emanate from culture, as do appropriate means "to get people what they want" (p. 5). Wildavsky saw variations among cultures in two ways. The groups with which people identify or to which they "belong" have more or less strong boundaries. These groups also have more or less emphatic prescriptions for members' actions. Thus, differences over ends and means (Cell 4) are defined by those involved as very basic, each preference "endogenous, formed through opposing and supporting institutions" (p. 5).

Best known among the analysts who subscribe to Cell 4 attributes, Clark and Ferguson (1983) have spent their careers showing that methods used by cities to deal with fiscal stress can only be explained with a cultural theory. They break down regimes into Democrats, Republicans, Ethnic Politicians, and New Fiscal Populists. Their definitions of these regimes and their analysis of the connections between these regimes and the unique policies for dealing with stress provide impressive support for the cultural hypothesis. Simply, all reforms will not "work" in every culture. My own research in cross-cultural reforms (Miller, 1980) adds support to this finding.

The differences among the principal cells, Cell 2 ends looking for means and Cell 3 means looking for ends, suggest different theories of change and different political theories as well. Cell 2 (looking for means) suggests Kuhn's notion of change (1970): Ideas (means) will work until something better comes along. Cell 3 looking for an end resembles Kaufman's battles among the forces underlying public administration doctrine (1956). Each interest, whether neutral competence, executive leadership, or representativeness, has control of the political universe in mind. Nonetheless, the battle exists over how control will develop.

Political theories change as well with the cells. In the Cell 2 looking for means situation, a council of experts is called for (elite politics) in which falsification (as with scientific method) is the major determinant of appropriate means. In the case of Cell 3 looking for ends, pluralist politics requires compromise in which a dominant set of groups achieves control.

The similarities between Cells 2 and 3 are equally remarkable. First, both theories are deterministic and exogenous. In Cell 2, events transpire that create anomalies which the working reform fails to comprehend, much less solve. In Cell 3, events transpire that create dysfunction. In both cells, events beyond reform's control have a crucial effect. Second, both theories have interpretive features; that is, ambiguity exists in Cells 2 and 3 about what happened to cause the apparent need for reform and why. The resulting anomalies or dysfunctions lead to competition among explanations.

The implications for the plausibility of the "gently unfolding succession" hypothesis could not be harsher. Even though Schick (1966) suggested that values evolve smoothly and cumulatively, such does not seem to be the case, either in the logic of events surrounding financial systems reform or in the evidence alone. Reform seldom represents a progressive accumulation of knowledge because it is so often prodded by anomalous events. At the very least, reform may come about because events create opportunities which vested interests exploit (Cell 3).

Reforms may also offer opportunities in which rationalization of the past or reinterpretation of the present changes the entire picture confronting all actors (Cell 4). In fact, the entire frame of reference changes so that no vested interest sees the world in the same way, no anomalous event can truly be said to be anomalous or not, and steady-state politics no longer exists. It is this last type of reform that leads to the plausibility of a "titanic struggle"—a struggle involving no less than the fight to change the entire premise by which individuals operate. This fight is over what Taylor (1961) called "vindication" or "the standards and rules that make up a value system" (p. 129).

The competition among value systems could not be keener, the implications for what we "know" more profound. The logic of events allows the conceivability that professionals battle, instead of slowly and peacefully giving way to each other. Their norms are pitted against each other in a manner that their entire reason for existence may be called into question. The threat to jobs, livelihoods, and even conceptions of self lurks.

Events themselves suggest that change comes with conflict, and this view is not new. Morstein Marx (1957) portrayed the fierce battles that took place, as far back as the Brownlow Commission in 1937, between the orthodox Brookings

Institution members and the more insurgent New York City group from the Bureau of Municipal Research. Kaufman (1956) described many similar ideological battles in the second Hoover Commission. Evidence from Mosher (1984) comparing the development of the U.S. General Accounting Office (GAO) and the U.S. Office of Management and Budget (OMB) and from Walker (1986) on GAO leads one to believe that the successions of points of view taking place as these departments evolved did not take place in a deferential way but in circumstances just short of force.

The logic of events and the events themselves support the idea of a titanic struggle for dominance of the premises behind public financial management and lead to an analysis of current thinking in these terms. Who rules?

Since the antigovernment campaigns waged by Presidents Carter and Reagan, a premise has gained ascendance in which positive government has become "part of the problem rather than the solution." The premise has had substantial effects on public financial management, as I discussed in identifying privatization, supply side economics, and cutback management. The issues faced in financial management have mirrored the fundamental change in premises. To take only four issues, consider how premises have changed to force a new frame of reference in top-down budgeting and in market allocation.

Top-down Budgeting

Emerging in the privatization movement is a new coalition of neutral competents and fiscal conservatives. Neutral competents are intent on pursuing top-down budgeting, which Schick (1986) said was a way to even the balance between the "bottom-up" agency-dominated interest-group liberalism of the recent past (Wildavsky, 1964) and the more ideological and insurgent politics of the 1980s (Ferguson and Rogers, 1986). Fiscal conservatives have taken the mantle of executive leadership; their lock on the Presidency has provided initiative in a battle over who will govern; a battle in which fiscal issues become major tests of will and offer chances for one side of the other to threaten a stalemate and bring the government's fiscal machinery to a halt. In any event, executive branch budgeting no longer rests solely on the base and fair-share norms that underlie a bottom-up budget system of an administrative agency, a Congressional appropriations subcommittee, or an interest group alliance. Top-down budgeting places the President on a continual collision course with Congressional leaders.

Market Allocation of Private Goods

The loss by the positivists in the emerging conflict is the loss of faith in pluralism as a means of allocation as well as a means of formulating regulatory policy, and as a contributor to the redistribution. To its adherents, privatization is a means by which private interests, which are served by government programs, can become actual, private, individual rights which the market can allocate.

To use an illustration taken from Linowes (1988, pp. 248–249), a small farmer, through government programs, received permission to use publicly provided and subsidized water for irrigation. The farmer could not transfer or sell this permission even if it had higher value to a municipality nearby. Privatizing this permission by granting the farmer the right of transfer or sale would bring markets into the decision about the highest and the best use of the water.

Market, Not Government, Allocation of Public Goods

Does government finance have a role in the emerging view of financial management or will the market allocate even public goods? What the new coalition of fiscal conservatives and neutral competents has provided is not only a more strident advocacy of businesslike government finance administration but the direct application of individualism as the assumed basis for decision-making in allocating such collective goods as industrial and debt market regulation.

For example, in matters involving the U.S. Office of Management and Budget, cost-benefit analysis has gained common use in guiding the review of the quantity and type of regulatory rule-making in agencies, to the point of creating a "regulatory budget" (Stockman, 1986, p. 103). The bias of cost-benefit analysis toward the individual (Meier, 1986) removes the public good aspect of regulatory rule making and, with privatization, reinterprets regulation as a private, market-allocated interest.

The change of focus has affected municipal debt markets as well. The competitive market has been used as a guide to state and local government capital investment and infrastructure improvement, through reliance on taxable debt instruments, as Congress has curtailed tax-exempt market uses by these governments for economic development purposes.

Finally, cash management has been pushed to join regulation and debt. Some have urged cash managers to define professional competence less in terms of fiduciary responsibility and more in terms of business principles in which risk and return guide all decisions (Girard Miller, 1987).

The Retrograde Movement in Rights-based Budgeting

Finally, as a countermovement of sorts, the courts have begun insisting that individuals have rights with fiscal mandates attached to them. These rights, which are often a matter of setting standards in prisons, mental hospitals, and in schools, are deemed to be private so that the courts have even taken the initiative in forcing orders for the expenditure of the necessary funds to accommodate these rights (Harriman and Straussman, 1983).

The emerging conflict is one in which the courts enforce what has been called interest-group liberalism (Linowes, 1988; Reich, 1964, 1965, 1966) while fiscal conservative forces push these private interests into the market through various privatization programs. The courts which are nominally acting on the side of the unrepresented stand in the way. Inexorably, fiscal policy and public financial management seem destined to enforce a move away from the provision of broadly defined classes of public goods and the redistribution of income. Thinking has sided with, and now helps guide, the implementation of the premise that government is a part of the problem and not the solution.

SUMMARY

Different points of view exist at each point in the American federal, state, and local political-administrative systems. Unlike parliamentary governments that control a permanent bureaucracy, American systems are not easily and comprehensively reconciled through elections and legislative votes of no-confidence. The distribution of influence—or more likely the determination of ends and means linkages—is highly randomized. As a result, problem-solving is piecemeal. On a problem-by-problem basis, the connection between how the problem is defined and what technologies (including organization and management knowledge) are used in solving it are highly contextual.

In the larger scheme of things, the problems and solutions are randomly connected with each other (Cohen and March, 1986). How do we make sense or gain meaning from a piecemeal fragmented system? We construct meaning, according to ambiguity theorists. After the fact, we rationalize information to make it meaningful. We interpret the situation beforehand in defining problems and in choosing solutions, but, because of the fragmented nature of problem-solving itself, we often make sense of it all after the fact in ways that provide continuity with the past. We ignore the essentially random nature of the relationships.

The role of financial management in ambiguous situations, then, is to interpret and to act based on this interpretation. Financial management is a repository of language; of processes in budgeting and revenue projection that reconcile; of networks that establish legitimacy; and of categorization devices. Language, reconciling devices, legitimacy-granting structures, and tables of classification are the tools of meaning construction. For financial-management theorists, the job is to conceive of which ways are used and to investigate these ways, their contexts, and their representation for the people who are served by them.

The emerging thinking represents the victory of parsimony over equity and efficiency. The three values have competed for control since financial management became a topic of serious study. The victory is one of reconstructing meaning through the control of the premise that guides thought, as the "government is a part of the problem, not the solution" so vividly captures.

For once, the implication of theory-building is *not* the capture of financial management by economics and market devotees. Rather, it is the imperative to base public financial-management theory on a foundation of meaning construction.

For the successors to the Bureau Movement analysts, the question of theory is largely left unanswered. During the Progressive era, the analysts could cope using a theory which, at the time of the Brownlow Committee, was thought to be the leading thinking in the field of management. It was orthodoxy at its height yet based on strict deductive logic. Its successor, during a period of government growth, was incrementalism. Connected ineluctably to pluralist theories of politics, incrementalism served to counter the pretense of hierarchical power and executive leadership with an "invisible hand" of policy selection based on a give-and-take among interests. Yet incrementalism's resemblance to individualist theories of market behavior led to a counterrevolution in which the market forces apparently rebelled over the cost of government growth based on the pursuit of private gain by public interests.

At present, an alternative view has developed to challenge the orthodox and incrementalist approaches in two different ways. First, ambiguity theory (Cohen, March, and Olsen, 1972) reflects the idea that neither planning/control theory nor pluralism provides a conceptual structure to qualify either alone as a full-fledged analytic approach with the three requisite parts: technique, management theory, and institutional value structure (Selznick, 1957; Parsons, 1960). This problem is of such a magnitude that I will have more to say about it in Chapters 3 to 5.

Second, social construction theorists (Berger and Luckmann, 1966) argue that developing an institutional-level approach is possible, even though it is no small task. The elaboration of an institutional level of analysis—the level of belief structure and values—on which to base a conceptual structure and from which we infer techniques in specific financial management systems comprises my task in the rest of the book.

NOTES

1. This chapter elaborates an argument that I made in a paper delivered at the annual meeting of the Southeastern Conference on Public Administration (SECOPA), in Jackson, Mississippi, on October 5, 1989.
2. This imperative comes from the "vault system" (Advisory Commission on Intergovernmental Relations, 1962) which suggested that prudence in the safekeeping public funds requires that money thus held might not circulate for fear that the bank holding the funds might fail.
3. The time value of money suggests that the value of a given sum is greatest at the present and that, foregoing its present use, it should be priced as interest. Opportunity cost calculations are those in which one use of money is compared to another and the difference between them is defined as a cost or the cost of an opportunity not chosen.
4. Supporting this political coalition argument, Adrian (1987) called all the groups, other than the Progressives, "urban conservatives." Schiesl (1977) and Elkin (1987) took the more conventional, political science route to describe the composition of the coalition, placing forces on either the promachine side or in the antimachine block.
5. See Chapter 9 for a discussion of this system.

6. Private goods are defined in the context of market failure and nonappropriability, and the term *private goods* refers to those goods produced and sold by either government or private business or both. Since market failure comes about as a result of the inability of a provider of goods to receive all the returns from the purchase of a service, "market success" is an instance of appropriability, or the ability to exclude nonbuyers of a good from its use and to prevent the concurrent use of a good by buyers and nonbuyers. What private goods are in practice and who should provide them is the subject of much speculation (see Wolf, 1988, for the best balanced analysis).

7. The large literature on cutback management has consumed thinking in public financial management for almost a decade. The apparent source of thinking on cutback management began with Simon (1962). For more of the bibliography on cutback management, see McCaffery (1981) and Levine (1980).

8. Later, these beliefs would be spelled out in implementation measures that developed into iron-clad principles, each viewed as good in and of itself.

9. For an explanation of put-and-call options as well as many other new debt management techniques, see Chapters 7 and 8 in this volume.

3

Orthodox Theories

This chapter and the next three examine the theories that have vied to influence research in public financial management: orthodox, incremental, and interpretive. In this chapter, those approaches are again outlined briefly, with the chapters building on financial-management history (Chapter 2) and showing that the political coalitions which attained power fundamentally influenced the pursuit of knowledge by altering financial-management research: namely, the topics chosen, the methods used, the explanations given, and the problems solved.

The four dimensions of financial management that develop each variant were chosen because of their historical importance. Yet they also permit the distinction to be made among the three theories, providing an idea of the breadth of activity encompassed in public financial management. Consequently, orthodox, prevailing, or alternative thought links 1. the technology of financial management (variously referred to as corporate financial theory, strategic management theory, or interpretive theory) with the basic preoccupations of financial managers. 2. It links the role managers should and do play, such as that specified by legal options underlying their fiduciary role, the conflict reduction role they play as either guardian or spender, or the emergent rules that provide them with an interpreter's role. 3. It focuses on financial managers' actions, particularly, their output-orientation in public administration, their political economy orientation toward work organizations, their ability to develop cognitive or decision-making theory, and so forth. 4. Lastly it focuses on an organization theory or a guiding principle that lies behind financial managers' efforts to cope with internal and external organizational phenomena—to cope with, in a word, *uncertainty*. I will show that these three variants—orthodox, prevailing, or alternative thought— have made it possible for managers to differ in the way each has handled the four dimensions of management and, yet, managers' decisions, emerging from different perspectives in orthodox, prevailing and alternative thought, have had a cumulative effect on theory.

CHAPTER OUTLINE

Table 1 provides a description of the three theories developed as a three-by-four relationship relating orthodox, prevailing, and alternative theory to technology, role of the finance office, organization theory, and decision-making model. Competing theories that exist to guide public financial-management research and practice specify the role of the finance office in financial management, the technology to use, the common elements each has with a broader theory of organization and interorganization dynamics, and, finally, each version's model of decision-making.

Orthodox Theory (Synopticism)

Orthodox theory is a normative approach to utility maximization. That is, its technology follows closely that of modern financial theory—the maximization of shareholder wealth—in a government and nonprofit framework, usually relying on techniques designed to create a "Pareto optimal"[1] distribution of benefits and burdens. The role of financial manager is to guide the agency to maximization with financial-management theory being the primary means of casting organization goals and determining their achievement. Management analysis goes no

Table 1 Comparison of Three Theories of Choice

Theory	Technology	Role theory	Organization process model	Decision
Orthodox	Corporate finance	Business model	Closed system	Rational
Prevailing	Strategic management	Interest group model	Coping with uncertainty	Disjointed incrementalism
Alternative	Process design Rule design	Symbolism Myths Language	Loosely coupled system	Garbage can Retrospective rationality

further than the internal mechanics of the organization; structure is pyramidal. Finally, the techniques relate to a rational decision-making model which specifies that preferences can be ordered and should direct the search for the most efficient means to satisfy them.

Prevailing Theory (Incrementalism)

In almost all respects, prevailing theory relies on the intended rationality of managers to guide thinking. Although denying that actors have the ability to find the Pareto optimal distributions, for example, the theory nevertheless requires that they intend to do so. This technology is based on a modified corporate finance model, a strategic management model, the aim of which is to guide nonmaximizing behavior in at least partially rational ways by specifying the use of techniques as heuristics or aids to decision-making. In a well-known passage, Wildavsky described the phenomenon (1986, p. 10):

> Those who . . deal with their overwhelming burdens [of calculation] by adopting heuristic aids to calculations . . . simplify in order to get by. They make small moves, let experience accumulate, and use the feedback from their decision to gauge consequences. They use actions on simpler matters (which they do understand) as indices to complex norms.

Moreover, roles act as the primary techniques. In fact, as interest groups, the various participants in financial management are expected to differ, and the collision among interests that results provides information. The varying fortunes of interests create a sort of continual change in the broad consensus that permits concerted action, creating what appears to many as "learning" (Moscovici, 1976; Braybrooke and Lindblom, 1963). The organization theory prescribes structures that cushion against the unknown, permitting the element of strategy to dominate financial managers' worlds with the question of "what if . . . ? Finally, the decision-making scheme is referred to as "disjointed incrementalism" (Hyneman, 1950) and described as "the mutual adjustment of ends and means" serially to continual changes in the knowledge of factors that a decision-maker can never fully understand (Braybrooke and Lindblom, 1963, p. 98).

Alternative Theory (Ambiguity)

Alternative theory jettisons the others' foundation of rationality. Financial managers must be humble. Cohen and March observed in their study of educational institution leadership (1986, p. 203),

> It is a mistake for a college president to imagine that what he does in office affects significantly either the long run position of the institution or his reputation as president. . . . few presidents achieve even a modest claim to attention 20 years after their departure [from office].

Most managers can expect to be remembered for little and what they have achieved may have resulted from happenstance, particularly results that ensue from good or bad times generally.

Techniques, therefore, tend to side with persistence and unobtrusiveness and a commitment to produce much but with realistic hope for only some. Ultimately, this may be called "sensible foolishness," the notion that goals are not necessary to choice, but that such things as imitating those with whom a manager holds common values, judicious use of coercion through such methods as deadlines and contracts, and rationalization of events to fit new views can be helpful to choice (Cohen and March, 1986, p. 223).

The role of the financial manager under ambiguity is far less concerned with achieving goals than in establishing meaning. Different in critical ways from posing prevailing theory's "what if . . . ?" questions, the manager creates evocative language, symbols, myths, and even routines with which to make a particular construction of reality meaningful to all others. As I explain later, accounting languages, the symbol of the credit-rating agencies, the myth of budget review, and the routine of cash reporting express a reality for organization members. Creating this reality or meaningful view is the primary role of the financial manager.

An organization theory fitting such needs for the unconventional is one based on the idea that units within an organization typically are only loosely coupled. Unlike the interest group interpretation in prevailing theory, or even less, the pyramid in orthodox theory, the organization as a whole is not swayed by dominant coalitions of interests. Rather, subunits tend to have few links or vulnerabilities to other units. Their links tend to be weak if they do exist. However, the disconnectedness allows for independent generation of preferences and alternatives, which come together in a sort of random meeting so that problems, solutions, participants, and choice opportunities reconcile randomly.

Loosely coupled systems create "garbage cans" in which the elements of choice (problems, solutions, participants, and choice opportunities) meet haphazardly. Unlike the other theories, the four elements are disconnected and their correspondence is strictly random. Managing the flow of elements or determining their juncture may have far greater power in decision-making than objective analysis. In fact, a poor decision is often one that excludes or ignores some important decision-maker rather than one that fails in any ordinary sense (Boss, 1976, p. 108).

ORTHODOX THEORY IN PUBLIC FINANCIAL MANAGEMENT

Orthodox theory has enjoyed remarkable longevity, owing in no small part to the willingness of its adherents to overlook its problems. In fact, prevailing theory, which followed chronologically the development of orthodox theory, may be viewed as successive efforts to solve orthodox theory's problems by relaxing the theory's rigid assumptions. Orthodox theory, then, has importance because most, if not all, of its key parts remain in the theory that prevails today.

In this section, I first develop this classic model, through the approach already outlined: portraying the method and stress orthodox theory takes in describing the role of the finance office, finance technology, the decision-making model employed, and the theory's implied theory of organization and management. In a succeeding section, I argue that two basic problems exist in following this approach to financial-management theory: delegation of authority and uncertainty.

Organization Theory: The Closed System Model

Public financial managers deal with an internal and an external environment. The decisions they make depend on the determinants and reactions of a turbulent outside world and a complicated internal set of relationships among organization members.

The public financial manager's method of operation, therefore, has a basis in general management thinking as expressed in an understanding of organization behavior. The approach Caplan (1966) provided another rationale:

> The operation of the [public financial managers' system] requires them to be constantly abstracting a selected flow of information from the complex real world and using these selected data as the variables in their "model" of the [organization]. It seems clear that accountants [for example] exercise choice in the design of their systems and the selection of data for admission into them. It also seems clear that the entire management accounting process can be viewed from the standpoint of attempting to influence the behavior of others. It follows, therefore, that they must perform these functions with certain expectations with respect to the reactions of others to what they do. In other words, their model of the [organization] must involve some set of explicit or implicit assumptions about human behavior in organizations.

If public financial managers carry behavioral assumptions around in their heads, what are these assumptions? For a thumbnail guide to the assumptions, see Table 2.

Organization theory, embraced by the orthodox approach to financial management, rests on assumptions from three related conceptual sources: industrial engineering technology, classical organization theory, and the economic "theory of the firm," (Caplan, 1966, pp. 496–497). Thus, orthodoxy has tended to borrow rather than develop theory, and much of what has been borrowed developed originally in the study of business organizations. For our purposes, three conceptual bases, being very similar in the business organization literature, can be referred to as close relatives here as well: they share essentially the same view.

Table 2 Behavioral Assumptions of Classical Organization Theory

A. Assumptions with respect to organization goals

1. The principal objective of organization activity is productivity maximization.
2. This principal objective can be segmented into subgoals to be distributed throughout the organization.
3. Goals are additive—what is good for the parts of the organization is also good for the whole.

B. Assumptions with respect to the behavior of participants

1. Organization participants are motivated primarily by economic forces.
2. Work is essentially an unpleasant task which people will avoid whenever possible.
3. Human beings are ordinarily inefficient and wasteful.

C. Assumptions with respect to the behavior of management

1. The role of the manager is to maximize the productive use of the factors combined in production in the organization.
2. In order to perform this role, management must control the tendencies of employees to be lazy, wasteful, and inefficient.
3. The essence of management control is authority. The ultimate authority of management stems from its ability to affect the economic reward structure.
4. There must be a balance between the authority persons have and their responsibility for performance.

D. Assumptions with respect to the role of management accounting

1. The primary function of management accounting is to aid management in the process of productivity maximization.
2. The accounting system is a "goal-allocation" device that permits management to select its operating objectives and to divide and distribute them throughout the firm, i.e., assign responsibilities for performance. This is commonly referred to as "planning."
3. The accounting system is a control device that permits management to identify and correct undesirable performance.
4. There is sufficient certainty, rationality, and knowledge within the system to permit an accurate comparison of responsibility for performance and the ultimate benefits and costs of that performance.
5. The accounting system is "neutral" in its evaluations—personal bias is eliminated by the objectivity of the system.

Source: Adapted with permission from Caplan, 1966, p. 49).

First of all, industrial engineering's contribution helped in the assembly of a rudimentary organization theory through detailed studies of factor costs, stimulating the development of management and cost accounting. In 1911, foremost among these shop floor consultants was Frederick W. Taylor whose concern with the relationship between technology and organization produced the realization among government agency heads that maximizing productivity could be thought of as the real goal of public management, as government organizations shared this goal with business organizations. In fact, both could share the goal of increasing efficiency and reducing costs.

Classical organization theory, developed in a number of areas by Max Weber (1947), provided a theoretical framework for what was essentially a practical solution to a shop-floor problem encountered by Taylor and the industrial engineers. Authority resting in a single superordinate provided a substantial method of control in creating accountability and maximizing productivity. This authority's power rested in the ability to influence the economic reward structure. The organization's efforts came from the coordination of primary work efforts (line efforts) the planning, evaluation, and financing of which fell to advisors (staff assistants) to the authoritative head of the organization. Substantial amounts of planning and evaluating were carried out by control agents who later became accountants.

This organization theory's major contribution was internal structure and the process of management accounting. The hierarchical structure, including unity of command and a narrow span of control permitted the work of the parts of the organization to add to the good of the whole. The structure permitted the equitable and balanced distribution of authority and responsibility. And, finally, structure allowed the organization-wide interest to come before the interest of individual "lazy" employees.

The management accounting system—in one sense the early manifestation of financial-management technology—provided the basic methods for productivity maximization. Planning activities allocated goals among subunits. Evaluation activities compared performance of subunits to goals, providing information on how well the organization was doing and what needed attention if the organization was failing to do as expected.

Decision-Making Model: The Economic Theory of the Firm

Caplan suggested that until the new entrepreneurial class of the eighteenth century emerged, the traditional determinants of human behavior in organizations, either custom or physical force, were satisfactory. This new class, however, needed "not only a social philosophy to rationalize its actions, it also sought practical solutions to the immediate problems of motivating, coordinating, and controlling the members of its organizations" (Caplan, 1966, p. 497). The need to develop practical solutions led to the development of organization theories. Rationalization efforts promoted the incorporation of what is now known as "the economic theory of the firm" into organization and management logic.

The economic theory of the firm referred to maximization as profit maximization. Maximization required the manager to face a series of alternatives that were subject to market and technological limits. Thus, success in this method of thinking depended for its success on the assumption of fully informed and exhaustive analysis. The method of decision-making also rested on an economic base whereby the individual whose behavior the analysis predicts is motivated by economic incentives, including the value of leisure. Thus, more economic rewards convince the "lazy" worker to perform.

A flowchart of the decision-making model moves from goal to decision, shown in Table 3. A goal drives the action, which ultimately moves through the exhaustive search for alternatives that maximize the achievement of that goal. A decision is reached when the manager finds the most suitable alternative.

Unequivocal action within an organization, in which organization members agree on both ends and means, stems from a branch of orthodox theory known commonly as the *rational comprehensive model of decision-making*, which includes five major parts (Boss, 1976, pp. 105–106) (see Table 3). Consider that the decision-maker faces a specific problem that can be isolated from other problems or that can be considered meaningfully in comparison with all other problems. The goals or values to be achieved in solving the problem are selected and ranked according to their importance. The decision-maker then searches for and finds all possible approaches for achieving the goals or values, and the consequences and costs of each alternative approach are predicted. Next, the decision-maker compares the consequences for any approach with that of all other alternatives. Finally, the decision-maker chooses the alternative that has consequences most clearly matching the predetermined goals.

Microeconomics and, in large part, public finance, political economy, and public budgeting theories rest on rational decision-making assumptions. These

Table 3   A Rational Comprehensive Model of Decision-Making

1. Values or objectives are determined and clarified separately, usually before considering alternative policies.
2. Policy formation is approached through ends-means analysis, with agreed-upon ends generating a search for ways of attaining them.
3. A "good" policy is, therefore, one that provides the most appropriate means to some desired end.
4. Every important relevant factor is taken into account.
5. Theory often is heavily relied upon.

Source: Lindblom (1959); Golembiewski and Rabin (1975).

theories provide normative approaches to the process of choice and require clarification of values or objectives prior to an empirical analysis of alternative policies. Therefore, rational theory requires a decision-maker to follow the steps outlined in Table 3 explicitly in each decision sequence to maximize return from effort and resources in meeting objectives.

Role of the Finance Office

The orthodox theory predicts that staff advice (management accounting) provides planning and evaluation for the organization. Management accounting's place provides the role of the finance office[2] (see Figure 1).

Recall that the "principles" for Figure 1 in organization theory included these propositions.

1. Work must be specialized in terms of functions at upper levels of organization and in terms of processes at lower levels.
2. Authority must be delegated by a single head to a sharply limited number of subordinates.
3. Supervision must be detailed and continuous.

Golembiewski (1964) emphasized the internal reporting aspect of the finance office, but his argument can be generalized to all parts of the public financial-management role. For example, the purposes of internal reporting according to Simon and his collaborators (1954), relate to three basic types of questions:

1. Score-card questions (control as an emphasis): "Am I doing well or badly?"
2. Attention-directing questions (the management of the enterprise as an emphasis): "What problems should I look into?"
3. Problem-solving questions (a planning or analytic exercise): "Of the several ways of doing the job, which is the best?"

The questions are those that a "line" manager might ask herself and those that an internal accountant could help to answer.

The relationship between the questioner and the answerer provides the basis for understanding the financial-management role. Golembiewski (1964, p. 340) described the classical model's line-staff relationship as the "neutral and inferior instrument" (NII) concept, because

> it prescribes that the "staff" person is outside the line of command, that she merely provides neutral advice or expertise. The internal accountant commonly does not report "across" to a lower-level "line" official at his own level. In contrast, he reports *up* his own "staff" hierarchy of one or more superiors, the "staff" superior then reports *over* to the appropriate higher level "line" official, and the latter in turn communicates *downward* to the "line" official directly concerned, the communication going through one or more levels of intermediate "line" supervision.

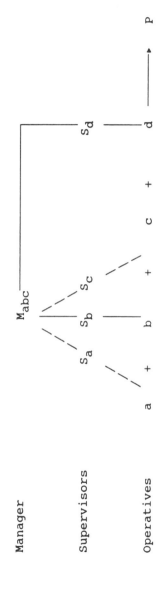

Figure 1 Orthodox organizing principles for financial management. Source: Golembiewski, 1964.

The NII concept requires that the "line" specialize in "doing." "Thinking" or planning and evaluating are reserved to the "staff," thereby avoiding a challenge to the unity of command by claiming both neutrality and inferiority.

The role of the finance office under the assumptions of an orthodox model most clearly resembles the role of finance in any organization that is bent on optimizing goals. The traditional theory prescribes that the role of staff and line be clearly distinguished. Even though commonly separated in public/nonprofit- and private-sector organizations, finance may, nevertheless, become the first among equals. In private organizations, wealth maximization provides a strong basis for finance officers' claims for leadership in investment decisions, dividend policies, and in financing approaches—the three major policy decisions in a private-sector, wealth-maximizing firm.

Although public/nonprofit organizations separate substantive matters (what the organization actually does) from financial matters (how it is paid for), orthodox theory would still prescribe optimization. What the organization does depends on how much money it will bring in.

Consider a few illustrations from orthodox theory. Major strategic planning by agencies revolves around efforts to build a supportive clientele which will go to bat for the agency at appropriations time. The agency focuses programs toward the desires of strong committee chairs in the legislative bodies that will review the programs. At the local level, budgeting is often called a revenue exercise (Wildavsky, 1986; Meltsner, 1971) in which inflow dictates outflow.

At the federal level, Congressional authorization committees commonly take a back seat to the Appropriation committees, allowing finance to dictate substance in legislative matters. The rational voter literature (see Pomper, 1968) suggests that rational voters are the persons who pick candidates who will maximize their financial returns; candidates who win will vote to maximize their constituents' returns; legislative committee chairs steer their committees to maximize their committee members' returns; and administrative agency heads advocate programs that maximize appropriation members' returns (as well as those of their own departments).

Finally, the rational budget movement (Lewis, 1952; Novick, 1968), the costing out government services movement (Kelley, 1984; Eghtedari and Sherwood, 1960), and the privatization movement (Savas, 1982; Murin and Pryor, 1988, p. 37–70) provide evidence that there is concern for optimization by fairly straightforward means.

Technology: Corporate Finance Theory

The technological basis for performance in finance offices at all levels of government and nonprofit organization lies in theory, which guides organizations that are bent on maximization, especially wealth maximization (see Table 4).

Table 4   Corporate Finance Theory

A. Utility theory
1. People are rational and seek to maximize expected utility under uncertainty. Utility is built on the assumptions of greed and risk aversion.

B. State preference theory
2. People calculate the payoffs associated with given states of nature (risks) and choose the mix that maximizes their portfolio return, given the mirror calculation by firms offering returns.

C. Mean-variance theory
3. Choice is a measure of the ability to hedge risk in keeping return at its highest possible level.

D. Arbitrage-pricing theory and capital asset-pricing method
4. The price of an asset is related to its relative sensitivity to risks affecting all assets. These risks may be broadly or narrowly inclusive for analysis.

E. Option-pricing theory
5. Price and, in turn, choice are related to the value of contingent claims and related to the uncertainty of a future price and the cost of establishing that fact for the firm.

F. Modigliani-Miller theorems
6. When taxes are not considered, and, in many views, even when they are, the leverage of a firm does not change its value. Value is based on rate of return.

Sources: Sharpe (1964, 1963); Lintner (1965); Ross (1976); Black and Scholes (1973); von Neumann and Morgenstern (1955); Williams (1964); Modigliani and Miller (1958, 1961); Markowitz (1952, 1959); Tobin (1956); Fama and Miller (1972); Hirshleifer (1970, 1964, 1965, 1966).

First and foremost among the principles in this approach is the directive in *utility theory* to optimize. This notion lies behind *individual* decision-making. It is also assumed of collective activity in a "for-profit" wealth-maximizing organized entity as well.

Second, the approach assumes a cutoff date. Waiting forever for results of a decision will not do. Setting an arbitrary point at which time a person can assess the effects of a decision directs attention to continuing or to stopping and changing the current finance policy being evaluated.

Third, the approach includes a selection of alternatives or "strategies." There might be a finite or infinite number of apparent strategies. The number actually considered depends, according to the approach, on the person enumerating them and the knowledge and experience that person has accumulated.

Fourth, each strategy has a payoff. Considerable lack of knowledge creates a lack of predictability. Are the resources available? Will they combine to yield the desired outcome? Will the result have a market?

Fifth, conditions often elaborate the individual decision-maker's knowledge and experience. These conditions come in three types. Certainty yields knowledge of the payoff from a given strategy by a cutoff date. The risk condition allows for numerous known variables that affect payoffs; the long run relative frequency of their occurrence is assumed to be known. Uncertainty provides no knowledge of long-term frequency of the variables (see Figure 2 for a comparison). The most prominent conditions are risk and uncertainty. Under conditions of risk, the manager calculates the expected value under each strategy. The expected value is the sum of each payoff multiplied by its respective probability. Each strategy has an expected value; optimization, as *state preference theory* would dictate, forces the choice of the strategy with the highest expected value.

An alternative method is *mean-variance theory*. Thus, if individuals find that payoffs (expected values) and variability tend to increase together directly, they would choose the expected value of the strategy that they thought maximized their own utility. At the level of a portfolio of strategies, they would want some hedge against variability to optimize payoff. In such a case, they would "balance" two strategies that had opposing variabilities (i.e., uncorrelated movements) or follow the dictates of *arbitrage-pricing theory* and the capital asset-pricing method.

Finally, decisions are affected by knowledge of probability. Risk carries greater understanding of the probability of an event by relying on sampling. That is, sampling a population provides a substantial estimate of the probability of a payoff, attached to a reasonable estimate of the error that is due to sampling. *Option-pricing theory* explains that the cost of taking a position under uncertainty is related to the value of the information needed to establish certainty; therefore, the price of an option is directly related to the error estimate of the sample.

As the sample becomes smaller in relationship to the population, the amount of uncertainty grows. At some point, the manager finds no reliable objective measures of variability and is left to judgment or some other means of establishing probability subjectively to gain any notion of the degree of certainty.[3] Finally, at some point, there is no information; there is ignorance of the variability.

PROBLEMS WITH ORTHODOX THEORY:
DISAGREEMENT AND UNCERTAINTY

No more than common sense need be used to challenge the rational approach to decision-making. For example, Lindblom (1959) argued that rational models tend to hide a number of underlying principles, including the model's requirement of (a) a comprehensive overview of the factors relevant to the decision; (b) clarity of definition of social objectives; (c) a means-end approach to policy-making; (d) a

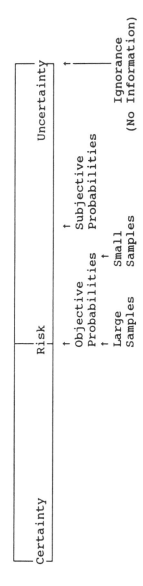

Figure 2   A comparison of conditions of certainty, risk, and uncertainty. Source: Archer, 1964.

deliberate and explicit choice among policies; (e) a calculation and minimization of cost; (f) reason and cooperation rather than arbitrariness, coercion, and conflict; and (g) a unified decision-making process for decisions that are highly interdependent.

The model's requirements are vast. Its use forces centralization, and users brook no compromise.

Yet, consider a condition under which orthodox theory may fail, a condition under which there is disagreement among actors about causation, but a singular preference prevails. The problem confronting competing interests is not what to do; rather disagreement is over how this end might be brought to fruition. For example, note a local municipality's economic development effort. Creating great local wealth, on almost any terms, finds wide agreement. Disagreement within the financial management community exists over how. Conflicts pit traditional, general obligation, bond-financing adherents against those who support such other methods as revenue bonds, leases, or private sector efforts (Sbragia, 1983; Sharpe, 1986). Disagreements rage as well between finance and other groups over substantive goals—infrastructure rehabilitation versus affordable housing (Adams, 1988)—and over timing with some persons advocating that the city provide infrastructure to stimulate development and others advocating a wait-and-see attitude, willing to offer services after development takes place when the needs are clear (Pagano and Moore, 1985).

Yet no city council, for example, can pursue economic development without delegating the investigation of means to experts or competing interests for study and resolution. Thus, decision-making is a matter of delegation. No matter how simple the decision or how prescient the decision-maker, some decisions must rely on the expertise of specialized, subordinate managers. Golembiewski (1965, p. 256) argued that delegation is so critical there can be no organization without it. Nevertheless, such delegation opens up a complex series of occurrences to which, orthodox thought says, theory must attend.

The first series of consequences usually amounts to a positive factor in organization dynamics. Selznick (1949) and March and Simon (1958) suggested that delegation increases the amount of specialized competencies, since the restriction of employees' attention to a relatively limited number of problems increases their experience within these limited areas and improves their ability to deal with these problems. As more hands become adept at such problem-solving, achievement is increased. Similarly, as delegation decreases the distance between organizational goals and their achievement, even more delegation is stimulated.

Bifurcation of Interests

Delegation of authority often results in unanticipated consequences at least two of which threaten organizational effectiveness. First, delegation's encouragement of specialization also leads to the bifurcation of interests among the subunits of an organization. Bifurcation is attributable to the increased personal commitment to the subunit goals which delegation suggests as well as to the specialized training that must exist for delegation to work. Specialized training maintains bifurcation of interests by increasing the costs of changing personnel.

Second, the bifurcation of interests can also lead to intraorganizational conflict. Thus, the content of decisions from differentiated subunits increasingly resembles subunit goal achievement rather than organization goal optimization, particularly if there is little internalization of organizational goals by participants. Boss (1976) depicted a spiral of sorts: "As the congruence decreases between the organization's goals and the individual achievement of those goals," he argued, "increased delegation follows within the subunits, and the cycle is repeated and reinforced" (p. 115).

Furthermore, internalization of subunit goals at the expense of organization goals can occur. Subunits fit their sometimes fragmented policies into the official policy of the larger organization (often displacing official policy). Daily decisions or routines based on subunit goals create a system of precedents and subvert the goals of the larger organization.

March and Simon (1958) advocated orthodox theory's approach to reducing the dysfunctional effects of delegation. They suggested that the solution would lie in the greater operationality of organizational goals. Therefore, the extent to which it is possible to observe and test how well subunits achieve organizational goals affects the degree of internalization of organization goals as opposed to subunit goals. Also, organizational incentives could reinforce attention to organizational goal achievement by influencing decision premises and by reinforcing observed performance.

Whether purposeful action is taken or not, the delegation of authority creates a bifurcation of views between managers and specialists that may lead to either good or ill. When any action is counterproductive it is denounced as a goal displacement; when it is unexpectedly beneficial, it is applauded as an innovation (Maynard-Moody and McClintock, 1987, p. 132). The critical datum is the definition of productivity, and that definition is an ideological or a belief problem, one calling for no less than meaning construction or interpretation.

Uncertainty

In reality, there are often constraints on management's ability to influence specific decision premises.[4] An inability to influence creates much uncertainty with which a manager must cope. Thus, in continuing the economic development example, some alternatives have little predictability: (a) tax laws may change thereby affecting financing methods; (b) interest rates or inflation may change, thereby creating lower demand for housing and/or higher costs for materials for infrastructure; and (c) some industries may be enticed with improvements that already exist whereas other industries may dictate what improvements are necessary later, only to make any improvements that were constructed in anticipation already obsolete. Assuredness about positions on causation—what will create local wealth most quickly—begins to unravel in the face of uncertainty about causation.

Generally, managers may force an agreement in the case of bifurcation but are hamstrung by uncertainty. Why? First, the most obvious reason for the inability of management to specify the cause/effect beliefs to be used in decision-making is incompleteness in existing knowledge. Although complex organizations are not established when knowledge is totally absent, they frequently do operate with incomplete knowledge. For example, this would be true of organizations that work on the edges of established knowledge, such as new areas of surgery, new phases in a national space program, or basic research. Even though all variables that are known to be pertinent are under unilateral control and may be specified by management, imperfections or gaps in knowledge call for some other management strategy to overcome the lack.

Second, perhaps a more pervasive constraint on management occurs when the object worked on is itself dynamic, for here some of the pertinent variables are not unilaterally under the control of the organization. Thus, the outcome of an educational program may hinge in large measure on the student's desire to learn, and therapeutic programs designed to modify basic personality are greatly affected by cooperation or antagonism of the human targets.

Still a third type of constraint on management's ability to dictate cause/effect relationships arises from competition between the organization and others. Competition is a situation in which the decision unit retains unilateral control of its preference hierarchy but must behave toward prospective customers, suppliers, or "judges" in light of its expectations about the behavior of rivals and prospects. Where outcomes are determined in part by the behavior of others, cause/effect relationships are uncertain, and this factor leads us to expect use of other types of strategies.

How can we differentiate degrees of uncertainty? Major sources of uncertainty tend to vary in different ways. Information can be scarce, and its accuracy and clarity often questionable. Unclear cause-effect relationships, which are always difficult to discern, make preferences obscure. Definitive feedback comes slowly or unpredictably, and, finally, no probability table exists to connect alternatives with likely outcomes, whether they are preferable or not.

An Example of Causes of Uncertainty

Consider how financial managers perceive uncertainty. One approach to specifying perceptions of uncertainty, and used by budgeteers and financial managers, comes from political economy. Wildavsky (1975) created a matrix of determining factors based on wealth and predictability.

Wealth refers to the ability of a government to mobilize sufficient resources or to control expenditures. Related to this variable is Caiden's notion (1978, p. 540) of political capacity to tax:

> The concept of the political capacity to tax is a difficult one to operationalize, but it appears to be a factor which has considerable impact upon governmental financial policy and the pattern of budgeting. The pattern of budgeting we are familiar with assumes a high level of both economic and political taxing ability—i.e., that resources are there and are open to direct government access; however, not all governments are so fortunate.

Predictability relates to differences in perceived certainty, similar to our volatility variable posed earlier. This concept identifies the ability on the part of a financial manager to calculate the flow of expenditures, revenues, or both in the immediate past and present and to project them into the future.

The result is four cells in the matrix. They are (1) poor and uncertain, (2) poor and certain, (3) rich and uncertain, and (4) rich and certain. Each cell or condition, according to Wildavsky leads those who budget and manage financial affairs to proceed about their work and to cope in different ways through no choice of their own. Orthodox theory fails to specify more than one condition, presumably rich and certain. Wildavsky shows that much of the world, if not all, operates in the three *other* cells, leading to the conclusion that certainty has little relationship to the behavior of these variables.

To summarize, orthodox approaches to financial management do stress procedures that follow logically a rational model of decision-making. The model has appeal because of its simplicity and its deductive elegance. The model's problems stem from practical problems of management: bifurcation of interests as well as the effects of chronic uncertainty.

With these failings in mind, I turn to the thinking that has developed in reaction to the orthodox approach. I call this reaction "prevailing theory" because I argue that it is that approach which still guides much of financial-management thinking at present.

NOTES

1. No one is worse off, as a result of a given distribution, and at least one person is better off.
2. From Golembiewski (1964).
3. See Chapter 10 and the bibliography in Wright and Ayton (1987).
4. This section is based on Miller (1983).

4

Prevailing Theory

Unlike orthodox theory, prevailing thought about government financial management relaxes the assumption of closed systems. Organizations instead would not only manage internal matters but interorganizational matters as well. Such an open system implies a different organization theory and a revised decision-making model, a new role for the finance office, and a technology that differs from that of the simple utility-maximizing, organization goal-optimizing methods that are associated with orthodox theory.

Despite major differences, the two theories share the assumption of preference ordering and intent as they relate to individuals' motives or collective endeavors. Thus, individuals and groups of individuals have preferences for certain outcomes of their work. They *intend* that their efforts produce something which they foresee as a direct result from their behavior.

ORGANIZATION THEORY

Farsightedness is the coping mechanism most financial officers would probably believe to be an important individual trait which they bring to their jobs (Coe, 1982). However, prevailing theory suggests methods of coping with uncertainty at two different levels of the organization, specifically at the level of the organization subunit—the finance function in the government, for example—or at the interorganizational level, where might be observed the relationship of a finance officer acting with vast uncertainty for the organization as a whole.

At the subunit level, prevailing theory's moving principle, from the so-called behavioral theory of the firm, holds that individual actors operate to create slack (March and Simon, 1958). Thus, budget share, hedges, arbitrage, and insurance create, by whatever means, extra resources or guard against loss of resources that already exist.

To some extent, the perception of uncertainty must lead to anxiety and to its reduction. In organizational terms, reduction translates into action by decision-makers to prevent, forecast, or absorb uncertainty.

Consider that among organization subunits, some rise to prominence when they attempt to gain information to cope with uncertainty, thereby allowing organization structure to follow coping ability and success (Perrow, 1970). The organizational need for information and subsequent action to reduce uncertainty can illustrate the point. Producing relevant information becomes a major competitive activity among all subunits that have similar information sources.

Subunits vie for influence over interpretation of relevant stimuli, each attempting to apply its unique view and capture the initiative in coping with uncertainty. The incentive for activity rests in the successful unit's ultimately receiving the organizational resources and rewards for doing so. Therefore, the "counter to uncertainty" is the ability to attain information and apply expertise or *to cope*; the motivation to cope rests on greater resources and greater rewards.

In a sense, coping is the organization's shock absorber, and three types of shock-absorbing activities exist (Hickson et al., 1971):

1. Coping by prevention: activities that are aimed at reducing the probability of input and output variations, such as legislative liaison around budget time.
2. Coping by information: activities that provide prior warning of variations in inputs and outputs, such as district offices or representatives on interdepartmental committees. Coping by information is an extremely powerful mechanism because it acts to define the situation, to set the agenda, thereby allowing a unit to take the initiative in coping by absorption.
3. Coping by absorption: activities that offset the effects of the variations in inputs and outputs, such as finding alternative revenue or countersuing in liability cases.

Routinization ultimately obtains when a subunit copes and creates patterned uncertainties successfully. Paradoxically, success in coping can encourage failure. Discerning patterns, coping, and routinizing procedures can reduce the rewards and the subunit's coping motivation. Routinizing coping efforts through *prevention* reduces power quickly when uncertainty is also reduced. For instance, worker's compensation sales and service by a state agency in a volatile insurance market may result in power, but long-term contracts reduce that power. Usually, routines, created by subunit efforts to forecast or absorb uncertainties, are found in standard-operating procedures, in which case the subunit has increased its own substitutability or replaceability.

Structure, tactics, and strategy constitute the organizational response to perceived environmental uncertainty. Structure may emerge as intentional intervention to segment environments or may result from the prominent rise of one or several competing subunits. Tactics become useful as the organization differentiates production functions from functions whose sole purpose is interaction with a volatile environment (Thompson, 19987). Finally, strategies prove effective in controlling or changing the environment in ways that make secure certainty and challenge, which are the original goals of the organization. Structure, therefore, has predominant importance as it impinges on the ability of organizations to discern patterned variability, to translate information into categories on which to base coping strategies, and to apply these coping strategies to uncertain situations to maximizes lack.

Duplication (strategies in which attention-getting questions get asked) (Simon et al., 1954) serves two purposes. It multiplies the amount of information that can be processed, assuming the capacity exists to process information of whatever quantity and quality, and it facilitates judgment about performance, allowing managers to sever a unit for failing to cope and to replace it without undue hardship.

Is such an arrangement efficient? As Jump (1968) argued, maximizing managers would be efficient as long as they covered every base in attaining slack: more programs would exist than could possibly be staffed optimally.

In information-processing terms, the salience of a given issue to the organization (its degree of uncertainty-causing potential) gives rise to competition among units to find ways to deal with the issues. Rewards flow to the unit that may solve the problem or reduce uncertainty. In financial terms, the salience or risk attached to the issue by the organization translates into potentially high payoffs for the unit that is to minimize the threat produced by the salient issue. The classic risk-return tradeoff is then created, much as in finance theory.

The risk and return forces guardians to ask attention-getting questions usually through comparisons among the subunits. Advocates are then able to pose "How am I doing" questions by drawing the issue into their own paradigmatic terms, thereby creating a standard as well as comparing their performance with other subunits doing the same thing.

Decision-Making Model[1]

A general model of decision-making draws wide agreement in the literature of financial administration to explain how these decisions are reached. The incremental/pluralist model, despite its limitations, serves as a prevailing theory in this subfield. Yet, as argued here, incrementalism is a well-defined special case of the more general model of rational decision-making.

Lindblom (1959) distinguished an incremental model (a type of rationality dependent upon individual initiative) from others that are far more comprehensive. He criticized the difficulty in identifying and isolating a given problem, which process the rational approach idealizes without describing the means of easing the chore. Often the specific challenge cannot be isolated, Lindblom asserts. Indeed, the cause or source of the problem is even more difficult to pinpoint. Also, rational processes demand time, methods, and information. Ironically, the decision-maker has neither the time, the capacity, or the information required for this method. Finally, the rational approach unambiguously relates means and ends.

Lindblom argued that the relationship is clear only to the extent that ultimate values can be agreed upon. The usual situation is that one person's goal may be another person's means to achieving an entirely different goal.

Lindblom proposed the incremental approach to decision-making as an alternative to the rational method. Briefly, incrementalism greatly simplifies the task of making decisions. The model holds that a policy maker can consider only a limited set of policy alternatives that are incremental additions or modifications of a broader set of policies that differ only marginally. Basic policy is a given; narrow parameters confine the choice.

The model implied by incrementalism suggests specific limits: limited intelligence, limited reasoning powers, limited time, and limited information. Thus, the satisficing model of Simon (1947) can be inferred: the model (1) generally seizes on the first satisfactory alternative when deciding, rather than looking for the best; (2) rarely changes things unless they get really bad and, even then, continues to try what had worked before; (3) limits the search for alternatives to well-worn paths and traditional sources of information; and (4) remains preoccupied with routine. These notions specify cognitive limits to rationality. Consequently, the model does not optimize or maximizes, argues Simon, but does satisfice.

Lindblom's model, translated by Wildavsky (1964) permits a psychological rather than a microeconomic approach to strategic choice. Wildavsky (pp. v–vi) argued that (a) setting objectives and ascertaining resources occur together, (b) choosing the mix rests on what is known to work from at least some experience and (c) providing organizational incentives to get the objectives achieved with available resources. The degree to which parties agree to an alternative may have far greater power in decision-making than analysis in objective terms. In fact, a poor decision is often one that excludes or ignores some important decision-maker rather than one that fails in any ordinary sense (Boss, 1976, p. 108).

Lindblom argued that the incremental approach has value, and its greatest virtue is that it makes agreement possible. With incremental methods, differences in values seldom reduce the chance of agreement. Concerning themselves with only actual choice situations, decision-makers can consider values, not alone, but in light of practical constraints. Such reconsideration can prompt agreement on programs. Finally, individuals can often agree on policies or programs even if they hold conflicting values.

Much of the discussion thus far concerning decision-making suggests a model that varies from the rational/comprehensive ideal. Actually, the variance is only superficial, because as argued earlier, the two theories share the assumption of preference ordering and intent as they relate to the motives or collective endeavors of individuals. Whether alone or in groups, individuals have preferences for certain outcomes of their work. They *intend* that their effort produce something which they foresee will result directly from their behavior.

ROLE OF THE FINANCE OFFICE

Within public organizations, Wildavsky (1986) has observed the conditions that encourage the development of roles reflecting clear and divergent positions on the topic of decision-making. Classic spender-guardian roles profoundly affect government expenditure decision-making, Wildavsky has argued. However, the logic can extend further; these roles may also exist in other areas of financial management, including risk, cash, and debt management. Given conditions of scarcity, a "ubiquitous division of roles between advocates and guardians" develops in all areas of financial management (Wildavsky, 1975, p. 15). On one side, advocates in government budgeting make expansive claims on resources by using programmatic criteria to satisfy constituencies. Guardians believe that advocates have narrow biases in the preparation of budget estimates and feel a personal responsibility to serve as the watchdog of the Treasury (Schick, 1964).

Risk, cash, and debt management practices provide evidence of the same clash of priorities. First, in risk management there are advocates among those wishing greater decisiveness in policy making who risk liability suits (Hildreth and Miller, 1983); those pursuing performance goals single mindedly, such as police officers who risk property damage; and those in dangerous jobs, such as fire department personnel who risk their own lives. Moreover, in each case, some guardian exists in the person of an attorney, risk manager, or safety officer.

Second, cash management succumbs to a similar risk prone-risk averse splitting of views. Those program officers advocating greater services, as well as those arguing for use of more speculative investments of idle cash and pension funds, become the "spenders." The investment officer, often acting as the fiduciary under pension law and as a conservator of capital in the role of cash manager, acts as guardian.

Third, debt management closely resembles the budget roles as well. In the capital spending and budgeting process, advocates of more capital expenditures take aggressive, prospending roles, often advocating risky financing techniques. The finance director, who is ultimately responsible for the financing plan for the government unit, often plays the role of the guardian by opposing unusual financing plans and defending the conservation of revenues for debt service or operating-budget uses.

The roles in all four processes (budgeting, cash investment, risk management, and capital goods financing) have value. "Governments run out of money when no one plays guardian; vital operations run down when no one plays advocate" Wildavsky has argued (1975, p. 15). The tension between policy and project activism and resource conservation provides the essential "bottom up" conceptualization of countervailing forces struggling for decision not only government budgeting but also in public financial management (Mowery, Kamlet, and Crecine, 1980; Bozeman and Straussman, 1982).

TECHNOLOGY

Although traditionally viewed in terms of reactions to scarcity, the roles dictate positive action to cope with uncertainty. If an advocate is considered a risk taker and a guardian as a risk averter, the process can be observed as part of the traditional and technology based process of handling risk. Thus, as part of the process of analyzing risk and dealing with it, financial managers use one or a combination of three strategies, (a) avoidance, (b) assumption, or (c) transfer/ shifting.

First, public officials can avoid risks by simply foregoing the activities where risks occur. Second, risks can be assumed; that is, losses due to risks can be retained by the government unit. Assumption may also mean living with uncertainty and being willing to accept fate. Third, a government unit can transfer risks to a third party. In the case of risk management, the third party is usually an insurance company; in cash management, it is a futures or options contract; in debt management, an underwriter.

Perhaps the key question about risk handling in the context of roles is not whether one or the other role "wins" but when should one take precedence. When should a manager avoid risks, or assume them, or shift them to a third party?

Another way of looking at the technology of financial management, prevailing theory style, is to elaborate the various coping tactics and strategies suggested by this theory.

Tactics

Besides structural approaches to the equivocality problem, managers can pursue three sets of tactics: buffering, leveling, and forecasting (Thompson, 1967). First, managers attempt to buffer the organization from uncertainty by absorbing the necessary resources to promote continuous production. They stockpile raw materials at the front end. Personnel offices, for instance, hold files of qualified individuals for jobs. Organizations also warehouse products at the back end. The best example of warehousing was J. Edgar Hoover's legendary collection of

FBI-generated gossip about celebrities and political figures which he may have ladled out as needed to powerful individuals (Lowenthal, 1950).

Second, organizations gauge the level of their input and output to prevent overloading productive capacity. For example, each year the Internal Revenue Service offers quicker income tax refunds to those who deserve them if their returns are mailed early. Moreover, the Postal Service annually warns patrons about the Christmas rush, so that individuals will spread their mailing over a longer period of time. Often, leveling can take the form of reciprocity in organizations (Perrow, 1970), illustrated by federal budget practices that encompass almost inviolable base appropriations and fair-share division of additional increments, and presupposes reciprocity, conscious or unconscious, among competing budget actors.

Third, organizations attempt to forecast needs to avoid surprises and to anticipate peak or low-demand periods. For example, the Internal Revenue Service, despite warnings about April 15 rushes, forecasts worker demand and schedules part-time workers for data input and other assorted tasks.

Strategies

Common attempts by agencies to gain some control over the effect of constraints and contingencies in the environment involve important strategies, such as mergers, expansion of clientele, co-optation, and diversification (Thompson, 1967). First, an agency can merge functions with other agencies, ensuring a vertical or horizontal combination of activities. The grant-in-aid system illustrates a vertical merger or functions in that state and local governments, and even private organizations, "merge" with the federal agency through a financial transaction to pursue a given policy goal.

Horizontal mergers also exist. For example, the passage of laws ensuring antidiscrimination efforts in *all* federal programs, particularly through contracting and subcontracting regulations, profoundly merged the functions of federal civil rights agencies with other agencies' financing initiatives.

Second, an organization can expand its clientele. The Veterans Administration advertises to attract more beneficiaries of services, and the U.S. Department of Agriculture draws new clients, such as grocers, food distributors, and the poor, through its food stamp program.

Third, agencies can co-opt clients. The Tennessee Valley Authority absorbed local officials into its decision-making process to guarantee support and goal achievement during the 1930s and 1940s (Selznick, 1949).

Fourth, agencies can diversify. For example, the Department of Housing and Urban Development (HUD) began as the Housing and Home Finance Agency with a goal of financing new housing construction. Upon gaining cabinet status, the Secretary of HUD began pursuing the task of guiding urban development and "solving," among other things the urban fiscal problem of the 1960s. Then, in the

1970s, HUD grew even more diversified with programs to provide technical assistance to state and local governments in the financial management of the public sectors HUD had encouraged to develop.

The uncertainty may be elaborated in conceptual terms. Selecting the appropriate coping strategy derives from a knowledge of the frequency of risks and their severity. In normally understood strategy development, the greater the severity, no matter what the frequency, the more likely would an attempt be made to avoid or transfer the risk (Snider, 1964). The knowledge of frequency and severity mask the complexity of uncertainty. Coping effectively, in organization theory terms at least, depends on an ability to discern "patterned variation" (Hinings et al., 1974).

Patterned variation lies at one pole of a continuum, which reflects the vast reaches in which greater uncertainty may be found. Thus, uncertainty may be characterized as a continuum combining at least seven variables (see Figure 1).

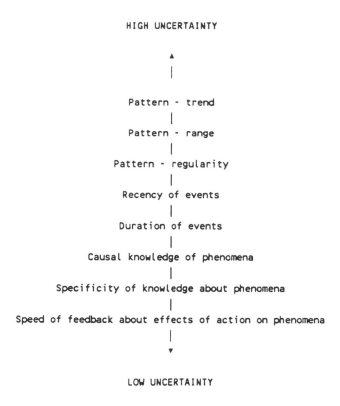

HIGH UNCERTAINTY

Pattern - trend

Pattern - range

Pattern - regularity

Recency of events

Duration of events

Causal knowledge of phenomena

Specificity of knowledge about phenomena

Speed of feedback about effects of action on phenomena

LOW UNCERTAINTY

Figure 1   Conceptual dimensions of uncertainty. Source: Hinings et al., 1974.

PREVAILING THEORY AND PROBLEMS OF
ORTHODOX THEORY

Evidence provided by Wildavsky and Barber yields answers to the orthodox approach's two problems—bifurcation of interests and uncertainty. Simply defined, bifurcation and uncertainty feed off each other; each serves to exacerbate the other's dilemma, leading to the adaptation of ends to means (rather than vice versa) and analysis that continually redefines the problem at hand.

For bifurcation to occur, there must be uncertainty.[2] Fragmentation of interests occurs as a result of the lack of agreement about causation or technology, and, lacking any agreement, the organization effort proceeds uncertainly and in doing so, creates still greater uncertainty. For example, a finance officer delegates authority for capital asset financing, for numerous reasons,[3] to an assembly of different interests; that is, a large team of experts with particular specialties.

Bifurcation arises as a method of dealing with uncertainty but creates its own uncertainty, which requires accommodation. In capital finance, a finance officer cannot state with certainty the costs of financing or the consequences for these costs of disclosure of past financial practices. The need for expertise—in the form of adding experts who can help gain more certainty—creates its own uncertainty. A certified public accountant, in light of demands of a credit-rating agency or even with regard to generally accepted accounting standards (GAAP), may view past reporting practices as deficient and may call for their change. Thus, the finance officer, in order to finance a project, changes reporting practices. The end—in this case, the interest rate the market demands based on information disclosed—is adjusted to the means, namely, improved reporting practices. All interests are "adjusted"; the accountant gets compliance with reporting standards, the finance officer gets market support for a debt issue.

Taking the Thompson and Tuden (1959) model we introduced earlier in Chapter 1, Burchell and colleagues (1980) provided some graphic detail of what might be inferred from Lindblom's "intelligent" system (see Figure 2).

Because either objectives or cause-effect relationships may have high uncertainty that is due to bifurcation of interests, Lindblom's system adjusts ends to means in a serial process. The search for ends is a matter of partisan mutual adjustment; the search for means, trial and error. Thus, as the organization "learns," certain goals are accommodated: their methods of achievement become more obvious and their value grows to a greater degree than other goals. Unlike "answer machines" that provide structured solutions to structured problems, ammunition machines provide arguments for given positions, and learning machines[4] provide assistance in strengthening the position of some arguments.

The combination provides a glimpse at "the art of the possible." Thus, if means are known (if, say, a computer and software are available), some ends are more likely to be supported (designing the accounting system to support the goal of the software rather than the goal of the organization's leaders).

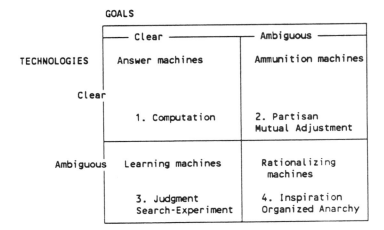

Figure 2 Organization choice theories as degrees of ambiguity. Source: Thompson and Tuden, 1959; Burchell et al., 1980.

Ammunition machines provide the fodder for partisan mutual adjustment; the results may be quite different than what the partisans envisioned. As Lindblom indicated (1965, pp. 30–31):

> Partisans emerge in mutual adjustment in the pursuit of their own perceived interests, which are not assumed to be either the same as, or harmonious in some sense with, the interests of others. As they play out their moves in partisan mutual adjustment, however, it may turn out either that what one gains another loses, that everyone gains, that everyone loses, that some gain more than others, or that some lose more than others gain. As will often be the case, a "solution" reached is to the advantage of all participants, yet the distribution of the advantages is a point of conflict in the settlement. Although the partisan is defined as one who does not assume that an adequate greed criterion is discoverable and that it should be found and applied, there will nevertheless sometimes exist such a criterion in a partisan mutual adjustment situation; and it will sometimes be found and applied as the result of the partisan moves of the participant decision makers.

Among the forms, Lindblom defined the twelve that are found in Table 1 as partisan mutual adjustment. So far, prevailing theory neatly solves the problems of orthodox theory. The bifurcation of interests springs from uncertainty reduction efforts, but it creates another source of uncertainty as an unintended consequence. This uncertainty is lessened when the trial-and-error process of learning makes it more likely that some goals can be attained than others. As a

Table 1 Methods of Partisan Mutual Adjustment

I. Adaptive (X seeks no response from Y.)

    A. *Parametic*, in which the decision maker, X, adapts to Y's decisions without regard to consequences for Y.

    B. *Deferential,* in which X seeks to avoid adverse consequences for Y.

    C. *Calculated*, in which X does not wholly avoid adverse consequences for Y but nevertheless adjusts his decision out of consideration for adverse effects for Y.

II. Manipulated (X, as a condition of making a decision, induces a response from Y.)

    A. *Negotiation*, in which X and Y, in a variety of ways, induce responses from each other.

    B. *Bargaining* (a form of negotiation), in which X and Y induce responses from each other by conditional threats and promises.

    C. *Partisan discussion* (a form of negotiation), in which X and Y induce responses from each other by effecting a reappraisal of each other's assessment of the objective consequences of various courses of action. (Where bargaining alters the consequences, partisan discussion exchanges information about unaltered consequences.)

    D. *Compensation*, in which X induces a response from Y by a conditional promise of benefit; and bargained compensation (a form of bargaining), in which X and Y make conditional promises to each other.

    E. *Reciprocity*, in which X unilaterally, or X and Y symmetrically, in negotiation or otherwise, induce a response by calling in an existing obligation or acknowledging a new one.

    F. *Authoritative prescription*, in which X prescribes a response to Y, who concedes X's authority.

    G. *Unconditional manipulation*, in which X induces a response from Y by unconditionally altering the advantages or disadvantages to Y of various responses.

    H. *Prior decision*, in which X takes a prior decision to induce Y to respond rather than forego the advantages of coordination with X.

    I. *Indirect manipulation*, in which X uses any of the above forms of manipulation to induce a third decision maker to induce Y to make the desired response.

Source: Lindblom, 1965, pp. 33–34.

result, the mutual adjustment of partisan goalseekers stems from the serial adjustment of ends and means.

PROBLEMS WITH PREVAILING THEORY

There is a great deal of disagreement over many facets of prevailing theory. These differences or controversies exist in at least three areas: the nature of ends, goals, or preferences; the limited validity of incrementalism; and the concepts not explained by prevailing theory that, as a result, create a conservative bias.

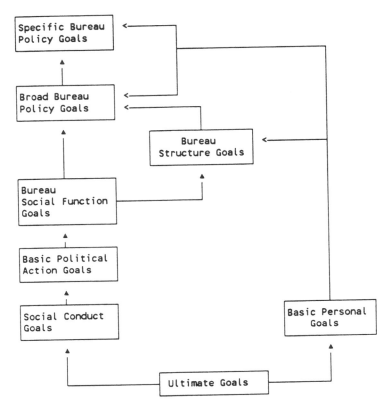

Figure 3 Layers of goals in an individual official's goal structure; deepest layer at the bottom, shallowest at the top. Source: Downs, 1967, p. 86.

The Nature of Ends, Goals, or Preferences

If orthodox theory established the ends-then-means sequence of decision-making, prevailing theory cautioned that, just as often, the sequence operated in reverse and worked to create "intelligent democracy." Nevertheless, both suggested that ends, goals, or preferences were known or knowable explicitly and that some relationship did exist between ends and means.

Much thought sides with counterviews: the no-preferences and the no-relationship positions. First, the no-preferences argument rests on a well-respected lineage of concepts. Most prominently, Barnard's theory of authority (1968), Berelson, Lazarsfeld, and McPhee's research on public opinion (1954), the subsequent development of theories of political authority and bureaucratic control

(Downs, 1957, 1967), and the public choice school's explanation of explicit and implicit logrolling (see Buchanan and Tullock, 1962, pp. 134–135) each argue that "the assumption that objectives are known, clear, and consistent is at variance with all experience" (Wildavsky, 1987, p. 215).

Wildavsky pointed out the value of breaking and keeping broken the links between policy objectives and budgets; that a common feature of such budget reforms as PPBS is their concern with ranking policy goals and assigning budgets to them (1964, pp. 220–221). Much of this effort resembles the exercise of setting goals and searching for the one best way to achieve them. Wildavsky argued that the narrow applicability of this approach to budgeting makes the use of a budgetary no-preferences strategy more appropriate:

> Thinking about objectives is one thing, however, and making budget categories out of them is quite another. Of course, if one wants the objectives of today to be the objectives of tomorrow, if one wants no change in objectives, then building the budget around objectives is a brilliant idea. But if one wants flexibility in objectives (sometimes known as learning from experience), it must be possible to change them without simultaneously destroying the organization. . . . Because it is neutral in regard to policy, traditional budgeting is compatible with a variety of policies, all of which can be converted into [organizational terms].

Budgets without policies attached represent a no-preferences position, one inherently more flexible for situations of flux.

The no-relationships position is somewhat more complex. Consider two approaches, one that rests on some concept of rational action, the other that is imputed to a situation. First, rational allocation of attention among a variety of interests or problems depends on the opportunity costs of alternative choices. Downs' layers of goals (1967, p 86) illustrates how an individual official's goal structure allows for competing foci for attention (see Figure 3). Over a range of officials in a bureau, with each official having a similar set of choices, the individuals who will make *the* decision about a specific bureau policy goal will be

> over disproportionably [sic] those who have nothing better to do. The problems that end up being attached to the choice are disproportionately problems that have no better place to go. The solutions that end up being appropriate for the problems are disproportionately solutions that have no other problems to solve (March and Olsen, 1986, p. 47).

The solution is not a lack of structure as orthodox theory would prescribe. We have very little idea of who is a partisan for what; therefore, the solution is not to be found in a partisan mutual adjustment process because prevailing theory would suggest either one.

Second, if even the smallest of assumptions is made about the use of such scarce resources as time or attention, little relationship can be shown between ends and means over a population of bureau officials. Long (1958) and the ecology of games model give some flavor of what takes place:

> A particular highway grid may be the result of bureaucratic department of public works game in which are combined, though separate, a professional highway engineer game with its purposes and critical elite onlookers; a departmental bureaucracy; a set of contending politicians seeking to use the highways for political capital, patronage, and the like; a banking game concerned with bonds, taxes and the effect of the highways on real estate; newspapermen interested in headlines, scoops, and the effect of highways on the papers' circulation; contractors eager to make money by building roads; ecclesiastics concerned with the effect of highways on their parishes and on the fortunes of the contractors who support their churchly ambitions; labor leaders interested in union contracts and their status as community influentials with a right to be consulted; and civic leaders who must justify the contributions of their bureaus of municipal research or chambers of commerce to the social activity.

Each game includes a different choice, and the sum of the choices is the highway grid. Imputing a relationship between end and means would be simplistic. However, trying to understand the highway grid as an instance of partisan mutual adjustment would understate the grid's complexity as well, for there is no single decision in which all partisans mutually adjust their ends to means.

Validity of Prevailing Theory

The major problem with incrementalism lies in its validity. Can trial-and-error processing lead to small incremental changes occurring anywhere? Generally, Dror (1964) has led the opposition. He argued that prevailing theory lends explanatory power to decisions made in government *only* when there is general satisfaction with existing policies, continuity in the nature of problems, and continuity among available means. He stated that

> the three conditions essential to the validity of the "muddling through" thesis are most likely to prevail where there is a high degree of social stability. Under conditions of stability, routine is often the best policy, and, change being at a slow rate, incremental policy change is often optimal. But even in the most stable societies, many of today's qualitatively most important problems are tied up with high speed changes in levels of aspiration, the nature of issues, and the available means of action, and require therefore a policy making method different from "muddling through" . . . Lindblom . . . does not realize that there is no country, including the United States, stable enough to fit his analysis. (p. 154)

In addition, Dror criticized the inertia inherent in prevailing theory, especially when contrasted with orthodox theory; orthodox theory stimulates budgeteers to get out of established routines, but prevailing theory justifies making no effort at all.

More specifically, whether there is an increment even in places of social stability concerns others. These arguments deal with the Davis, Dempster, and Wildavsky (1966) findings, the related findings of Crecine (1967, 1969), Fenno (1966), and Sharkansky (1968), and the inferences drawn from them. For example, Wanat (1974), most prominently, has shown that high statistical correlations could be derived from data that "were generated that fitted the constraints [prevailing theory] but which varied randomly within those constraints (p. 1222). The regularity with which the incremental changes that actually occurred in real appropriations and budget request data Wanat found to be explained by other nonstrategic variables,[5] from which can be inferred that Davis, Dempster, and Wildavsky's mechanics do not necessarily hold. Specifically, changes in appropriations resulted from far more independent determinants and less from strategic choice: changes in population, economic activity, and social circumstances, for instance.

Does an incrementalist strategy necessarily follow from evidence of incremental outcomes? Look at alternative explanations. First, remember that, implicitly, incrementalism (or any decision-making model, for that matter) assumes that budget participants have control over the budget. If they wanted to do so, they could spend in radically different ways and depart from traditional choices. Yet, participants have only limited control over budget authority or outlays, or decision alternatives, in the larger realm.[6]

Incompleteness of Prevailing Theory

In conclusion, prevailing theory fails to come to terms with phenomena that lie at the basis of financial management. For example, how does prevailing theory comprehend disagreements over objectives or methods of achieving them? As we have seen, substantial differences exist over the government's role in society: many financial theorists subscribe to the positive government approach, many to the privatization approach. Because they are so radically different, how can we expect prevailing theory's intelligent adjustment to work in the ways in which it is expected when such radically different approaches threaten stability? Otherwise, prevailing theory fails to come to grips with determinant effects of such things as changes in population, economic and social circumstances that substantially diminish strategic choice. Since prevailing theory depends for its power on the expression of interest, knowledge of these determinants is presumed as the basis for the interest in the first place. These determinants, however, are unpredictable, creating for prevailing theory a problem of surprising oversight. How can persons know their own interests when the bases for them are uncertain and highly unstable?

Prevailing theory's value lies at the managerial or tactical level of organization life. Managers may state within limits the interests that may depend on relatively stable determinants. The manager's scope in financial matters is sufficiently limited that certainty is not the prime requirement for predictability. Thus, prevailing theory may describe the way managers think and act. It fails, however, to describe how the financial management system (the institutional level of organization life) functions as a whole.

With the limits to both orthodox and prevailing theory, there is a significant lack of theory to explain the system and its functioning. Through orthodox theory, the level of technical prowess financial managers can develop. At the managerial level, prevailing theory provides similar detail on tactical considerations. However, the strategic, institutional, or system level lacks a basis on which to explain the relationships among values, behavior, and change. For this basis, as well as a way to link the technical, managerial, and institutional levels of financial management, an alternative body of theory will be treated in the next chapter.

NOTES

1. The argument in this section closely follows that in Miller (1984a,b).
2. The train of thought goes something like this: the top managers demand greater control to increase reliability of behavior (Merton, 1940), implying uncertainty to begin with. Demand for control leads to increased delegation of authority—subordinates are held responsible for acts which they have authority to act, in turn leading to departmentalization and bifurcation of interests (Selznick, 1949). According to March and Simon (1958, p. 41), "the maintenance needs of the [organization] subunits dictate a commitment to subunit goals over and above their contribution to the total organizational program."
3. Basically because the financing requires more reasoning power and insight than could be programmed in a computer.
4. An example of "learning machines" is that produced by Wildavsky (1987, pp. 212–232). The self-evaluating organization is one in which there exists rival teams of organization policy evaluators:

> A rough equivalent of a competitive market can be introduced by letting teams of evaluators compete for direction of policy in an area. the competition would take place in price (a specified objective accomplished at a lower cost), quality (better policies for the same money), quantity (more produced at the same cost), maintenance (we can fix things when they go wrong), experience (see our proven record), values (our policies will embody your preferences) and talent (when it comes down to it, you are buying our cleverness and we are superior). The winning team would be placed in charge until it left to go elsewhere or was successfully challenged by another team. The government might raise its price to keep a talented team or it might lower it to get rid of an incompetent one. The incentives for evaluators would be enormous—restrained, of course, by ability to perform lest they go bankrupt or lose business to competitors. . . . [Leaders of self-evaluating organizations] must select organization activities,

not only with an eye toward their analytic justification, but with a view toward receiving essential support. Hence they become selective evaluators. They must prohibit the massive use of organizational resources where they see little chance of success. They must seek out problems that are easy to solve, and changes that are easy to make, because they do not involve radical departures from the past. They must be prepared to hold back the results of evaluation if the times are not propitious; they must be ready to seize the p roper time for change whether or not evaluations are fully prepared or wholly justified. Little by little, it seems, the behavior of the leaders will become similar to that of officials of other organizations who seek also to adapt to their environment. . . . The self-evaluating organization would be well advised not to depend too much on a single type of clientele. Diversification is its strategy. the more diverse its services, the more varied its clientele, the less self-evaluating organization has to depend on any one of them, the more able it is to shift the basis of its support. Diversity creates political flexibility.

5. Wanat (1974) suggested that as constraints are relaxed, variation in appropriations nears randomness, throwing doubt on the strategically incremental nature of agency requests and Congressional action (cf. pp. 1221–1228).

The mandated increases in budgets alone allow explanation of the incrementalism that has characterized much of budgetary phenomenon. . . . What typically happens is that the agency's request is somewhat larger than it was in the previous year because some increase is mandated by such forces as wage increases, inflation, and growth of entitlements and also because the agency seeks to expand or enrich its programs. Thus, it is obvious why an agency's request for a given year exceeds its previous year's appropriation. The legislature is aware of the mandatory nature of some of the agencies' requests and knows that those increases must be honored if faith is to be kept with the clientele of the agency. At the same time the legislature knows it can cut the requests for the new Programs, and it usually does that to some degree. Consequently, because it allows the mandatory requests to pass practically untouched, each year's appropriation usually surpasses its predecessor. But since the programmatic portion of the increase is usually reduced, the appropriation is less than the request. Finally, because the mandated increases were caused by demographic changes or economic changes, both of which are generally marginal from one year to the next, and because revenue changes are not radical from one year to the next, all of the inequalities express slight or incremental change (Wanat, 1978, p. 125).

6. See Chapter 6 for a discussion of this point.

5

Alternative Theory

Despite repeated instances in which financial reforms have failed to provide the results reformers expected, most current efforts at change do not reflect any of the wisdom the failures impart. New reforms, including those in financial strategy (Hildreth, 1989; Wetzler and Petersen, 1985),[1] fail to consider the contradictory beliefs of members of coalitions that brought about reforms (cf. Chapter 2) or the nature of the organization belief systems in which reforms were to take root, which is the subject of this chapter.

Both orthodox and prevailing theories have dealt with unique variations of rationality. I extend this notion to the point of viewing belief systems as a range of different rationalities and describe and set norms for choice for each of them. This argument joins with recent work by other researchers in describing organization structures and decision models, finance office roles, and technologies to provide a new direction for financial-management theory. No longer content with the prevailing notion that organization complexity stems from conflicting, but known, interests, present-day researchers have developed a body of thought large enough to hold not only orthodox and prevailing views but other variants as well.

As a larger view than either the orthodox or the prevailing ones, alternative theory provides a full blown answer to problems inherent in ambiguity. These problems are those that relate to choice under conditions in which there are no consistent shared goals; in which unclear technology marks how work is done; and in which the fluid participation of members bedevils leaders.

In defining such a condition, Cohen and March (1986; 1974) labeled it an "organized anarchy" and used the American university as a prototype, which they claim "does not know what it is doing. Its goals are either vague or in dispute. Its technology is familiar but not understood. Its major participants wander in and out of the organization" (1974, p. 3). They go on to point out that these factors do not make a university a bad organization or a disorganized one; "but they do make it a problem to . . . lead."

The new view implicitly categorizes the degree of ambiguity in the organization and among its members, a variation that directly bears on the ability of any leader to provide direction and meaning. As contexts differ, the view holds that interpretations of environment data differ as well, making judgments about what are difficulties for organizations and what are opportunities extremely variable. Furthermore, ambiguity affords (even necessitates) a special role for structures, which focus attention, and for myths, symbols, and rituals, which enable members of the organization to cultivate a meaningful attachment to what they do, to the institution through which they do it, and to each other.

As a result, financial managers have special responsibilities in the management of choice. Theirs is the job of interpreting financial data—organization financial problems and financial contingencies outside the organization—and justifying courses of action that are legitimate in metaphorical terms as well as rational and predictable in the context in which the organization operates.

The upshot of it all is that there are alternative rationalities that suggest organization theories, choice strategies, roles, and technologies different from those in either orthodox or prevailing theory. To give some indication of the thinking encompassed in alternative rationalities, consider the three major alternatives to the conventional rationality presented in orthodox and prevailing thought (March, 1978).

First of all, *contextual rationality* is an alternative that refers to the tendency of people, problems, solutions, and choices to be joined by relatively arbitrary accidents of timing rather than by their relevance to each other (Long, 1958).

Another alternative, *process rationality*, suggests that explicit outcomes are secondary. Decision-making has real meaning only through the intelligent way it is orchestrated (Edelman, 1988; Cohen and March, 1974).

Third, *posterior rationality* juxtaposes preferences and action. Action-creating experiences form meaning, and, in a real sense, preferences, after the fact (Hirschman, 1967; Weick, 1969).

These three "other" rationalities[2] form a group of alternatives to both orthodox and prevailing theory but which together with them forms "ambiguity theory." This larger whole is the alternative financial management theory.

In this chapter, I explore ambiguity theory by employing the same framework used to describe orthodox and prevailing theories. Once again, the model covers organization theory, decision models, the role of the finance office, and technology. Next, I look at the ability of ambiguity theory to solve basic problems that are confronted by orthodox and prevailing theory. Finally, I present the research design that is followed in later chapters.

CONCEPTS

In this section,[3] I describe the theory of organizations which ambiguity theory suggests, the decision-making model inherent in the theory, the role of the finance office, and the technology the theory prescribes as appropriate for the tasks performed.

Organization Theory

Ambiguity theory views organizations as superimposed structures (Weick, 1979, p. 11). This position develops from the fact that individuals perceive what goes on among themselves as equivocal and act to bring order by structuring their relationships (Daft and Weick, 1984). What results is not an organizational life based on some set of preconceived relationships that are created to achieve an ordained goal; this ordering is based on a reality discovered after the fact. Putting it simply, an organization theory under conditions of ambiguity is *posterior rationality*.

The emergent nature of reality under these conditions is a bottom-up phenomenon. The ordering that arises in organizations comes of cycles of interaction among individuals. Contingent response patterns or double interact cycles emerge when action taken by actor A evokes a response in act B which is then responded to by actor A (Weick, 1979, pp. 89–118).

Stable organizations come into being through the emerging linkage of many double interacts. The architecture of complexity (Simon, 1962) builds from the bottom-up notion that organizations have greater likelihood of flexible response to contingencies when subassemblies (double interact cycles) are stable and when their linkages are flexible or not tightly and irrevocably linked. In fact, his "empty world" hypothesis notes that high interaction within and among small sub-organization systems has greater prevalence than the interactions among larger subsystems or large systems.

The term *loosely coupled systems* denotes these stable subassemblies and their frequency of interaction with all other subassemblies. Following an early use of the term in the literature (Glassman, 1973), Weick (1976, pp. 3–9) used the term to convey the image that while coupled organizations or units of an organization are responsive to each other, each also preserved its own identity and some evidence of its physical or logical separateness. He illustrated this by arguing that in an educational organization, the counselor's office is loosely coupled to the principal's office:

> The image is that the principal and the counselor are somehow attached, but that each retains some identity and separateness and that their attachment may

be circumscribed, infrequent, weak in its mutual affects, unimportant, and/or slow to respond. (p. 3)

The example might be taken further with the reform-minded city government organization (Petersen, Watt, and Zorn, 1986). With a city manager at the helm, this type of organization would usually place a budget office in the Office of the City Manager with instructions to frame overall operating budget policy from year to year. Yet the Chief Finance Officer would ordinarily have equal status but would also have a genuine staff position as opposed to the budget officer's position within the Office of the City Manager. Likewise, comptroller functions might be separated from treasury functions by establishing separate staff departments, depending upon the degree of fiscal checks and balances the procedures demanded. In either case, there is attachment but considerably different roles and technologies.

The description of loose coupling resembles only partially our previous discussion of bifurcation of interests. Loose coupling is meant as the larger concept of which bifurcation or interests in organizations is one part. In the larger scheme, consider loose coupling as a description of the relationships that exist within five aspects of financial management. First, in revenue administration, intention is loosely coupled with action. For example, when Congress passed the oil windfall tax during the Carter administration, it was meant to prevent oil companies from reaping windfall profits from the decontrol of the price of oil; the effect, however, was an excise tax that dampened the consumption of oil products.

Second, in cash management, effort is only loosely coupled with reward. Normally, markets dictate that a direct relationship exists between the risk of an investment and its return; however, in public sector organizations, risk is to be avoided in any case, including return.

Third, debt management loosely couples knowledge with action. For example, competitive bidding for municipal bond issues minimizes the amount of knowledge required over and above basic categorical accounting data that are provided in disclosure statements. Negotiated municipal bond issues, based on the idea that the more the buyer knows about the seller, the more accurate the price of the issue, are thought to be profligate.

Fourth, budgets couple those who have information with those who make decisions very loosely. The bottom-up budget request process would usually yield timely and precise estimates of budget need; however, top decision-makers may choose to ignore these sources of information to make macrobudgetary decisions.

Finally, categorization in accounting may be loosely coupled with control. Creating accounts and tending them closely coincides with the need for focused attention and careful scrutiny ordinarily demanded of an accounting system. However, by the very act of creating accounts, the categorization may not anticipate events that occur later to jeopardize control.

In each case of loose coupling in financial management, a method must be sought to exploit the benefits of loose coupling. Of necessity, the concepts that are loosely coupled would, if tightly joined, lead inevitably to rigid reactions to unfolding events.

Weick argued the overwhelming advantage of looseness. First, loose coupling allows some portion of organizations to persist. Second, it may provide a sensitive sensing mechanism. Third, it may be a good system for localized adaptation. Fourth, in loosely coupled systems where the identity, uniqueness, and separateness of elements is preserved, the system potentially can retain a greater number of mutations and novel solutions than would be the case with a tightly coupled system. Fifth, if there is a breakdown in one portion of a loosely coupled system, this breakdown may be sealed off to avoid or lessen the breakdown's effect on other portions of the organization. Sixth, there is more room available for self-determination by the actors. And seventh, a loosely coupled system should be relatively inexpensive to run because it takes less time and money to coordinate people.

Loose Coupling and Independent Streams

Although loose coupling preserves the idea of free will in the management of organizations (I interact with another to achieve a purpose through it), aggregations of these subassemblies resemble randomness. Whether interaction or coupling occurs at all is a matter of recognizing the possibility of constraints or contingencies, a matter of interpretation in light of "nature of the answer sought, the characteristics of the environment, the previous experience of the questioner, and the method used to acquire it" (Daft and Weick, 1984, p. 284).

Interpretation is far more contextual than is suggested by synopticism's approach in finding the one best way. Ambiguity theory argues that there is no such thing as a right answer; rather, answers are achieved through the random interaction of variables that form an interpretation (Daft and Weick, 1984), as well as the random interaction of choice opportunities and people who want to make choices (Cohen, March, and Olsen, 1972).

Randomness dictates the importance of structure, personnel, and, to a much lesser extent, timing (Padgett, 1980). Since people, solutions, choices, and problems flow independently in a continual stream, context dictates which will interact with what—what the perceived issue will be and what information, broadly speaking, will be brought to bear—to produce a decision.

The management of loosely coupled systems or organized anarchies (March and Olsen, 1976) is primarily a matter of structure and people. Using a U. S. Housing and Urban Development budget simulation, Padgett (1980) has argued that less prescription of behavior or low structure has the effect of moving attention from old programs with long histories to highly salient new programs with no history at all, because the more an analyst knows the less information influences interpretations. Add to this the policy of putting inexperienced analysts with new programs and experienced analysts with old programs and the effect increases.

Low structure and inexperience also have the effect of creating more differences or conflict. The less settled the issues or modes of interpretation, the more these differences may exist. In turn, these differences or conflicts require movement of issues up the hierarchy for resolution, creating the need for coordination that only a head, with standard operating procedures and policies, can provide.

In summary, with ambiguity theory the view of an organization can make virtuous what synopticism and incrementalism view as vices. Loose coupling results in the coordination that could never be achieved by principled hierarchy's central control and standardization. Managing and creating are examples of *nonlinear* thinking with the imperative to view phenomena in ways that are opposite in synopticism and incrementalism. The imperative succeeds in putting the natural tendencies of individuals to creative use by placing individuals in contexts where we would normally not think them appropriate.

Decision-Making Model

In an organized anarchy, a decision is an outcome (or an interpretation) of several relatively independent "streams" within an organization (Cohen and March, 1986, p. 81). Thus, a decision is a product of *contextual rationality* or the tendency of people, problems, solutions, and choices to be joined by relatively arbitrary accidents of timing rather than by their relevance to each other.

The accidents of timing emerge as "interpretations." There is no such thing as a right answer; answers are achieved through the random interaction of variables that form an interpretation (Daft and Weick, 1984), as well as the random interaction of choice opportunities and people who want to make choices (Cohen et al., 1972), as already argued.

Interpretations are borne out of metaphors that are carried around in the minds of leaders. Cohen and March (1986) studied university governance and found seven possible metaphors that are imposed on the organization by the work of university presidents. These metaphors are adapted to government organizations and are listed in Table 1.

Each metaphor carries with it a reasonably independent method of management and resource allocation for decision-making. For example, the anarchy metaphor provides that the leader be the catalyst who brings together independent streams of only partially interested parties in choice situations that make use of superior information. The university president "gains . . . influence by understanding the operation of the system and by inventing viable solutions that accomplish . . . objectives rather than by choosing among conflicting alternatives" (Cohen and March, 1974, p. 39).

Table 1   Metaphors of Governance

1. Competitive market metaphor. Government organizations provide a bundle of goods and services in a free market. All needing these goods and services select among alternative providers and chose those which come closest to serving perceived needs.
2. Collective bargaining metaphor. Assuming fundamentally conflicting interests within the organization, citizens, managers, politicians, and other interested parties resolve conflicts by resorting to bargaining, often through representatives, using formal "contracts" and social pressure for enforcement.
3. Democratic metaphor. The organization can be viewed as a community with an electorate of organization members and clients. Major decisions are made by resorting to voting, and votes are swayed by promises of one sort or another.
4. Consensus metaphor. To achieve agreement, organization members resort to some procedure, including discourse and assembly, which have typically relied on those with high interest and large amounts of time for involvement and participation. Unanimity is possible because of the relative lack of both interest and time among organization members.
5. Independent judiciary metaphor. Authority is bestowed by some relatively arbitrary process—birth, co-optation, revelation—on a group of current leaders. This method assumes that "there are substantial conflicts between the immediate self-interests of current constituencies and the long-run interests of future constituencies" (p. 84). It is possible to train a judge to recognize the long run interests and to convince constituencies to accept judgments made in this way.
6. Plebiscitary autocracy metaphor. An autocrat makes all decisions on behalf of the organization until such time as a plebiscite is called for to ratify the autocrat's performance. The autocrat serves with the overwhelming approval of the electorate or abdicates. Decisions to be made are technically complicated relative to the amount of time and knowledge available to organization members, and the variance of objectives among participants is so small that small amounts of time and interaction may make up for it.
7. Anarchy metaphor. The organization's members make autonomous decisions. Resources are allocated by whatever process emerges but without explicit accommodation and with explicit reference to some superordinate goal. Decisions produced in the organization are a consequence produced by the system but intended by no one and decisively controlled by no one. The statistical properties of a large number of these autonomous decisions are such that they will reliably produce jointly satisfactory states.

Source: Cohen and March, 1986, pp. 81–84.

Subtle adjustments in the form of managing unobtrusively, giving more time, exchanging status for substance, facilitating opposition participation, overloading the system, and providing many opportunities in which problems, participants, solutions, and choice situations come together, work to the catalyst's interest in making choices (Cohen and March, 1974, pp. 209–211).

According to Cohen and March (1986), organizations vary in the metaphor-ical requirements they have. In most regards, variance is a matter of the amount of attention the organization members can a give a choice situation as well as the flow of problems and solutions. The patterns underlying the apt application of a metaphor might be a matter of how independent, exogenous, and rapid the flow of the streams of problems, solutions, participants, and choice opportunities might be.

The application to financial management's unique problems follows these premises. Budgets represent simultaneous flows of information through various choice structures. Picture an ecology of games as an appropriate way to suggest the various interpretations involved (Long, 1958). My problem, for example, may be another's solution. Many solutions, indicated by the number and type of participants on a given day, swamp the number of problems. Moreover, the number of choice opportunities, the times in which a formal decision should be rendered, may vary from time to time.

> A particular highway grid may be the result of a bureaucratic department of public works game in which are combined, though separate, a professional highway engineer game with its purposes and crucial elite onlookers; a departmental bureaucracy; a set of contending politicians seeking to use the highways for political capital, patronage, and the like; a banking game concerned with bonds, taxes and the effect on the highways on real estate; newspapermen interested in headlines, scoops, and the effect of highways on the papers' circulation; contractors eager to make money by building roads; ecclesiastics concerned with the effect of highways on their parishes and on the fortunes of the contractors who support their churchly ambitions; labor leaders interested in union contracts and their status as community influentials with a right to be consulted; and civic leaders who must justify the contributions of their bureaus of municipal research or chambers of commerce to the social activity. (Long, 1958, p. 58)

March and Olsen's model illustrates two points that need to be kept in mind when discussing alternative theory. The first is the contextual nature of decisions and, especially, the role of timing in decision results. A decision is not made in the abstract but in the context of real people interpreting the events on a given day and determining an outcome with the information they have at the time and the metaphor they used to define the problem and to structure the problem-solving process.

The second idea relates to the role of institutions (Kaufman, 1960; Selznick, 1957). Permanent procedures and organizations make the randomness associated with contextual decision-making a little easier to understand. Institutions provide stability where none may otherwise exist. Institutions also epitomize enduring values and attachments that members recall as they make decisions. With these values, and the procedures that go with them, institutions act as homogenizing influences, thus helping to gain conformity in an otherwise fragmented system of attachments and work.

Role of the Finance Office

The role that financial managers embrace is based on the question of organizational culture but is a form of *calculated rationality* that I call a *serial logic strategy* (Miller, 1989). According to ambiguity theory, as dominant subcultures differ, so do the roles that are played by administrative actors, such as finance officers (Maynard-Moody, Stull, and Mitchell, 1986). Only at the highest level of generality is there a description of the work of the finance office in a public organization that is commonly shared by organizations.

Cultures depend on values, and values dictate what is considered important and what norms must be observed in carrying out the goals of the public organization. However, values come from different places. The law plays an important role in determining what a public financial manager must pay attention to as well as the nature of that attention. The context itself, the institutional values as developed through the backgrounds, the socialization, and the shared experiences of members, is also an important source (Golembiewski, 1989; Berger and Luckman, 1966).

In this section, the sources of these values are explored. I try to establish the constants and variables among values as a method of contrasting this contextual approach in alternative theory with the roles for finance officers that are suggested by orthodox and prevailing theory.

Orthodox and prevailing theory models cannot cope with the ethical values that public sector managers must obey, particularly those from liability law. In fact, liability law prescribes a fiduciary role for public managers, a role that seems to prevent the use of devices that tend to capitalize on opportunism, which is the antithesis of the fiduciary role.

In addition, existing models cannot be reconciled with managers' preferences for strategies. Typically, managers conform to a strict constitutional interpretation of their role, holding a conservative view of the tools available to them in their jobs, a narrow view of the tools' appropriate uses, and a sophisticated but realistic view of the determining factors, over and above their choices of policies (Miller et al., 1987).

Finally, the view of existing models differ from the view that is held by public managers. With existing models, there is a tendency to equate risk with a return on investment, the two strategies varying directly, risk being an opportunity that defines gain when exploited. Public administration theory derives ethical connotation of the meaning of risk such that risk-taking violates the fiduciary role (Lovrich, 1981).

Agency-level and individual-level research is generally in agreement with the serial logic proposition; that is, a deliberately realized strategy, in either linear or nonlinear forms, is a fundamental starting point for view of action. Yet strategies emerge from this starting point that are determined by ecological and cultural factors which are sometimes evanescent but often embedded in the fabric of collective effort.

The values that seem to underlie synoptic (or hierarchical) cultures as well as pluralistic ones (see Fischer, 1980) do not necessarily underlie all cultures. In fact, one view of culture looks quite different: "a nonrational concept stemming from the informal values, traditions, and norms of behavior held by the firm's managers and employees" (Greiner, 1983, p. 13).

Greiner would likely agree with Burgelman (1983) that concrete financial plans (to take one example) are not the forward looking clarion calls for action and achievement that the finance office develops through analysis but are "the more or less explicit articulation of the [organization's] theory about its past concrete achievements" (p. 66).If anything, plans are *not* a created focus for action, in a sense, a place to go or a direction from which to move; the financial officer's role is not that of the analyst, the scout, or the bugler.

A more useful view lies in seeing planning as an internal communications device (Waterman, 1987). As such, a plan has very little importance except for the information the process reveals, as individuals talk and negotiate, opening up new vistas and hopefully showing potential crises or opportunities that are looming for the organization and its members. The role of the finance office may lie in its careful attention to the processes that enable communication and marshal competence, content and relevance.

The finance officer's most important role may be that of timing: helping focus attention on truly relevant issues at just the right time to gain the power to interpret events important to the organization.

In another way, financial plans, and the role of the financial manager in formulating and implementing them, become an emerging manifestation of basic agreements among people in a work organization—agreements that may never be recognized as such. These agreements arise through simple interactions, like conversations or even meetings in which each person confirms whether or not the meaning attached to objects and processes is similar enough to that of others to get through work relations appropriately (Gregory, 1983, p. 364).

The manifestation of basic agreements appears in a number of symbolic ways, including financial procedures, financial programs, and budgets, all of which are routinized and categorized as shared experiences in working together. Again, they appear to be deeply embedded in organization life and serve as manifestation of culture. Thus, according to Weick (1985) "culture can substitute for plans more effectively than plans can substitute for culture" (p. 383).

Technology

So far, I have described public financial management as loosely coupled with other elements of the organization as well as loosely coupled with other elements of financial management. I have also described decision-making as the role of the finance office, and the output of the finance office as the interpretation of randomly associated ends and means. I described the source of interpretations as a set of values that create the fiduciary role for financial managers.

As a result, the argument follows that with only ambiguity in both organization and decision-making with which to contend, finance officers apply their fiduciary values to their own work as well as to larger organization issues. These are usually referred to as strategic technologies. This section identifies and tentatively describes these technologies.[4]

As ambiguous as government organization phenomena appear to be, finance is forced into competition over reinterpretation of these phenomena to achieve a consensus over means and ends; thus, technology reflects a *process rationality*. As I related earlier, process rationality refers to "the ways we act while making decisions, and in the symbolic content of the idea and procedures of choice" (March, 1978, p. 592). The components and framework for the process-rationality approach build on work interpretivism, as Carter (1985) uses the term in the context of constitutional lawmaking.

A fundamental metaphor is derived by those with common fiduciary values. *Categorization* of types of expenditures into accounts and transactions becomes the metaphor, essentially the work of accounting and management information systems. The metaphor represents the *language* that all concerned agree to use for descriptive words and definitions. The metaphor and language are given life through a set of *rituals* in which the various concerned actors amplify and subtly apply the language in new contexts. Moreover, these rituals are supplemented by day-to-day processes of interpretation, such as management information systems, which must be self-correcting systems closely resembling a *cybernetic process*. Two of the methods of self-correction lie in the *networks* (the range of interpretations of the rules) that form the sources of comparison and information and in the process of *forecasting* (the degree of divergence from conditions foreseen in the rules). Therefore, the technology of financial management, as ambiguity theory suggests, involves the use of those methods that derive from the creation of meaning. At the bottom, there lies a metaphor around which emerges a language that is developed and guarded by the networks. Through rituals the language unfolds and, when it is successful, creates an interpretive system that is cybernetic because it is internally and logically consistent and, thus, self-correcting.

Alternative Theory and the Solution of Orthodox and Prevailing Theory Problems

The comparison of the three theories is now focused on the comparative handling of two problems: the bifurcation of interests and uncertainty. First, the bifurcation of interests problem comes about as an unforeseen problem of orthodox theory, that more than one preference could exist in an organization despite rule or force. Differentiation in organizations relates directly to size, and orthodox theory, whereas dealing with differentiation, does not predict differentiation as a consequence of organization growth.[5]

Prevailing theory solved the bifurcation of interests problem through *game rationality*. Game rationality refers to multiple interests that are reconciled, often through partisan mutual adjustment, or coalition formation, sequential attention to goals, or the development of mutual interests, *without* necessarily a change in any one of these various interests.

Yet the idea has remained that known preferences fueled the action in organization. Preferences are properties of individuals, and the bifurcation that occurs through organization growth may be reconciled or amalgamated, so prevailing theory has argued.

In addition to a known preferences condition, ambiguity theory posits an unknown preferences condition. Ambiguity theory, therefore, foresees not only those conditions that are foreseen by orthodox and prevailing theory but also those necessary to describe the full scale of variation.

The second unforeseen problem in orthodox theory is an assumption of certainty. Certainty is a special case of organization environment and technology, the other and dominant cases being risk and uncertainty. Although size is a controlling force over diversity inside the organization, diverse elements of the environment and diverse technologies also tend to be forces also creating uncertainty. With orthodox theory, neither various different and conflicting forces such as other organizations, nor time, in the form of technological development, has some sway over an organization.

With prevailing theory, the problem of uncertainty is solved through limited rationality. Through such methods as simple search rules, incrementalism, and organization slack, uncertainty, according to prevailing theory could be controlled.

Ambiguity theory, in contrast, centers attention on uncertainty. Theory is built on the various shades of uncertainty—more and more or less and less rather than on a special case.

The comparison of orthodox, prevailing, and alternative theories tends to be based on the notion that it should be comprehensive in its coverage of the phenomena that are depicted. By this measure orthodox theory is least comprehensive, and alternative theory is the most and prevailing theory somewhere in the middle.

Another method of comparing the theories—especially the more comprehensive alternative and prevailing theories—is the parsimony and plausibility each brings to the explanation of the same phenomena. The first competition exists to explain how innovation occurs. Prevailing theory tends toward a clash of preferences in which competition produces the fittest survivor (selected rationality), the most powerful survivor (game rationality), the first satisfactory alternative to the present course (limited rationality), or the most experienced course of action (adaptive rationality). The key to understanding innovation is the size of the competition; the more entrants and the larger the contest, the better. The risk facing innovation is a one competitor condition.

Having postulated a no-preferences assumption, ambiguity theory explains innovation in terms of "the apparent tendency for people, problems, solutions, and choices to be joined by the relative arbitrary accidents of their simultaneity rather than by the *prima facie* relevance to one another" (March, 1978, p. 592). Since ends and means operate in independent streams, the fact that we even see something we desire and something that will fulfill that desire at the same time is convoluted (contextual reality). The former does not lead to the latter; in fact, seeing the latter may make the former come into focus (posterior rationality). Even more, since preferences may not exist, the *process* of decision-making may be an end in itself (process rationality), providing as it does continuity, attachment, and purpose.

With ambiguity theory, it is possible to explain innovations as a fortuitous mating of ideas. Fortuity depends on having a multitude of items in the stream as well as artistry in "seeing" the patterns develop as one looks back.

The major difference with prevailing theory is ambiguity theory's parsimony. In effect, no idea ever loses a struggle as would be the case with prevailing theory. Every idea is recycled through the process of random, fortuitous mating of ideas in the stream.

RESEARCH IN AMBIGUITY THEORY: THE RESEARCH DESIGN OF THE BOOK

As we related earlier, process rationality refers to "the ways we act while making decisions, and in the symbolic content of the idea and procedures of choice" (March, 1978, p. 592). The components and framework for the process rationality approach build on Carter's work in interpretivism (1985) and forms the model which we investigate in the remaining chapters of this book.

Recall that Carter's model included a fundamental metaphor derived by those with common fiducial values through *categorization*. The metaphor represents *language* (words and definitions) that all concerned agree to use. The metaphor and the language are given life through a set of *rituals*, especially investiture rituals, in which actors signal new uses for old words and procedures in existing contexts. Moreover, these rituals help form self-correcting systems of interpretation. Two other methods of self-correction lie in the *networks* (the range of interpretations of the rules) which form the sources of comparison and information and in the process of *forecasting* (the degree of divergence from conditions foreseen in the rules).

Therefore, ambiguity theory involves the creation of meaning. At bottom, there lies a metaphor from which emerges a language developed and guarded by networks. The language unfolds through rituals and helps create and develop an interpretive system that is logical and self-correcting.

Categorization

The shared meanings or understanding that grow to embed the "organization's way of doing things" in the minds of members usually arise from a metaphor that governs thinking in basic and subtle ways. For finance officers, this basic metaphor is a set of categories in which all financial transactions fit by definition. These categories represent definitions about priority ("the funds were available" for this but not for other things), timing (this expenditure falls into this fiscal year and not in that one), and agency (this expenditure is charged to this account and not to that one).

The metaphor remains the basis for these definitions long after the organization has changed. Accounting manuals, as one unresearched hypothesis states, continue to exist functionally long after the organization structure has changed. As a basic guide to meaning in finance, the metaphor is constantly reinterpreted with differences of view over accounting terms and meaning flowing from audit to audit.

Language

From the metaphor, language develops to convey the organization's understanding of its shared meaning. In the choice of words used and not used and in the definitions of the words and the contexts which draw together word use and definition, this language expresses what the metaphor actually isolates as important.

If language expresses basic values, it also makes them legitimate. Highlighting certain meanings gives them stature. Associating an important action with basic values justifies the action and develops a commitment to the value.

Financial management's understanding of the fiduciary role has also led to the creation of a language—a language that is vital to conservatorship (Wildavsky, 1964) and to risk averseness (ACIR, 1961), especially in cash management.

Rituals

Rituals provide the appearance of certainty, and the mere repetition of rituals as meaningful events creates an attachment to the organization. For example, the annual budget hearings lend a business-as-usual air to organization life. Also these hearings tend to force the defenses of programs that are included later on, and that event creates an attachment to the budget.

Rituals also provide continuous ceremonies for change. The budget reform attains the standing of an "investiture ritual" in which the old administration and particularly its *budget system* no longer are viewed as legitimate ways of making decisions. The budget reform is then an investiture of the ritual that ratifies the new way of making decisions and often, indirectly, those who have such important skills (Schick, 1966; Walker, 1986; Mosher, 1984, 1979).

Networks

The creation of meaning is the province of those whose view of the world predominates. These groups or individuals are often called the *ruling coalition*. In political terms, this coalition maintains power through various attempts at providing side payments (Cyert and March, 1963), through their liaison or representative role (Bachrach and Lawler, 1980; pp. 105–140) with important constituencies, and through their authoritative knowledge (Cartwright, 1959; French and Raven, 1959), which is based on specialization and centrality in the work process (Hinings et al., 1974).

Networks dominate interpretation because of the discretion their access to resources allows. Command of resources enables network members to make side payments, or, as is more likely, to gain and marshal knowledge and centrality, making them essential to their own organizations in interpreting outside events. Networks of interorganization forces provide more comfortable interpretations of an ambiguous environment and help the network members feel that they dominate that environment.

The network assumes a social construction of reality. Members in the network tend to create a common view of the world that helps them function. Networks created for a long-term finance project, for example, tend to devise unique methods with which they interpret the markets for the particular financing, interpret the law as it pertains to the procedures used with the project and the financing, and interpret organization resource sufficiency for backing the project.

Cybernetics

Because the function of networks is to provide interpretation, the system that is used is one in which the process of interpretation is made to seem self-correcting. Thus, various cybernetic systems are known because of their functions, such as providing early warning (forecasting systems such as the Troika at the federal level), coordinating activity (such as the role the former "A-95" system played in the intergovernmental system), or detecting error (financial-management information systems).

Investiture Rituals and Budget Reforms

First, I take up the idea that a budget is part of the glue that holds together the social system inside a government organization. Budget reform (using balanced base budgeting in Kansas as the case study in this chapter) is a highly ritualized technique that signals change as well as continuity, as I see it. Using ethnographic methods, I will look at the important efforts to achieve a new emphasis in budgeting through reform.

Language and Cash Management

Most observers have wondered why public sector managers have a love/hate relationship with chance, especially when the rewards in the financial markets could be so large. I examine the place for risk-taking in cash management as a surrogate for the entire financial-management system in the next chapter. I test the idea that views of risk are widespread and also try to establish the various goals of investment that are held by managers to determine whether these goals are independent of each other.

Networks and Long-Term Finance

In the next chapter, I look at the question of why conservative public servants would enter into some of the most innovative financing deals that are seen in either public or private sectors. I conclude that in coping with uncertainty in the bond market, the parties involved in capital asset financing create a political economy of incentives and deference and, in the end, socially construct a reality with which all parties to the deal feel comfortable. Using economic "cobweb theorems," I try to explain logically why competition may not provide a guarantee of success in avoiding risk. I try to show that financing techniques, not members of a financing team, provide better coping methods.

Cybernetics and Management Information Systems

In Chapter 6, I look at the financial-information systems that exist, not as inherently control oriented systems, but as measures of the social construction of reality. The inventor of the system usually has a model in mind, and in the case of the A-95 system, the model is that of the U.S. Office of Management and Budget. I retest Padgett's assertions (1980) that greater innovation comes of less centralized direction, under conditions of ambiguity.

Forecasts and Revenue

In the last chapter, I looked at the various views of reality that come into play in forecasting economic and revenue data. I look at the efforts made by the Troika, the federal forecasting effort made up of the U.S. Office of Management and Budget, the Council of Economic Advisors, and the Department of the Treasury. The struggle among these three units illustrates the rough and tumble of social construction which I find is constructed through the sequential attention of participants; the structure of this process dictates the outcome.

NOTES

1. To relate this idea to previous discussion, financial strategy refers to a body of concepts purporting to enable managers to analyze the larger organization environment to detect patterns and trends and gain insight that helps them to predict opportunities for the reduction of risk in managing cash, using debt wisely, and generally making more productive use of scarce tax and revenue resources. Financial strategy can be generalized to efforts to cope with uncertainty across organizations and time. Strategy's major components suggest that understanding environments and classifying them properly affords a financial manager the insight to foresee difficulties and opportunities.

2. The three alternative rationalities join five others (March, 1978): two variants of orthodox theory, *calculated rationality* [the direct ends means calculation] and *selected rationality* ["rules of behavior achieve intelligence not by virtue of conscious calculation of their rationality by current role players but by virtue of the survival and growth of social institutions in which such rules are followed and such roles are performed" (p. 593)]; and two variants of prevailing theory, *game rationality*, or the partisan mutual adjustment of individuals, and *adaptive rationality* or organization learning.

   March's two types of orthodox theory—calculated rationality and selected rationality—can be related to two others: one based on the stimulus-response set in which organization members find themselves and Wildavsky's idea (1975) of fatalistic cultures.

3. The material in this section is adapted from Miller, Rabin, and Hildreth (1987).

4. In the context of power, Pfeffer (1981) found this line of research particularly useful.

   > One productive research task involves taking . . . general [technologies], and delineating specific examples of each. Then hypotheses could be developed and tested concerning the conditions associated with the [technologies'] use and the circumstances under which each is likely to be effective in mobilizing support and quieting opposition to decisions. To this point, there has been little empirical comparative study of these forms of symbolic action and political language, but this type of comparative analysis is clearly feasible and necessary to further understand the use of political language in organizational politics. (p. 211)

5. As Meyer (1971) showed, increasing organization size and holding spans of control leads logically to greater horizontal and greater vertical differentiation.

6

Executive Budgeting Vindicated Through Sign, Symbol, and Ritual

In this chapter, I describe budget theories and argue that only one satisfies the requirements that I adopt as necessary for a theory. With such a theory, I would ask three questions: What role does the government budget play in relationship to the economy? To what principle is government action held accountable? and How do budget actors make decisions?

In the past, the answers to these questions have been found to reflect the positions on fiscal matters that are held by dominant political coalitions existing at the time. Thus, budget theory, being normative, has traditionally tended to elaborate the positions of coalitions rather than describe their actual practice.

I survey the literature and divide it along normative, descriptive/empirical, and interpretive dimensions. For economic and accountability questions, the interests described in Chapter 2 have specific views. For the decision-making questions, analysts are divided among themselves as to the actual or appropriate methods. I survey the opinion in all three areas in the sections that follow.

ECONOMIC QUESTIONS

In the case of the role-in-the-economy argument, both market proponents and positive government advocates stake positions. Will the government budget process act as (1) a special case of the *free market*, specifying the proper amount and distribution of collective goods as well as the equitable allocation of their burden through voting rules and analytical procedures, the market proponents' view, or will (2) government officials *manage the economy* as a whole through the rational use of fiscal policy in stimulating or contracting the macroeconomy, the positive government view. The resolution of these differences lies in deciding the proper role of government in the economy.

ACCOUNTABILITY QUESTIONS

Arising as almost a matter of belief is the accountability issue: To what principle shall government action be held accountable? Shall it be *responsive* to external clients, as both market and positive government proponents argue, or shall it be responsible to principles of internal control and efficiency, which analysts would hold? The accountability issue arises as a matter of belief, rather than fact, in the same way that tools, procedures, and technologies have often been viewed as ends in themselves. In contrast to the free market versus government management level of analysis over the ends of budgets, the accountability debate is argued over means, pure and simple, as Morstein-Marx would say (1957, Ch. 3).

The debate cannot be dismissed quickly as one of misplaced interest in means rather than ends, to characterize budget theory's fascination with accountability. The development of budget theory, through the study of budget reforms, is much like a learning curve. Taking Schick's view of budget theory's development (1966), we can place the ends-means debates alongside to show what has happened, as seen in Table 1.

Table 1 Budget Views of Budget Theorists

	Budget Views	Schick	Waldo
Means	Budgets as devices for accountability to outside interests	Control	Muckrakers
	Budgets as responsibility devices to responsibility principles such as performance and efficiency	Management	Bureau movement
Ends	Budgets as a method of planning and attaining macroeconomic and social goals	Planning	Positive government movement
	Budgets as the market's rules for burden and distribution of collective goods		Business interests

Sources: Schick (1966); Waldo (1948).

DECISION-MAKING QUESTION

Individuals who are trying to build budget theory in public administration have spent most of their time lately in setting budgets in decision-making theory. From the orthodox position, much principled argument holds to the ends first and then the means position, based on an individual level analysis of rationality. The prevailing wisdom among others holds to the plural interests model of rationality in which ends adjust to means.

The ends-means debate has partisans who would argue a randomness in the way the two relate (Cohen and March, 1986). The direction of the causal arrow

ENDS → MEANS *or* ENDS ← MEANS

may be more a matter of which episode was chosen to illustrate the argument, much as it is at what frame the film critic chose to stop the film in illustrating a point, rather than relying on something called an objective reality of what the film is to be. The choice lies more in the construction of the event than in the event itself.

This point of view follows an emerging argument among interpretive theorists about social science in general. First of all, events have an unrelenting ambiguity; reality is subjectively viewed, being what we say it is. Second, organizations, meant at creation to be sources of unequivocality in viewing reality, tend to be composed of loosely coupled segments for reasons that benefit the members and the organization's chances of survival. Third, the social sciences rest on the idea that truth in the portrayal of phenomena lies as much in the mind of the scientist as in the phenomena themselves. Fourth, ambiguity is resolved most often after the fact, in post hoc view of an event or of phenomena, through the interaction of loosely coupled segments of organization in predetermined choice opportunities in which participation may be random.

In the three sections that follow, I look at three approaches that compete to explain budgeting in public financial management theory. First, an approach that assumes prospective, intendedly rational, created action called *normative budget theory*; second, another based on the idea that action is externally constrained or situationally controlled (a descriptive budget theory); and third, a view of budgeting decisions as almost random, emergent processes; a view that leads to interpretive budget theories.

NORMATIVE BUDGET THEORY

From its early reform period to the present, the budgeting literature has elaborated a normative model of what should take place among government agencies and between branches of government as well as within government agencies. In this section, I briefly review this model, in the forms it took in the municipal reform movement, the state reorganization movement, and the national government's executive budget movements.

Municipal Reform Movement

It is safe to say that the traditional history of the reform period from 1890 to 1920 generally drew a picture of reaction. Reformers reacted to a situation in which immigrants voted on long ballots for bundled groups of machine candidates who assumed office in a fragmented structure and then went about processing voter demands and lining their own and their cronies' pockets, driving up taxes and expenditures to the detriment of the middle- and old-monied patrician classes (e.g., Hofstader, 1955; Schiesl, 1977; Adrian, 1987).

The response provoked in the reaction was a call for representativeness in political structures of a different sort. A genuine political community, not merely coalitions on both sides of a partisan struggle, was to be achieved (MacDonald, 1988, p. 707). Specifically, according to Lineberry and Sharkansky (1971, p. 73), the reformers had

1. an aversion to "politics" as a means of arriving at public-policy decisions and specifically to political parties and organized interest groups;
2. a holistic conception of the community, a belief that there is a single interest of the "community as a whole" to which "special interests" should be clearly subordinated;
3. a strong preference for professional management of community affairs, implying preference for public policy-making by technical experts like the city manager;
4. a strong faith in the efficacy of structural reform.

At the root of the problem of partisanship was the ward election system in city governments of the time. Through divisions of the area, machine candidates could directly cultivate and exploit the new immigrant blocks, usually in homogeneous blocks of people who arrived from the same country. The machine politicians could then bundle their own ward candidates and run them without fear of their being able to be contested as a slate (Adrian, 1987).

The reformers tackled the problem head-on. They proposed at-large political offices that would be filled through nonpartisan elections. The reform produced the desired results—a dramatic fall-off in participation (Lineberry and Fowler, 1967).

The reformers also proposed a centralization of power in the form of strong mayors with executive powers. These powers included the ability to appoint, through a combination of political appointments and a merit system, the most qualified experts and specialists to run city departments. This departmentalization of expertise would be coordinated through principles of orthodox management, narrow spans of control, and a chain of command. The work of the city government would be financed by a budget in which the various needs of departments, as determined by experts, would be presented and deliberated over by the mayor and a council of at-large elected council members. The responsible administration that was created as a result would be held accountable on the basis of economy and efficiency by the electorate (Schiesl, 1977; Adrian, 1987).

In summary, the municipal reform model is the clearest normative model of budgeting today. The model views a genuine political community as operating with leaders elected at-large to represent the community's interest as a whole, an administration staffed by experts headed by a strong mayor with executive powers, including a budget through which process the work of the city could be financed economically and efficiently.

State Reorganization Movement

At the state level, the reforms generally reacted to legislative supremacy and its problems. As White has pointed out (1933, pp. 207–208), before reform, "the typical state agency or institution prepared its own estimates, submitted them directly to the appropriations committee, ultimately received an independent appropriation, and spent its funds without supervision other than that provided by the auditor." Such a system had led to an increase in total expenditure of the states by almost 650% over two decades, to muckraking that revealed public ineptitude and corruption, and to a growing following for "the new gospel" being spread by scientific management proponents (Schick, 1971, p. 15).

The new gospel's provisions included an executive budget that resembled the municipal reform movement budget and included three perspectives. The first or planning perspective enabled the governor to use the status of sole representative of all the people to produce an authoritative statement of policies and programs (Cleveland, 1915; Schick, 1971). The second or management perspective provided that the governor be the chief coordinator. The executive would "standardize and consolidate agency estimates . . . ensure that the budget facilitated the efficient conduct of the public business" (Schick, 1971, p. 16). The management perspective linked the budget with the reorganization movement itself, the chief goal of which was to functionally consolidate fragmented agencies and strengthen the executive's appointive and removal powers.

The third or control perspective would deter waste and fraud. The governor would become the state's chief controller, installing centralized purchasing, accounting, personnel, and internal audit controls to protect against corrupt or inept officials.

The tradition that developed as executive budgets were installed, however, limited executives' roles in the process. The legislative bodies guarded their constitutional duty and prerogative to appropriate by trading some of their former financial powers for control over expenditures. As Schick observed (1971, p. 18):

De facto, the governor became the control agent of the legislature; his [sic] job was to present the budget accounts in a way that facilitated detailed legislative scrutiny of agency requests and enabled the legislature to intervene when it wanted to. The conception of the governor as active policymaker fell by the wayside, although his [sic] potential for this role remained.

Schick in fact argues that prior unfettered agency initiative in the preparation of estimates did not change; rather, it provoked the creation of a centralized control role for the executive in checking unconstrained spending requests. Unchanged agency initiative and the new centralized check over it also displaced a policy and planning role.

National Executive Budget Movement

The federal executive budget followed lines similar to that in the municipal reform and state reorganization movements. The movement at the national level came into being as a result of the confluence of seven factors. First, Progressives wanted to head off the agrarian radicals and their proposals for greater levels of government spending (Savage, 1988, p. 145). Second, Republicans wanted but did not have enough support to pass the Payne-Aldrich Tariff. Third, Progressives wanted but did not have enough support to pass the income tax. Fourth, Republicans blamed the Panic of 1907 on spending and on the deficits of 1908, 1909, and 1910. Fifth, the populism of the Agrarians led to a widespread demand for schools, roads, and other government services. Sixth, the idea of centralized administration as being essential to promote efficiency and accountability caught on as a result of the efforts of members of the Bureau movement (Waldo, 1948, p. 32). Finally, alarms were raised over spending during World War I.

In reaction, over a period from 1907 to 1921, four major financial management events cascaded. First, centralization developed in the Treasury and in the Congressional appropriations process in the collection, reporting, and consideration of expenditure and revenue measures. Second, Congress passed parts of the Payne-Aldrich tariff that placed 1% tax on corporate incomes above $5,000. Third, Congress passed the individual income tax. Finally, Congress passed the Budget and Accounting Act of 1921.

For budgeting, the 1921 Act brought centralized management into being and created a balance between the legislative and the executive branches in pursuit of financial management as a whole. Mosher (1984, p. 33), following Stourm (1917), divided the ideal budget process into four steps and assigned responsibility in this system to one branch (see Table 2): The ideal system balanced the branches and provided checks of one department over the other. The creation of the income tax, despite its later dilution and laggardly implementation (Savage, 1988, pp. 147–150), complemented the budget act and led to the maintenance of balanced budget symbols. The ideal budget system created an answer to the economic question in providing that the Chief Executive steer the economy. The ideal also answered the

Table 2 The Ideal Budget System

Step	Branch	1921 Act
Preparation	Executive	Bureau of Budget (BoB)
Appropriation	Legislative	Congress through appropriations committees
Execution and control	Executive and legislative	Agencies, BoB, General Accounting Office (GAO)
Postaudits	Legislative	GAO

Source: Mosher (1984).

accountability question in providing responsible, hierarchically oriented management. Finally, the rational decision-making approach offered a technically elegant way of joining steering to responsibility.

DESCRIPTIVE BUDGET THEORY

Incrementalism (Lindblom, 1959) best typifies the descriptive approach to budgeting. Even though there is relatively little disagreement about the ability of incrementalism *to describe* the budget process or the decision-making process for the vast majority of policies that are made in government at all levels, there is much disagreement about how much incrementalism actually *explains*. Rather, the problem seems to lie in the different views of incrementalism. One view of incrementalism in this incarnation holds it to be a set of adaptive techniques and decision rules which individuals and groups use to deal with an uncertain and often turbulent environment. Another view of incrementalism is that of empirical phenomena. Incrementalism, then, is a happenstance, an event, a set of decision-making outcomes that result from, or are caused by, the application of or use of particular strategies.

We can therefore think of incrementalism as either a description or an explanation of reality. As such, incrementalism *appears* to those who are naive as a powerful element in decision-making. But let us look at this difference more closely. First, descriptive incrementalism has a rather large base in the case studies of governmental decision-making and resource allocation. Much evidence exists to explain the interaction of actors at all levels and between branches of government to confirm the view that actors make only marginal changes in past decisions.

The decision process becomes very simple and elegant. Thus, in the federal government's budget process, descriptive incrementalism reveals that agency requests in any year are marginally greater than that agency's appropriation for the previous year. The appropriation in any year exceeds the previous year's appropriation by a small amount relative to the size of the appropriation. Lastly, the appropriation for an agency is somewhat less than what had been requested.

Although descriptive incrementalism became well established (cf., Wanat, 1974), quickly, major disagreements developed over not only the estimates of the increments but also whether incremental outcomes exist at all. Moreover, *major* disagreements also burned over the reason for incrementalism or why incremental changes seemed to prevail, if at all.

What then is explanatory incrementalism. It is the idea held by some individuals that marginal changes in the budget figures of agencies from year to year can be explained by human behavioral dynamics. Thus, the lack of resources and the need for a consensus put a limit of what changes can be proposed or approved.

Consider Barber's research with Connecticut's local boards of finance (1966). Barber convened members of Connecticut local boards of finance in a small group laboratory and gave them a budget-reducing task. Each group looked over its own most recent budget figures "to determine where and by how much the total could be cut if this were necessary" (Barber, 1966, p. 35). Barber tape recorded the deliberations, read the typed manuscripts, and analyzed the content of the materials "to determine what criteria were actually employed as the members approved and rejected reductions" (pp. 35–36). Five criteria emerged (see Table 3). First, the members distinguished between controllable and uncontrollable costs. According to Barber,

> certain expenditures have been committed by previous long range decisions, or are tied in closely with basic legal requirements, or are mandatory accompaniments of other fundamental costs such as retirement funds or wage levels. Excluding these from consideration enables the board to devote its efforts to those matters on which it has discretion in the short run. (p. 37)

This was the most frequently noted criterion for decision-making.

Second, the boards rejected across the board cuts and focused instead on the large items in the budget and requests that have increased over the previous request and/or appropriation. The comparisons are made horizontally (this year versus last year) rather than vertically (Department A versus Department B). Barber noted that "the operative assumption seems to be that stable expenditure levels are *prima facie* valid and need not be closely examined (p. 39). Raises are "suspicious" and need "detailed scrutiny." As a simplifying device, this technique to Barber "reflects the much more general tendency for a person to notice objects in motion amidst a collection of fixed objects" (p. 39).

Third, the board members, usually business persons, tended to grasp quickly the practical implications of budgetary details, overlooking certain less tangible

Table 3   Decision-Making Criteria Used in a Laboratory Experiment

	Reasons for cuts
Magnitude and change of expenditures	Appropriation was increased in last budget
	New item
	Large item
	Account shows surplus; current expenditure rate
Effects on operations	Cuts will not hamper services
	Expenditure can be postponed
Uncertainty	Original appropriation based on rough estimate, was not considered carefully by board earlier
	Funds may not be needed; can correct later
Other	Effect on tax rate
	Comparison with other departments
	Probable public reaction to cut
	Probable reaction of department to cut
	Comparison with other towns
	Competence or sincerity of requester
	Reasons against cuts
Uncontrollable items	"Can't be touched"
	State requirements
Appropriation already minimal	Board cut from last request
	Board considered last request carefully
	Appropriation has decreased
	Request was minimal; tight
Effects on operations	Cut will hamper services
	Effect uncertain, perhaps harmful
	Urgent; cannot be postponed
Other	Probable public reaction to cut
	Effect on tax rate
	Competence or sincerity of requester
	Probable reaction of departments
	Comparison with other departments
	Comparison with other towns

Source: From Barber (1966). Categories and criteria within categories are ranked from most often observed to least often observed.

but relevant matters. Consider Barber's example of the recreation budget. Board members had little trouble dealing with such questions as the variety of fencing available and best for playgrounds or grading costs for ballfields. Little was said or considered in programmatic terms: Which teenage sports programs lead to the health and welfare of youngsters? or Where should the balance be struck among programs and among groups? Thus, members tended to concentrate on the concrete, the nuts and bolts questions rather than on more abstract ones.

Fourth, pressure of time tended to focus members' attention on the here and now. The long-range picture or the memory of things past tended to be downplayed; "the member . . . may be made to feel that he is interrupting an emergency meeting to introduce irrelevancies" (p. 41). Few members used experience in other towns to decide questions of budget reductions.

Although concreteness often served the members in decision-making, past decisions did come into play in reminding members about the past confidence in their decisions. Thus, according to Barber, members

> will (a) not reconsider decisions about which the members have been certain in the past, and (b) make new decisions, without feeling entirely certain about them, only if such decisions can be taken tentatively and any ill effects can be corrected later. . . . The board looks back at its prior deliberations and recalls that in some cases decisions were made with considerable confidence and in others with considerable doubt. The more uncertain they are, the more willing they are to consider.

Therefore, members used some decision rules to reduce uncertainty about their decisions, but uncertainty itself often served as a major criterion of budget reductions.

Sharkansky's research (1968; Thompson, 1987) builds on that of Barber and leads to similar conclusions. Sharkansky measured the short-term success and budget expansion of state agencies as determined by

> the amount that was recommended by the governor and the amount that was appropriated by the legislature as compared to the state agency's current request and as compared to the agency's present appropriation.

Sharkansky found that the governor cut the request but that the governor's recommendation remained larger than the present appropriation. As for the legislature, he found that the members, short of time, staff, and expertise, tended to defer to the governor, leaving much of the recommendation intact. The dynamics of budgeting revolved around many of the same time-saving heuristics that Barber had discovered. Moreover, the result of the budget deliberations from year to year differed only incrementally.

In addition to Barber and Sharkansky, the team of Davis, Dempster, and Wildavsky (1966) examined agencies the budget results of which resemble the incremental changes found in other studies of budget results. They demonstrated that Congressional action on agency requests usually conforms to an equation:

APPROPRIATION = b X (AGENCY REQUEST) + Slight Variation

where b is a number less than but close to 1, such as .96. We can interpret this to mean that Congress usually allows an agency 96 percent of its request. This research had compelling statistical backing, since the Davis, Dempster, and Wildavsky findings explained a large amount of the variance in the budget—approximately 90 percent. The authors of this study explained the strategy/outcome connection by inferring that the b factor results from strategic considerations on the part of a Congress that feels an agency's request is a good estimate of what the agency needs but that the request is padded a bit and, therefore, can be cut somewhat.

There is a great deal of disagreement over the Davis, Dempster, and Wildavsky findings and over the inference drawn. For example, as discussed earlier in Chapter 4, Wanat (1974) has shown that the high statistical correlations among agency requests and Congressional appropriations could be explained by relatively random variation within broad constraints.

The research question for empirical test becomes obvious. Do incremental outcomes necessarily result from an incrementalist strategy?

An alternative explanation sheds some light. Implicitly, incrementalism assumes that budget participants have control over the budget and that they could, if they wanted to do so, spend money in radically different ways as a departure from traditional choices. Ordinarily, however, participants have only limited control over budget authority or outlays, or in the larger realm, decision alternatives.

If we include these sources of uncontrollability in the analysis, we see a much different picture than the one painted in traditional commentary (Wildavsky, 1964); that is, incremental outcomes result from the creep in uncontrollables. Costs associated with disaster assistance or with student tuition may increase without the number of disasters or students increasing or without any effort of agency budget officers either.

Uncontrollables and incrementalism are inextricably intertwined in empirical budget theory. In fact, agency strategy may require that budget arenas that have become hotly competitive—the normal route to budget success in the 1980s under budget constraint and revenue restraints—be forsaken for those less so. Those less competitive may be the arenas outside the areas of controllability—loan authority, contract authority, or entitlement routes (Ippolito, 1984; Bennett and DiLorenzo, 1983).

The incremental approach serves the cause of description well. By stipulating a psychology of budget motivations among actors, it creates a major opening for *management* theories to help explain organization behavior under conditions of both plenty and scarcity. The accommodation of actors to each other provides another competing answer to the accountability question raised at the outset in this chapter. Accountability relies on participation and competition; responsiveness to group interests, above all, with secondary interest in common goals spells success.

The economic question, and by implication the accountability question as well, are answered by an "invisible hand" theory of competing and accommodating interests. At an interorganizational level, however, incrementalism depends on this approach to withstand scrutiny and test. The deduced result of competition and bargaining—the small changes made over time to policy—do not have the convincing ring they had when supported by rapid economic growth.

Yet the actual value of incrementalism has been its spur to research by economists, organizational theorists, and political scientists. Not only has budgeting developed from a backwater left to accountants, it has also confounded all of the social science disciplines with its complexity and relationships to enduring questions. Incrementalism encourages interdisciplinary research and begs for additional explanation as anomalies unfold.

INTERPRETIVE AND EMERGENT THEORY IN BUDGETING

Finance officers and the procedures involved in financial management derive their reason for being in part from the values and culture within which they reside. Several intriguing research questions on public financial management can be posed: Why these procedures? Why these organization structures? and Why are these people in the places they occupy? In short, how does this world work? A curious student might look at financial management as a social process to provide a new frame of reference and a different interpretation of practice.

Generally, one can break down the world of the financial manager into two perspectives that serve as organizing devices. These two fundamental divisions are *affect* and *cognition*. By way of illustration, consider their meaning: If a financial manager solves a problem, the person must assume incomplete knowledge but a vast store from which to pull experience that is needed. What information does one use? Cognitive theory suggests some form of satisficing or intended rationality. Satisficing to a large extent also rests on prior actions, habits, and social comparisons. Affect can explain the necessity of these noncognitive aspects, particularly the feelings derived from social relationships, from valued ideas and routines, incorporated into cognition through symbols and rituals.

In this chapter I explored the cognitive side of budgeting in the form of incremental decision-making. Here I explore the affective side. Why this way? Why this approach? Indeed, why not more exploration of the cognitive side? The reason lies in what is often called the "folly" of systematic analysis. That folly, according to Herbert Storing (1962), lies in thinking that values, tastes, and other affective components of life have no connection with what we choose to do and how we choose to do it.

Financial management has never laid serious claim to "finding the best means to a given end" but has considered "isolating alternative behaviors and their consequences" (Simon, 1976). Storing views the latter as still forcing one to ignore criteria for "good" consequences: What are good? What are bad? What makes one better than another? Edelman argued, over a review of Mead's work (1934), that one seldom knows good from bad consequences, and, by that, appropriate behaviors, until one has experienced them. Said another way, having experienced a consequence, one can then rationalize or give meaning to what happened, calling it good or bad in terms of some other, socially derived or affect-based set of criteria.

That set of socially derived or affect-based criteria is usually thought of as "culture." Organization culture, or even a culture in which organizations interact, has prescriptive value. Culture implies "shared meanings, shared paradigms, and shared languages" (Pfeffer, 1981, p. 11) as well as an ideology, rituals, myths and knowledge that "prescribes what work is to be done and how it can be changed over time" (Walker, 1986, p. 7).

Two alternative approaches to the study of budgeting, the ritualistic ceremonial approach and a random-choice approach, relate to each other and explain how culture can transmit criteria of "good" consequences. I consider each in the sections that follow as concepts. Then I apply each empirically. Finally, I draw conclusions about their applicability by comparing them to the cognitive approach attributed to more traditional ways of thinking about financial management.

The Symbols and Rituals of Budgets

Consider for a moment the affective approach to understanding public life. We respond to symbols such as a balanced budget with concern. We believe in such rituals as the competitive bid process in awarding the sale of general obligation bonds. We listen closely to understand the language of economic forecasts because they tell us in their arcane way to be optimistic or not.

In all, we ascribe much importance to the pomp and circumstance that we see. This affect we feel comes from at least three sources that I want to consider here in an administrative context: symbols, rituals, and language.

Symbols are simple representations of complex matters. They may be defined as a stimulus object, "the meaning or significance of which is socially generated and cannot be inferred from its physical form" (Elder and Cobb, 1983, p. 142). Symbols focus attention in such a way that they bind people together through the shared attention that is brought about. Symbols also bring with them associations for people that create a discipline for individual behavior in favor of larger goals. This latter use of symbols is what I want to describe here—the leader's use of symbols to bind and discipline followers.

In addition to a leader's use of symbols, I also want to explore the rituals and ceremonies that take place in government organizations. These practices are accepted and desired by organization members as dramatic manipulation of symbols by legitimate persons, usually making those inside the ritual feel differently from those outside, and in so doing "structure, validate, and stabilize collective action" (Trice, Belasco, and Alutto, 1969, p. 42). Ceremonials provide cues, even explanations, for individuals confronted by novel or ambiguous information. Ceremonials also invest organization decisions with legitimacy.

Edelman (1964) defined a ritual as physical activity that gets people involved symbolically in a common effort; the ritual's efficiency is the way it *compels* attention to individuals' relatedness to each other and their joint interests. The result is conformity but also "satisfaction and joy in conformity" (p. 16):

> Men instinctively try to find meaning and order when placed in a confusing or ambiguous situation. In dances and other motor activity in which primitive man celebrates season changes, the basic order of the universe underlying the "blooming buzzing confusion" of sensations is reaffirmed and the individual reminded of the need to conform to a basic order himself. In rain dances and victory dances men achieve symbolically something they collectively need or want by reaffirming their common interest, denying their doubts, and acting out the result they seek. The motor activity, performed together with others, reassures everyone that there are no dissenters and brings pride and satisfaction in a collective enterprise. A simplified model or semblance of reality is created, and facts that do not fit are screened out of it. Conformity and satisfaction with the basic order are the keynotes; and the acting out of what is to be believed is a psychologically effective mode of instilling conviction and fixing patterns of future behavior. (pp. 16–17)

Moreover, Edelman argues, the ritual serves at least three purposes: to quiet resentments and doubts about particular political acts, to reaffirm belief in the fundamental rationality and democratic character of the system, and thus to fix conforming habits of future behavior.

Finally, language plays an important part in understanding as well. Edelman (1977, p. 16) argued that we "naturally define ambiguous situations by focusing on one part of them or by comparing them with familiar things." Language is useful in evoking those familiar ways of thinking about things. In fact, by using a particular language, we define what we see not only in understandable but often in believable and legitimate ways as well.

We can see the basic financial-management procedures pursued by governments as serving affect purposes. Decisions, such as those in budgets, may be better understood as part of a symbolic process. Symbols help managers communicate to their audiences the legitimacy of their decisions, showing their appropriateness and that of the process they used (no outcomes being measurable). Symbols also communicate that organizations are good decision-makers by showing that prized values are being honored; managers "consult relevant people, consider alternatives, gather information, act decisively" (March and Olsen, 1986,

p. 22). Decision-making processes also have rituals attached that assure society that human existence is built around intelligent choice.

The Chief Executive's attention to the ramifications of symbols, rituals, and language can spell the difference between successful and unsuccessful governing. In the research I report here, the attention to affect meant the difference between a consolidation of executive power after decades of slow reform in the executive branch and a slide to further fragmentation.

Role of the Financial Manager in Interpreting Fiscal Reality

I contend that a budget manager's major function is that of manipulating symbols, producing rituals, and employing a unique language to get the budget and impose it. It is the financial manager's job, and that of all managers, to give reason and meaning to the process of work. The process of work has larger meaning in public administration, for lacking the widespread notion of "making a profit" as do private sector organizations, each public organization must look for a unique vision that gives meaning to the processes each follows. That particular process can be "protecting the weak from the evil" or "defending the free world" but all have in common some notion of "doing everything possible with as little help from the taxpayer as possible," a shortened version of financial-management's fiscal vision.

I argue that finance departments create the reality that organizations have by symbolically, ritualistically, and rhetorically coping with the most critical problem each organization has, namely, resource constraints. Coping gives the finance department the clout to be able to enforce the use of a special language. In that language, *budget* becomes an overarching metaphor. Creating a reality in which resources are contingent and in which the finance department is the critical agency for commanding resources and wisely allocating them among uses, the financial manager provides much of the affective utility of financial-management procedures.

Reality Construction in Budgeting

To build this case for financial management as largely symbolic in nature, I survey the literature presently available. Most of the literature explains long held notions of administrative reform that assume a relationship between process and outcome. One authority claims that "the form in which information is classified and used governs the actions of [decision] makers, and conversely, that alterations in form will produce desired changes in behavior" (Schick, 1966, p. 257).

Linked to the idea of an executive budget, this idea has power. Process → outcome lends responsibility to the administrative organization and allows for the steering of local, state, and national economies. On the question, the evidence is mixed (Grizzle, 1986; Jernberg, 1969; Wanat, 1973). I look at existing studies and experience to illustrate both sides. The affirmative side—process dictates outcome—clearly believes that budget format decides outcomes (Grizzle, 1986), primarily because of the fact that decisions depend on information. Those who disagree tend to point out that process and format often diverge. An outcome oriented toward distribution of values or benefits cannot be pushed by a process that points out an optimal, goal-oriented distribution. Rarely does an evaluation report intrude in political decision-making, according to other researchers (Lauth, 1985; Lauth and Abney, 1986).

But can they both be true? If so, is there a point of reconciliation at which we find the two approaches actually working in harmony? My purpose here is to argue for integration, that the symbols, language, and rituals create and maintain a reality no longer sustainable with hierarchical relationships alone.

V. O. Key and the Continued Viability of the Metaphor of Choice

What are the ways of constructing reality? What is it that forms the budgeting and finance frame of reference? V. O. Key gets the credit for creating the first metaphor for budgeting—the metaphor of *choice*. His prescient contribution is the reigning paradigm of public budgeting: "On what basis shall it be decided to allocate x dollars to Activity A or Activity B?" (1940, p. 1138), and predicted later work of a more fundamental nature in organization choice by Simon (1948) and in policy analytic choice by others (cf., Quade, 1975).

Choice is the approach Key proposed as the basis for both the study and practice of government budgeting. Key's selection of choice fit his times. The early development of public budgeting did not provide an occasion for addressing choice in the administrative context, emphasizing as it did the control of expenditure rather than its exploitation. Yet with methods of expenditure control and analysis in place, with the ability to track where money went, and with increasing revenue at the federal level from the income tax, decisions about "whether the function is worth carrying out at all, or whether it should be carried out on a reduced or enlarged scale, with resulting transfers of funds to or from other activities of greater or lesser social utility" (Key, 1940, p. 1139) became Key's central considerations.

Later, out of the notion of choice developed the question of who gets what, when, where, and how as the basis for accommodation rules in Congress. The institutions that worked well under the politics of addition were those dominated by a few individuals the interactions and accommodations among whom "constituted the 'invisible hand' of the budget marketplace which acted to limit conflicts and also to restrain the rate of budget growth" (Caiden, 1983, p. 106).

The appropriations committees countered the tendencies of the others. The members reduced the president's spending estimates although they granted increases over the previous budget. They played the role of guardians of the public purse, and budget cutting came amid mutual expectations about budget growth and its limits.

Do We Have Choice?

Does choice dominate the field today? We have now in budgets less and less choice, some would say (Caiden, 1983; Gist, 1989). The survey in the previous section of this chapter illustrated the uncontrollables and off-budget items in the federal budget that have blunted choice. Major institutional changes then occurred to both promote and brake attempts to cut budgets. First, from the late 1960s on, leadership, seniority, and committee structure entropied as members of Congress urged greater decentralization, a factor that impeded cutting efforts while under the old system. Second, the appropriations committees lost the security—safe committee seats, closed hearings, larger membership, and democratized committee chair-selection procedures—that allowed the groups to act as cutters. In a democratized organization, members found incentives to play program advocate much greater than cutters. And, third, formulas began to drive spending: who would be eligible for direct payments, such as health benefits, was stated in the authorization of a program, by substantive committees, removing discretion over actual spending amounts from those interested in cutting or restraining the budget.

Therefore, as Wildavsky (1987) and Cohen and March (1986) have argued the budget exercise is fundamentally an act of governance oriented toward something other than analytical choice. The alternative candidates include competition, consensus, or autonomy. Thus, the critical questions over whether we have choice are: If not, why? and if not, What?

If Not Choice, Why?

Choice stopped being a major task of budgeting according to Caiden (1983), when Congress and the President began pursuing the politics of subtraction. The politics of decision-making in an era of scarcity have wrought both institutional and procedural attempts to bend the old politics of addition rules. The institutional changes are derived from the creation of the Congressional Budget Office (as well as new vitality in state legislative research and budget staffs and continuing development of legislative staffs at the local government level), as well as the Budget committees of both the House and the Senate. Procedural changes have continually developed from the formal tasks installed along with the budget office with legislation passed in 1974.

Those institutional changes that occurred to promote cutting began in earnest with the passage of the Congressional Budget and Impoundment Control Act (1974). The act provided for the creation of budget committees in each chamber to provide Congress with a view of the entire budget and to remedy the already fragmented system that had entropied through pressure for decentralization. The budget committees had staff members (the Congressional Budget Office) whose analyses would enable all members to compete with those in the "closed world" of alliances and triangles.

The procedural reforms were aimed to restore the guardianship role and to give it to the Budget committees. The act required the committees to set totals for the budget and enforce these totals through a series of two budget resolutions, the second of which reconciled all appropriations committee action to budget committee set limits.

The innovation initially failed to promote the politics of subtraction. Calculations tended to be biased toward accommodation, the hallmark of the old system. Deference toward appropriations committees tended to reduce the stridency of budget committee guardianship, especially in making reconciliation an adjustment of budget resolution figures to previous appropriations committee action rather than the other way around. Nevertheless, the cutting took place (Schick, 1980) and the general impression (LeLoup, 1980) reinforced it. But the real effect was the emergence of a "fiscal conscience" (Sundquist, 1981) in the House and in the Senate.

The promotion of cutting, however, fell under the spell of accommodation. Little effort to change authorizing legislation that drove automatic or formula spending took place. Moreover, agencies were created that did not appear in an otherwise unified and comprehensive government budget. Congress began allocating more through credit activities, such as loans to cities for sewer systems and guarantees for student loans granted by banks. Tax expenditures—tax concessions that Congress gave to organizations and groups of organizations—became a larger budgeting tool.

Strain demanded a cutting tool far stronger than what existed, and that tool came in two forms. First, reconciliation (the operation of the first budget resolution as if it were the second) of both spending and authorization to given targets and totals was mandated. Second, legislation which attempted to control the size of the budget deficit came into being with temporary or even contemporary effect.

The politics of subtraction is the politics of uncertainty; for example, consider this description of the politics of budget cutting by Caiden (1983, p. 102):

> As irrepressible demands continue to press on inadequate resources, the unified budget tends to disappear, fragmenting and splintering into myriad independent accounts and earmarked funds. In the absence of slack resources to cushion the effect of uncertainties, time horizons shrink so that the budget has to be made and remade throughout the year in accordance with the latest predictions for revenues and expenditures. In response to uncertainties and in an effort to conserve resources, central controls are reinforced over the areas that lie within their compass, leading to correspondingly greater effort on the part of spending units to increase their leverage and maintain their autonomy over sources of finance, information, and decisions. Budgeting—defined as the accurate implementation of a comprehensive annual plan for public expenditures—gives way to a desperate and repetitive struggle to maintain cash flow,

to the detriment of public accountability, consistent policy making, and unprejudiced information.

The description applies to nations, states, and localities that must come to grips with straitened circumstances.

The methods required by the politics of subtraction differ considerably from those in the politics of addition. Subtraction requires integration and not piecemeal decision-making, hierarchy not autonomy, inclusion not exclusion, clarification of issues not their blurring, and direct confrontation rather than avoidance of conflict. Such methods, Caiden argued, (1983) makes the executive rather than the legislative branch the suitable place for primary budget responsibility because only the executive branch has the high cohesion, the ability to force decisions in a strict timetable, and the capability to repeatedly ration claims. Congress has other responsibilities—representation of interests, vocalization of claims, melding of competing demands, and the negotiation and reconciliation of conflicting values. For subtraction politics, Congress faces a dilemma of choosing between the centralization necessary for budget cutting and the decentralization necessary for representation, negotiation, and reconciliation. Thus, the politics of addition and the politics of subtraction meet head on in Congress, as institutions and procedures are tried and replaced in the zeal to adjust to change.

If Not Choice, What?

The result of these new institutions and procedures is the politics of subtraction, which focuses on outright conflict, whereas the politics of addition invited gradual change, though not analytically induced decisions. We have less and less analytical choice and more and more need for methods and concepts of managing what is a loosely coupled system of individuals, subcommittees, issue networks, parties, and bureaucratic specialists.

Managing this apparent anarchy may mean employing affect-based strategies. Symbols, rituals, and language can guide the executive branch when nothing else might work.

Anarchy Metaphor and Executive Budgets

We should expect that organizations vary in the metaphorical requirements they have. As Cohen and March (1974, 1986) have pointed out, variance can relate to the amount of attention the organization members can give a choice that faces them. Then, too, the flow of problems and solutions can vary as well (cf. Chapter 5).

The patterns underlying the application of a metaphor might be a matter of how independent, exogenous, and rapid the flow of the streams of problems, solutions, participants, and choice opportunities might be. Metaphorical requirements relate to complexity. The more complex the structure, the greater the need for metaphor.

Picture, then, the making of budgets as simultaneous flows of information through various choice structures. Often, these flows contain one person's problem and another's skill at certain types of problem-solving. Thus, one person's problem is another person's solution. There may not be exact symmetry, however. Many solutions that are indicated by the number and type of participants on a given day may swamp the number of problems. The number of choice opportunities may also vary from time to time.

State governors face a fragmentary structure that they must somehow manage. Recall that managing an anarchy is possible, but managing may result in more than one decision style. March and Cohen (1986) found three styles prevalent among chief executives of major universities:

> Oversight. If a choice is activated when problems are attached to other choices and if there is energy available to make the new choice quickly, it will be made without any attention to existing problems and with a minimum of time and energy.
>
> Flight. In some cases, choices are associated with problems (unsuccessfully) for some time until a choice "more attractive" to the problems comes along. The problems leave the choice, and thereby make it possible to make the decision. The decision resolves no problems (they having now attached themselves to a new choice).
>
> Resolution. Some choices resolve problems after some period of working on them. The length of time may vary greatly (depending on the number of problems). This is the familiar case that it implicit in most discussions of choice within organization. (pp. 30–35).

Some choices involve both flight and resolution (i.e., some problems leave, the remainder are solved) but are defined as resolution. The three styles are mutually exclusive and exhaustive with respect to any one choice; but the same organization may use any one of them on different choices.

Strategic Budgeting

The strategy about choice style may depend on much that a chief executive cannot control. Nevertheless, March and Olsen prescribed some remedies in building a strategy (see Table 4).

Case Study of a Balanced Base Budget System

If we consider budget decision-making as an anarchy, we see vastly different sets of attention rules used by budget actors. Since process more or less formalizes the application of these rules, budget reforms come about as methods of forcing

Table 4   Remedies for Garbage Can Decision-Making in Organized Anarchies

---

1. *Spend time.* Since time is a scarce good, someone who is prepared to spend time is offering a valuable resource.
2. *Persist.* Losses and victories are partly fortuitous, due to the particular pattern of attention generated on a particular occasion.
3. *Exchange status for substance.* Symbolic issues are likely to be more important to participants than the substantive issues. Thus, someone willing to trade in the opposite direction is in a favorable trading position.
4. *Facilitate opposition participation.* The frustration of garbage can decision processes tend to reduce aspirations.
5. *Overload the system.* Any individual proposal may easily be defeated in a garbage can, but someone with a large number of projects will find some fraction of them being successful. Deadlines can also be used to manage the flow of problems.
6. *Provide garbage cans.* Deflect potentially irrelevant problems and solutions into innocuous choice situations—for example, discussions of long-term plans and organization objectives.
7. *Manage unobtrusively.* Sail the organization, rather than powerboat it, through the use of high-leverage minor interventions.
8. *Interpret history.* Control definitions of what is happening and what has happened to take advantage of the changing patterns of participation.

Source: Cohen and March, 1974, 1986.

budget actors to attend to budget decisions in particular ways along an agreed upon timetable. What these particular ways are, it turns out, are sources of competition. Budget actors evade those rules that bind them and abide by those that do not. In this section, I describe one instance of budget reform, using a case study method.

Executive Reorganization in Kansas

Until 1972, governors of Kansas had limited power. Their ability to appoint heads of departments had been superseded by the appointment of boards and commissions which then appointed the department heads. Moreover, the budgeting authority belonged essentially to the legislature and the agencies which together decided budgets without the two-year term governor having much say. The legislature met every other year for fiscal matters, leaving much of the oversight function in budget matters to a budget office jointly controlled by the governor and the legislature.

In 1972, the legislature passed and the voters approved a sweeping consolidation of management control in the governor's office. The governor gained responsibility for initiating and proposing an executive budget. In addition, boards and commissions were often abolished with appointment authority over department heads reverting to the governor, further strengthening gubernatorial power. For its part, the legislature created greater fiscal oversight with beefed up staffing in its Legislative Research Division and in its Ways and Means Committee.

The separation of executive and of legislative control over budgeting forced the passage of information through the governor's office. In fact, the 1972 law provided that the governor's budget agency stipulate the form of budget requests and that agency requests would be provided the legislative committees simultaneously with their submission to the governor. Such a form precluded some agency-legislative committee interaction because "no cabinet secretary relishes the prospect of appearing before a Ways and Means Committee to defend both his agency request and his governor's recommendation when the two do not coincide" (Rein and Brown, 1982, p. 33).

Balanced Base Budget (BBB) Process

From 1972 to 1982, the governor, the legislature, and the agencies worked through an annual budget accommodation. The legislature retained much control over budgeting. Not having full power over the executive branch, the governor let the budget director retain control over minutiae, influencing state agencies through wide-ranging efforts to increase federal aid, reform the tax system, and appoint personally loyal cabinet secretaries. The budget office, which was nominally a part of the governor's staff, remained a joint legislative-executive shop (Bibb, 1984).

By the beginning of the term of John Carlin, however, budgeting had become a routine, giving the new governor little strategic leeway. Legislative committees insisted on appropriating federal funds, such as revenue sharing, refused to reform the tax system by levying a minerals extraction tax, and used the budget to drive a wedge between the governor and his most loyal cabinet members (Muchmore and Duncan, 1982).

The BBB process was created to neutralize some of the legislative hegemony over the budget. The budget reform was meant to achieve two goals: provide strategic control and, in so doing, consolidate the governor's management control over the executive branch.

Muchmore and Duncan, the inventors of the BBB reform described it as an effort to gain the attention of executive branch officers.[1] This attention shift came about through scarcity production. Prior to the installation of a new budget system in Kansas, revenue estimates were made only after agency budgets had been prepared. They first came into play as the central budget staff began work with the Governor to reconcile requests to available resources.

Since the BBB system introduced resource limitations as a first step, the revenue-estimating schedule was advanced by six months—from November to

---

1. This section relies primarily on the research of Muchmore and Duncan (1982) and is used with their permission.

the preceding May. After the early projections had been reviewed, the Governor allocated the expected State General Fund revenues among agencies in order to create a "budget base," which became the centerpiece for all ensuing budget construction.

Each agency was directed to prepare a budget in which total general fund outlay equaled the assigned base level. Hence, the summation of all planned agency outlays exactly equaled expected revenues, and the base was a balanced budget.

To retain the characteristic of balance, gubernatorial recommendations for expenditures in any agency in excess of the allocated base amount had to be offset by a corresponding reduction elsewhere in the budget. The governor's base allocations applied at the agency level and not at the program level. Agency managers were left free to propose a distribution of the base amount across programs within their jurisdiction.

A critical element of the revised process was the information base available to the governor for deciding base budget allocations to agencies. In April, agencies were directed to prepare "issue papers" on major policy questions which they believed the governor should consider in dividing expected revenues among agencies. The issues and alternatives posed in the papers, accompanied by budget office analyses, constituted the data base for the governor's deliberations.

In the second year of implementation, the issue paper process was expanded to include input from private interest groups as well as state agencies. This broadened the array of issues and the variety of expertise available to the governor when allocations were made.

A form of zero-based budgeting also became part of the BBB system. It was felt that the governor would also need information on the changes in agency operations and public benefits that would occur if an agency received an amount of money that differed from the base allocation. Having assigned a *base allocation* and directed agencies to formulate budgets at that base level, the governor also assigned a *second allocation* at a higher level and a *third allocation* at a lower level. Agencies were then directed to prepare budget submissions at each of these supplementary levels to reflect potential agency adjustments to reduced funding and to express the priorities that might be executed if funding were raised above the base. Thus, the product with which the governor was presented, in anticipation of final budget decisions, was an array of alternatives that approximated the information required for optimal choices.

The array of alternatives focused not only on expenditures but also on variations in output. If the principles of constrained maximization were to be observed, it was thought, equal emphasis had to be placed on measurement of performance and service delivery. Therefore, the revised system obligated agencies to provide performance indicators and measures for each expenditure level. These measures provided a means of assessing progress toward achieving state program goals. Ideally, they also permitted a rough comparison of costs and benefits across a range of possible outlays, enabling the evaluation of adjustments either above or below the base allocation. In practice, the shift in emphasis from cost data to a combination of cost and benefit data was difficult to achieve in the short run. First, benefit and performance information was hard to obtain for some programs, and its reliability could be subject to challenge unless it reflected an established data-gathering process. Second, even when performance data were available, they were vulnerable to conflicting interpretations. Costs, on the other hand, were easily obtained, thoroughly documented, backed by extensive historical information, and were relatively unambiguous. Budgetary discussions, therefore, gravitated toward costs, particularly when the final fiscal plan adopted by the legislature was written in terms of cost control and not in terms of expected performance. The presumption in favor of cost data as the overriding element of decision-making was not easily countered.

The revised system also imposed a program structure and a program-planning requirement on agencies. The operations of state agencies were reviewed to determine how activities could be clustered more logically so that a budget unit was defined by reference to one or more common objectives and coherent management. The results were a breakdown of state government into approximately 350 programs. In some instances subprograms were defined as subsidiary but discrete activity clusters within programs. The fundamental unit for budget preparation purposes was the program.

The creation of programs logically preceded a second step; namely, the preparation of operations plans to spell out in detail the goals and objectives for every budget unit: (a) to describe the operational characteristics of the program, (b) to identify long-term factors affecting the need for the service, and (c) to provide indicators that could be used to monitor performance. Such program plans were commonly used in the central management and budget systems of the states from which members of the Division of Budget were recruited.

BBB Study Questions

As with any new official taking office, the investiture may provide considerable amounts of information to nominal subordinates and actual competitors. Thus, I wanted to determine what the components of the Kansas governor's investiture included. Specifically, what symbols and what rituals took on importance through the BBB system? Did they add to a plausible interpretation? Did the ritual leave the governor open to plausible alternative interpretations?

BBB Study Methods

The BBB system had constant scrutiny from the two executive branch agencies that experienced it and the legislators who contended with the governor for control of spending priorities. To ascertain the views of those who experienced the system, interviews and questionnaire surveys were conducted to assemble data.

Four sets of data on these budget actors and their reactions provide detail about what the budget system became useful for and how the system became implanted in the larger system of state government decision-making. One of these data sets came from a survey of agency budget officers, the primary officers who responded for agencies to the Division of Budget (Miller and Olson, 1983). Two surveys examined legislators and their views on the system (Tinkum, 1982; Solomon, 1983). A battery of face-to-face interviews with cabinet secretaries brought to the surface conclusions that were made by high-level managers.

The research design had one longitudinal feature. The questionnaires to agency budget officers and one of the legislator questionnaires (Tinkum, 1982) were administered within six months of the end of the first budget formulation cycle using BBB, as were the interviews with high-level managers. The second legislator survey (Solomon, 1983) was conducted after the second budget formulation cycle.

Findings and Discussion

The agency budget officials tended to see the new budget system as a sign of change. For small agencies, the writing was on the wall to begin responding to queries in programmatic terms rather than in service delivery terms. Large agencies, accustomed to a program view of the world, felt nevertheless that they gave away a source of leverage by surrendering problem analyses and policy initiatives *before* the budget season even got started.

In both cases, however, the governor, it appeared, had accomplished two objectives. First, he had consolidated executive power through the budget process, laying full claim to the values and imperatives of responsible administration. He may not have begun the executive reorganization movement in Kansas, but, it was said by a cabinet secretary, he did finish it with the BBB system.

It was in the BBB system that agencies felt the allocation power an executive budget brings to responsible administration. In this case, the allocation nominally resulted from decisions premised on agency policy papers, problem studies, and strategic environment scans.

In any case, the governor was able to achieve his second objective through the allocation decision. He was able to produce the political spectacle of a decision, and a major one at that, by announcing in grand style a direction for the budget to take before the first line-item form was ever filled out.

The grand allocation gesture came without the normal hearings process presided over by budget office officials. Previously, "cat and mouse games" had taken place. According to a previous budget director (Bibb, 1984, p. 126),

> Kansas law provided that the director of the budget review the requests of the state agencies and recommend a tentative budget to the governor from which the agencies could appeal to the governor for restoration. I had established the practice of periodically excluding programs from my recommended list so that,

in the appeal process, they would be evaluated and a decision made as to
whether each program should be continued and, if so, what level.

The budget director could force the agency to reveal data that would not ordinarily
come out in the budget-review process, and the director could hand the governor
the hot political potatoes that the budget director found it unwise to handle
himself. This scenario ceased! With BBB, the governor could ask what the agency
was doing to ensure his objectives. Even though it was still a game, the budget
hearing became a stage in which the governor could play by his own script and not
by that of the agencies, thereby holding them accountable for *his* agenda. Thus, on
the administrative side, symbols, rituals, and language were brought into play in
support of the consolidation of gubernatorial power. The allocation decision
symbolized initiative and decisiveness on the part of the leader. In so doing, the
allocation encouraged individual agency discipline in favor of larger goals, Elder
and Cobb's arguable primary role for symbols (1983).

The budget hearing, normally a ritual demonstrating budget office mastery
over accounting detail, was replaced by a ritual of a different sort. The hearing
ritual provided the governor with an opportunity to use the dramaturgy of probing
the agency budget requests and to play the roles of provider to the faithful and
punisher of the wicked. At once, the governor could ask for information in broad
sweeping terms, pointing out the value a program provided. At others, he could
command the damnation of those who failed his sense of vision and who allowed
events to take his initiatives in directions he did not want, all before an audience
newly enamored with gestures, scenes, and spectacle.

The governor's use of BBB fulfilled Edelman's three purposes for rituals. By
personally presiding and "leading" in his visionary way, the governor could quiet
the resentment his early allocation has stirred. Yet the allocation itself, which was
affirmed and defended by agencies in the hearings, became the grand gesture that
reaffirmed the role of the executive in the democratic system. Finally, by quieting
the resentment and reaffirming the governor's role, the hearing ritual in the BBB
gave the governor the ability to gain agency conformity.

BBB led administrators to talk a different language. The system encouraged
"cost control," program level responsibility for "priority setting," and an "early
spot" of problems. Most of all, the BBB system, temporarily perhaps, stilled the
agencies' claims to a common "fair share" of additional budget authority each
year, instead of pushing large, new-money budget increments toward single
objectives that the governor's strategy favored.

The legislative reaction was slow but stubborn. As both Tinkum (1982) and
Solomons (1983) found, legislators refused at first to believe that the reform had
any relevance for them. Only when legislators observed the way the system
consolidated the governor's power did they begin to encourage agency dissent.
That dissent came first from the state universities, a traditionally independent
group, experienced especially in the ways of legislative processes like budgeting.

Disgruntled university officials ultimately gained an attorney general's opinion of the constitutionality of the BBB process. The opinion lent support to the maintenance of some close agency/institution-legislative committee relationships, especially when these unique institutions had not been swept under the governor's full control through previous executive reorganizations.

The effect of the Balanced Base Budgeting system for theory was to demonstrate the potential applicability of investiture rituals in signaling a change in emphasis to important subcultures. Using the hearing ritual, the governor forced the allocation to be a symbol of executive power, and through the allocation, signaled change to all the executive agencies that could not escape his dominance through special legislative dispensation. These confrontations lent support to the budget process and its language under the new BBB regime. Ritual consolidated power, and through spectacle, quieted resentment, reaffirmed the budget allocation role, and gained conformity. The upshot was the final consolidation of a twenty-year centralization of management prerogatives in the office of the governor.

7

Network Political Economies:
Surrogate Markets for Debt

Budgeting, as the Balanced Base Budgeting (BBB) innovation portrayed, provides a way executives can structure and interpret reality indirectly for the people they manage. In this chapter, I explore municipal debt financing and the role of network political economies in defining and interpreting ambiguous situations for those involved, especially public financial managers.

Reality for public financial managers is often interpreted in careful and risk-averse ways; as I marshal evidence here to show. Competitive bidding for the sale of bonds often stands as the primary method by which risk is shifted to an intermediary. I argue that the competitive bid largely increases risk. Moreover, I argue that the innovative financing tools that cities now find it commonplace to use, although some call these innovations risky, have given cities little worry.

Why would anybody heedlessly follow a risky bid procedure but much more thoughtfully follow a risk-neutral financing strategy? I argue that innovations that take place in debt financing often come through the interaction of the financing participants—bankers, attorneys, accountants, and financial managers. This interaction is nothing less than a social construction of reality for those involved, and the resulting innovations appear to be quite radical in comparison with what I see as the values and reality construction of public financial managers.

This chapter has three sections, with each producing a part of the argument about innovation. In the first section, I outline research on the typical ways public managers encounter reality. In the second section, I argue that a network political economy is far more powerful in reality construction than individual financial managers. In the final section, I classify financing methods that belie the risk-averse manager thesis and lend support to the network political economy argument.

VALUES AND PUBLIC FINANCIAL MANAGERS[1]

Recent scholarship on public sector financial management has advocated the use of strategic planning and management (i.e., strategy) as the device worth considering for the improvement of productivity. Strategy provides a method with which a financial manager can analyze the larger organizational environment to detect patterns and trends. Having such foresight, the manager may be able to predict opportunities and then form a plan of action in areas of financial management concern: to reduce the risk in managing cash, employ debt wisely, and generally make more productive use of scarce tax and revenue resources.

The use of strategy heralds a reconsideration of values. In this chapter, I argue that the values underlying strategy tend to differ in many ways from those that prevail in government financial management at present. For strategy to have any value, its advocates must confront the problems in changing-value systems, however small these changes might be. When using strategy in a governmental as opposed to a private-sector setting, these advocates must similarly face inherent productivity problems. First, I outline the strategy position of these advocates. Then, I suggest the values that may lie behind their position. I then give one reading of the present values underlying government financial management, and furnish surveys of financial managers as evidence. The final section recapitulates my argument that existing values and the values that underlie strategy conflict.

STRATEGIC APPROACH

The primary vehicle for examining the values underlying strategy comes from the established periodical of the government financial-management community, *Government Finance Review*. Wetzler and Petersen (1985), following the typical route of those who proselytize on strategy, as well as the by now familiar litany that has historically preceded normative reform, have provided this explication:

1. Past management efforts and techniques have been appropriate for their times but not for present times, which are different.

2. Strategy is planning and analysis and both are good and fit to deal with problems of present times.
3. Strategy's track record so far is generally mixed, but the bad marks come from incompetent or inappropriate application.
4. Profound change comes with the acceptance of strategy as a mode of operation, change that might alter organization and procedure "to say nothing of politics."

But is this reform strategy unique? A new way of looking at management work? The development of strategy is not a short history although its recent rise to prominence suggests otherwise. After all, strategy has always been a management device for war-making.

Wetzler and Petersen's variations of strategy (1985, p. 8–9) parallel very closely those of others (see Table 1), which model the rational decision-making process. Finally, Wetzler and Petersen used strategy to introduce and urge acceptance in government circles of applied microeconomics and finance theory. They argued that strategy helps individuals choose between (a) capital markets and internal sources of financing; (b) projects with different rates of return on investment; (c) investments with different levels of risk; and (d) portfolios of various assets (resource or tax bases) (1985, p. 8).

The applicability of finance theory and concepts of applied microeconomics has limitations, as these authors and others (Methe, Baesel, and Shulman, 1983)

Table 1 Comparison of Models

Models of Strategy[a]	Models of Rational Decision-Making[b]
1. Examine the environment	Values or objectives are determined and clarified separately, and usually before considering alternative policies.
2. Assess the current situation	Policy formation is approached through ends-means analysis, with agreed-upon ends generating a search for ways of attaining them.
3. Set goals	A "good" policy is therefore one providing the most appropriate means to some desired end.
4. Identify the alternatives	Every important relevant factor is taken into account.
5. Analyze and select financial alternatives	Often theory is heavily relied upon.

Sources: [a]Wetzler and Petersen (1985); [b]Lindblom (1959); Golembiewski and Rabin (1975).

have pointed out. Yet the bigger problem lies not in transferring theory but in the singleminded insistence of advocates to set a course of action (*one* goal) that will stand as a criterion to which every other action will be compared.

Thus, Wetzler and Petersen and the strategists have confined themselves to the public sector road that leads to what is known as *organization engineering*. Selznick (1957) drew a distinction between organization engineering and institutional leadership. Strategy, Selznick (1957, p. 137) would say, operates much like engineering; that is,

> when the goals of the organization are clear cut, and when most choices are made on the basis of known and objective technical criteria, the engineer rather than the leader is called for.

Rather than employ engineering concepts—or applied microeconomics as is the case here—Golembiewski (1969) has argued the need to adapt to unique missions and roles, "to infuse technical structures with value" so that even "technically identical units of organization . . . have distinctive commitments to program, method or clientele" (pp. 218–219).

Values of Government Financial Managers

One set of values is that subscribed to by financial managers. In general, the greatest apparent contrast between finance theory/applied microeconomic prescriptions and the broad values that influence finance officers is the place for a guide to action. In positing wealth-maximization as the ultimate goal, finance theory creates a floor below which one may not fall. Whatever is done to maximize wealth is done to ensure survival. Fiducial values, I contend, create a ceiling—behavior will not go beyond a certain point.

To determine more specific referents for the values financial managers hold, we surveyed 824 financial managers about their knowledge and willingness to use prominent tools of economic development strategy: general obligation bonds, revenue bonds, leasing plans, private purpose bonds, and advance refunding stratagems (see Table 2). We expected the fiducial values of financial managers to play a large role in managers' acceptance of risky strategies.

All of the strategies were largely nonspeculative. However, three (leasing, private purpose financing, and advance refunding) were at least somewhat controversial.

In Table 2, the agreement about appropriate tools and uses tends to decline amazingly as the conservatism of the method decreases. Thus, general obligation bond borrowings elicit broad agreement with nothing else approaching this level of acceptance. Private purpose financings, at the time of the survey, had great notoriety; now this notoriety has given way to codified limits on its use. Yet the limited capacity to employ the technique underlies a contemporary reading of reaction to the technique.

Table 2   Willingness to Use Prominent Tools of Strategic Financial Management

[To respondents] "Please indicate which of the following instruments you believe government should or should not use as a long-term financing tool."

Instrument	Use	Not use	Not familiar
Revenue bonds	701	45	20
General obligation bonds	701	45	28
Leasing	556	113	85
Advance refunding	469	173	116
Private purpose financing	436	255	59
$N = 824$			

The values of public financial managers are largely opposed to maximization of returns on investment. These managers have a sophisticated sense of the legal obligations of their jobs and the legal consequences of mismanagement. Most feel that they dominate their organizations to a much smaller extent than private-sector financial managers. Finally, an understanding of strategy's tools, at least in the area of economic development and infrastructure rehabilitation, has its own limits; financial managers are not yet ready to chance the necessity to defend themselves against charges of profligacy.

NETWORK POLITICAL ECONOMY: ARBITER OF REALITY[2]

If financial managers were the sole arbiters of technique, we would find them choosing simple but not necessarily maximizing strategies based on their reported values. However, inferring a choice of strategy from only a debt issuer simplifies the process of financing beyond recognition.

As I and others (Miller, 1986; Hildreth, 1986, 1987; Sbragia, 1983) have pointed out elsewhere, financing strategies are formulated and pursued by issuers *and* others with whom they join in selling bonds. Research must focus on the team involved in the sale, not the issuer alone. Furthermore, I argue that the team members have different goals and the outcome of their team effort is more likely to be a least common denominator of these different goals than a rational pursuit of the issuer's end. The basic assumption made in this argument is that each organization represented on the team pursues a goal suited to that organization's survival and success. However, the more loosely joined or the more evanescent the team, the more unlikely the organizations will find a workable common denominator.

In this part, I outline a framework of research that would encourage a move to analysis. Specifically, I use an interorganizational network model that behaves as a political economy. Under some conditions, which I develop, the network members' stability or experience with each other becomes a major factor in the network's success. In turn, that experience depends on the various bargains struck within the network. These bargains, in turn, reflect the larger pattern of interaction among network members and the outside world.

In this part, I also provide an alternative view to the rational method showing that a bond deal is much more of a bargain struck among peer organizations in which the amalgamation of positions before and after the bargain are hard to reconcile along strictly means-ends terms. Rather, the appropriate theoretical framework might incorporate this network bargaining with surprising results.

Why study the bond deal or municipal debt financing? The politics of municipal debt financing has formed a part of the "lost world" of municipal government (Herson, 1957), although the role played by the network of institutions in providing funds to localities has important ramifications for the governance of cities, for their accountability, their efficiency, and their effectiveness. The general dynamics, processes, and uses of a capital market are well known; therefore, my effort is a closer examination of the financing process as a political economy in order to speed conceptual development of the micro aspects of the area, that lead to further research and professional development.

Consider Sbragia's (1983) position first. She observed that important links exist between the investment community, the professional finance community, and local policy making. These links suggest much greater interdependence and much less governmental initiative than would otherwise be the case considering the literature on municipal government decision-making. If we are to understand policy making, Sbragia has argued, much more must be known about these links and the causation they imply.

Sharp (1986) has noted that tax revolt movements seemingly limit the amount of taxes that may guarantee repayment of bonds; nevertheless, substantial areas of discretion and initiative still exist, especially in nonguaranteed debt and in off-budget enterprise debt. In fact, this area of debt (in contrast to general obligation debt) is the larger and is growing.

Moreover, Sharp pointed out that, in the last six years, substantial federal control over local government borrowing has now become apparent with federal law and Supreme Court decisions. The amount of control that will be exerted, as well as when it will be exerted, creates considerable uncertainty with which localities must cope. Their debt management decision-making is substantially geared toward reducing risk, and one way is to share the risk with a large group of professionals.

Finally, the research by Pagano (1982) and Pagano and Moore (1985) supports a line of reasoning which holds that, to some extent, public investment decisions have important effects on the economic decisions of private firms. When these economic development decisions encourage private investment, considerable economic and political development may take place, thereby changing the conditions and expectations of governance.

THE BOND SALE TEAM

In the sale of municipal securities, a fairly large group of experts may become involved in either of two types of sale: guaranteed debt and nonguaranteed debt (for a distinction of the two, see Sharp, 1986). Guaranteed debt underlies full taxing power of a government unit. Nonguaranteed debt is usually based on the repayment capacity of a revenue stream, such as a sales tax or water revenue. Guaranteed debt sales have become ever more tightly regulated by state constitutions and legal codes; in addition, federal law allows both banks and investment banks[3] to underwrite (bid for and purchase) these securities. As a result, these securities have become homogeneous, commodity-like instruments that require little distinction among advisors in their structuring. They rely for distinction on the credit worthiness of their issuers, as interpreted by rating agencies, and that the point in the business cycle when they are sold.

A nonguaranteed debt sale has become the place where advisors may actually use their creative talents. Because revenue streams may lack history or a basis for forecasting, "the market" must rely on an advisor to depict their earning capacity. Legal interpretations may also be required. Moreover, the market itself has to be analyzed to determine the likely purchasers of the securities both initially and in the secondary market.

Three basic groups of advisors form the team in a nonguaranteed debt sale: those whose efforts are made toward interpreting the market for the issuer, those who interpret the law for the underwriter/investor, and those who interpret the issuer for the underwriter/investor.

The financial advisor usually leads the effort to interpret the market for the issuer and determines how broad a market can be attracted to a sale or what part of a market is needed for a negotiated private placement. The determination of the market leads directly to the structuring of the security, influencing fundamentally its various features (see Hildreth, 1986, 1987; Moak, 1982; Lamb and Rappaport, 1980). The financial advisor may also be the underwriter (the buyer of the securities from the issuer for resale) if the sale is negotiated between the issuer and the underwriter.

The bond counsel leads the effort to interpret the structure of the security in terms of applicable law. Many individuals regard the bond counsel as the representative of the investors, who assures them that the issuer will not default on an obligation by pleading technical defects in the procedures used to authorize or issue the bonds. Petersen has observed (1988) that "additional roles of bond counsel in preparing transactions for market and [for] disclosure are extensive, flexible, and subjects of professional debate " (p. 4). If the structure's complexity demands it, the bond counsel may be assisted by counsel for an underwriter in a negotiated sale as well as for counsel for any other party, including the issuer.

Finally, the auditor or accounting specialist (CPA) interprets the issuer's financial status for the investor in terms of the structure of the security, typically as depicted through financial reports. If the revenue stream underlying the security must be forecast, the CPA may also verify the assumptions and calculations made to confirm the stream's contribution to the issuer's ability to repay principal and interest. Assisting or collaborating with the CPA, a consulting engineer, management specialist, or other expert may join in the interpretation of the issuer's financial status or the project being financed.

Disclosure

These separate areas of interpretation are disclosed primarily through the production of the official statement (OS). The OS is both official (i.e., the issuer's authorization of all interpretation made on its behalf by the team members) and a "direct exposition of information concerning the offering" (Petersen, 1988, p. 5).

The ultimate arbitering of the meanings ascribed to the offering, the issuer, and the market, however, remains the province of rating agencies. By considering the security's structure, the legal interpretation affixed to it, and the financial status of the issuer, as well as relevant economic and managerial information, the agencies determine essentially the likelihood that the issuer will repay the principal and the interest as scheduled.

Thus, the structure of the security and the disclosure of it and the legal status and repayment capacity of the issuer present the market with essential data regarding risk and reward. Theoretically, with these data, the new-issue market for municipal securities may achieve efficiency by allocating scarce capital among competing uses, assigning appropriate prices (interest payments to the issuer and bond prices and yields to the investor) to structures at particular levels of repayment capacity.

This outline of activity involved in bond sales has deliberately highlighted the range of discretion involved in an issuer's attempt to participate in an efficient market. Such discretion must exist to take account of the vast uncertainty with which an issuer must contend (and which I only hinted at in the first paragraph of this chapter); the bond sale team must guess. It appears that the type of team which must surround an issuer is the key to surmounting the vast uncertainty that often confounds a sale; consequently, we rely on theory as a guide, in determining the essential factors that comprise the team.

THEORY

If we consider the team-focused rather than the issuer-dominated framework as reasonable, we confront initially the lack of a workable concept. Public and private sectors relate bilaterally most often, as in the buyer-seller relations. In multilateral relations, most conceptions, such as the Triple Alliance/Iron Triangle (Freeman, 1965; Cater, 1964), tend to be simplistic or, as with issue networks

(Heclo, 1978), irrelevant. More recently, the concept of interorganizational networks has enjoyed revival and gained greater attention (Aldrich, 1979; Tichy, Tushman, and Fombrun, 1979). By a network, we mean the "totality of all the units connected by a certain relationship" (Jay, 1964, p. 138).

A network is constructed by discovering all the ties that bind a given population of organizations (Aldrich and Whetten, 1981). Typically, organization ties may be classified as organization-sets (Evans, 1966)—those organizations with which a focal organization has direct links—or action-sets (Barker and Jansiewicz, 1970)—a group of organizations that have formed a temporary alliance for a limited purpose—or both. The obvious difference between the two— organization- and action-sets—lies in the network stability and its consequences.

Network Stability and Its Consequences

Stability evolves through the work of linking-pin organizations that have extensive and overlapping ties to different parts of a network. Functionally, the links may be thought of as communications channels between organizations, resource conduits among network members, and even models to be imitated by other organizations in the population. Thus, an accounting firm might channel information about a reporting standard from rating agencies to bond issuers; the firm might direct clients to financial advisors the firm's members respect as a result of previous bond sales; or the firm itself, through one or more of its many services, might serve as a model for a municipal finance office.

All organizations within a network are linked directly or indirectly, and stability depends on the strength of these links. Aldrich and Whetten (1981) hypothesized that

> the ultimate predictor of network stability is the probability of a link failing, given that another has failed. This, in turn, is a function of the probability of any one link failing and two network characteristics: the duplication of linkages and the multiplicity of linkages between any two organizations.

Such hypotheses find confirmation in the literature on public management. Landau (1969) argues that redundancy tends to ensure performance. Golembiewski (1964) has argued that, in symbiotic interrelationships, duplication works to prevent the exercise of vetoes by powerful subunits. Lastly, the major result of stability is adaptability. Networks that are richly joined provide for greater opportunity for trial and error and for the spread of innovation.

For example, let us consider, as a simplistic situation, a small network consisting of a financial advisor, an accounting firm, and a law firm. The three are richly joined in the following ways:

1. The law firm acts as the corporation counsel to the other two organizations.
2. The accounting firm audits the transactions of the other two organizations.

3. The three organizations are active in the new-issue market for municipal securities with all other possible participants, and they serve together on a team for a bond sale for locality A.

Locality A becomes the beneficiary of knowledge about changes made by Congress in the tax laws that relate to municipal debt, about specific needs for information by rating agencies, and new debt structures that may be designed to appeal to specific segments of the market. Ultimately, the richly joined network results in the ability of locality A to adjust to complex and changing environments.

Now, consider a more complex sample. Assume that among a population of law firms that act as bond counsel, the firms tend, as a matter of each's ideology, to differ in their approach to interpret the law as it regards various creative capital-financing structures, some firms being indulgent, others strict. Assume, furthermore, that in a population of accounting firms asked to forecast the revenue stream that would generate principal and interest payments for various creative capital-financing structures, some would tend to be liberal, others tight. Finally, assume that among a population of financial advisors, the same sort of variation would exist among opinions about the applicability and marketability of debt structures.

Random selection of a combination of these firms by an issuer would yield a team that would advise the issuer to take a particular course of action, one in which the knowledge each advisor had, as well as the expectation each had of the other's interpretations and its effect on the market for the issue, would play a part. The result would produce a bargain in which a security configured in a unique way was rated and sold.

Now, assume a second random selection of firms by an issuer and a second sale. What knowledge does the second team have about the configuration of the first security? What keeps the second team from relying on an incorrect interpretation of what the first team did? What keeps the second sale from "missing the market"?

The situation is somewhat like the cobweb that economists used to explain market instability and the sellers' imperfect knowledge (see also Heilbroner and Thurow, 1984, pp. 126–127). Figure 1, a grower of crops plants quantity OA, but, under conditions of supply and demand at the time, could sell OA for price OB. The next year, the grower plants the quantity demanded the year before but finds that under the same supply-and-demand conditions, price OD. The result is a spiral of sorts. Yet, if conditions change as the two graphs show in Figure 2, the spiral could be successively more beneficial or it would be successively more explosive. The upshot of the random-selection notion with which we began is that, without gaining experience, the randomly selected team has a great chance of exploding and spiraling into an equilibrium.

On the other hand, given learning that a stable network would produce, a team, not selected at random, might have a better chance of understanding the

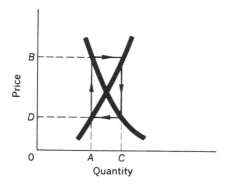

Figure 1 The cobweb. See text for the explanation. If expectations and information remain unchanged, producers will go on chasing their tails forever.

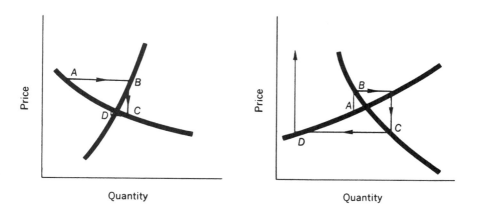

Figure 2 Stabilizing and explosive cobwebs. The cobweb on the left spirals into an equilibrium and the one on the right "explodes." The reason in both cases lies in the position and shape of the supply-and-demand curves. If supply and demand are favorable, a cobweb can lead to stability. if they are wrong, instability can result.

same market because they need less time to learn what to expect of each other—because they have duplicative ways of understanding each other—and more time to understand conditions in the market whether changing or not.

The Model

By combining elements of the bond deal with our hypotheses, we can build a model. From this model, we may draw conclusions on which to base advice for municipal bond issuers in forming teams.

Recall that the process of issuing debt involves four steps. Initiation of a sale rests on *the choice of the market*. Which investors will/should buy the securities? Tax laws, the economic cycle, and the habitual purchasing practices of individuals and institutions combine in reasonably predictable ways to encourage accurate choices.

The second step in the process involves *structuring an issue* to confront two problems: the predilections of the market chosen and the capacity of the issuer. The *structure* directly connects the market with disclosure.

The third step, then, is *disclosure of the issue and the issuer*. What facts will be disclosed? More importantly, what interpretation will be presented for these facts, whether in the OS alone or in the OS and to the ratings agencies?

The final step is the *sale*, at which time all parties decide the price of the issue. The sale confirms the assumptions made by the team about the structure of the issue and the level of demand for the quantity provided. In viewing the sale another way, it becomes a confirming piece of information about where the sale fell on the cobweb pattern. If the guess about supply and demand resulted in a spiral inward, we can say the team "learned."

Learning and Expectations

Consider what factors might encourage learning. Our hypothesis suggests that the number of links among members of the team leads to stability, and stability, in turn, leads to learning and adaptation. We use an expectancy approach to understand richly linked organizations in the bond team context; that is, each member of the bond team must be guided in an assigned task by expectations of the behavior of others. The financial advisor cannot select a market unless the advisor can expect to have counsel's positive legal interpretation of the structure that would most logically follow the selection of that market. Likewise, the advisor cannot select a market without the expectation that the CPA will interpret the various issuer capacities in such way as to support the structure the market suggests. In the end, no decision made by any member of the team can be made in a vacuum, without the knowledge of what the other members are likely to do. Otherwise, the decisions made by the members form an endless iteration—a loop—in which the market choice forces structure but is confounded by disclosure, thus leading to a new market and to a new structure with interpretations wedded to the previous structure, confounding this new market and structure.

Rich Links among Team Members

One solution to the problem of expectations is a richly linked network of organizations. Rich links lead to knowledge of likely behavior under varying circumstances. Assumptions at extremely general levels are shared, or at least, are made widely known through large numbers of activities in which the linked organizations jointly participate. Rich links also provide multiple avenues for the testing of expectations under widely varying conditions. For example, the legal interpretations a bond counsel is likely to submit may be expected because they are based on the legal interpretations the bond counsel has traditionally issued in the capacity of the corporate counsel, as the earlier illustration depicted.

Rich Links and Learning

If rich links lead to shared expectations of behavior, these links also contribute to learning. Consider the argument for specific types of teams in municipal finance. The negotiated rather than the competitive sale invites the sort of stability and exploitation of existing rich links among potential members of a team. Negotiated sales require the issuer to choose precisely those members who have apparently "learned" the market as well as each other in terms of the market. A negotiated sale provides an opportunity to choose the market (especially when the sale is privately placed), opening the way or creating the need for innovation (craftwork rather than routine technology) in the type of issue structure chosen. The negotiated sale also provides incredible overlap and duplication in the work involved.

Such rich links and the opportunities provided by the negotiated sale invite learning. Stigler (1961) indicated that buyers and sellers accumulate information from their experience in the marketplace which allows them to obtain more favorable conditions in each successive transaction. Specifically, Bland (1985) found that issuers using multiple negotiated sales received more favorable terms through each successive sale up to a certain point. He concluded that "local governments with previous bond market experience are capable of assembling a management team that can negotiate an interest rate comparable to what the most sought after competitive issues obtain" (p. 236).

Thus, a network's stableness or unstableness depends on the wealth of links among its members. The greater the stability, the greater the opportunities for learning; the greater the amount of learning, the greater the chance for innovation and adaptation.

Efficient Markets

Lastly, in the sale of municipal securities, achieving efficient markets is the broader goal of all participants. An efficient market allocates scarce capital among competing uses and assigns appropriate prices (interest payments to the issuer and bond prices and yields to the investor) to structures at particular levels of repayment capacity. Under what conditions does network stability lead to market efficiency? The answer lies in the reiteration of my model with one significant addition. Network stability develops through duplicative links among organizations in a network. Rich links open opportunities for learning. Learning leads to greater adaptability. Greater adaptability, of course, leads to better guesses about which market to choose and under what conditions. Moreover, adaptability helps shape disclosure, telling what to disclose to what market to provide its participants evidence of levels of risk and levels of reward.

SUMMARY

In this section, I have depicted the municipal capital-financing process as something more than the issuer-dominated activity researchers and public policy makers would have us believe. I argue that the process is much more a network activity which thrives when that network of participating organizations retains a large amount of stability. Such permanence allows the network to learn and its members to expect particular types of behavior from each other. More importantly, the network creates a dependence, especially for finance officers, who require the reality construction that the network can provide. The next section describes some of the results of the reality construction, and, later, I discuss the consequences of dependence.

OTHER ARBITERS OF REALITY

Not only does the network political economy play a major part in the social construction of reality through the imagery of riskiness absorption activities, the communications and rituals of debt management add their part as well. In this section, I briefly describe additional sources of reality construction, in the consideration of information activities. Thus, from activities that act to reinterpret the agenda of work or the roles of those involved, additional dimensions of a reality network which members can agree on are constructed.

Another method of dealing with the ambiguity of project finance has emerged as a reinterpretation of the agenda of issues (Kingdon, 1984). Agenda setting in the policy-making process encompasses the simple act of identifying a problem, thereby setting in motion the apparatus for solving it. The apparatus involves various institutional arrangements which act to aggregate resources.

The last, full national issue-attention cycle neared its waning moments at the beginning of the period from 1975 to 1990 that I have chosen for study. When the civil rights and urban disorders cycle of the late 1960s became exhausted, it was replaced by the fiscal crisis.

Actually, the fiscal crisis combined two issues: city financial emergencies and tax limitation. The financial emergency crisis began in New York City in 1975 with the tax limitation movement that was ignited by the passage of an expenditure "cap" law in 1976, which ultimately spread in 1978 to California in the form of Proposition 13.

In a sort of policy dialectic, the fiscal crisis gave way to a new issue-attention cycle of the 1990s—infrastructure problems and their repair and replacement. Fiscal crisis solutions tended to lead ultimately to proposals for higher taxes. But tax limitation and antigovernment solutions barred the rise in taxes. In the legislative standoff, the opportunity arose for resetting the agenda and for someone or a group not on either side to synthesize the proposals. Infrastructure provided the obvious candidate for synthesis, and public financial managers and investment bankers became the obvious issue entrepreneurs. The direct consequence of the fiscal problem was the declining facilities which cities had to face. At the heart of the tax limitation and antigovernment movements lay the question of the redistribution of wealth.

The infrastructure movement could solve the greatest fear of both sides' namely, that economic problems were not being solved. Economic problems of cities might not get solved through infrastructure replacement, but the multiplier effect of government spending on infrastructure would have an ameliorative effect (and those standing for election might have something to distribute). Economic problems of individuals might not be solved by infrastructure, but the new emphasis might produce productivity improvements and spark economic expansion (which to the middle class could blunt the redistribution of wealth carried on through the various social programs).

Likewise, infrastructure joined heretofore sparring institutions. Infrastructure repair could join the federal departments: specifically, Transportation for roads, bridges, and mass transit; Housing and Urban Development for general purpose development and public administration professionalism; and Environmental Protection for sewer and water systems. These departments, with infrastructure dominating the agenda, might appear to be doing what they intended—something "new," "innovative," or "pioneering"—even if it involved the most standard, traditional and mundane of activities and dealt with mere "upgrading of existing services." The infrastructure issue would also get the departments out of the "social engineering" morass and make managers responsive to the rising "frost belt" coalition of public officials.

The trick of getting infrastructure off and running in the face of tax limitation movements and federal budget contraction turned out to be financing. Who would pay for such a massive group of construction projects? With direct taxation or pay-as-you-go as well as direct federal aid eliminated, the only alternative left was long-term debt. Seeing such a demand, investment bankers and financial managers literally reshaped public capital financing as well as short-term cash management.

The entire "rebuilding America's cities" movement, as well as the budding "good schools" movement, represent agenda setting of a high order. Forces at work have reshaped the policy agenda, focusing direct attention on an issue other than tax limitation and blurring the deflate-the-government debate. The essential truth, however, lies in the notion that public financial managers have coped with uncertainty by information strategies, by seizing the initiative and resetting debate on policy in such a way that uncertainty may be absorbed and adjusted to in traditional, agreed-upon ways. Consequently, if reaction to risk captures the spirit of the decade, then *metaphors* give that spirit color, and have particular prominence.

The Administrative State

In the beginning of the period, the notion of an administrative state clearly signified the success financial managers had partially achieved and for which they continued to strive. Large social and community development efforts from Model Cities to Community Development Block Grants made financial managers the overseers of a larger and larger dominion.

The Besieged

Threats to dominion erupted quickly and violently. Fiscal calamities in New York City and in Cleveland, crises brought on by the initial tax-resistance movements in California and in Massachusetts, the growing willingness of the courts to allow personal liability of public officials (and later government liability and antitrust action against government activities), and, finally, the "energy crisis" itself placed the government manager in the role of "incompetent administrator" and the financial manager in that of "besieged servant." The financial manager's perseverance had to grow to take on the additional role of major actor in austerity drives or "cutback management."

The Magic Touch

If, however, the manager became something of a goat, he or she retained something of the magic associated with finance: managers, in a time when revenues were precious and tax increases rare, became known as prudent and successful investors, at times, providing the equivalent of a year's property tax millage increase in interest income from idle funds investments, while reducing the cost of borrowing through novel, consumer-oriented financings. These innovations, which were aided by federal budget deficits drawing in foreign capital, created enough new resources that, when added to the remaining public funds, helped end stagnation and spark a major economic renaissance in many states and localities, giving financial managers the image of "magicians."

The Financial Intermediaries

Not wanting to leave the job without completing it, financial managers did something about the shrinking resource base. Early on, studies confirmed the first major movement created from tax limitation, the increased reliance on user charges, or the creation of revenue streams based on exhaustible and excludable services. The market force reliance also generated the impetus for removing barriers to investment with idle funds. Moreover, new bond-financing techniques created the means to give the state and the local industrial and economic base some diversity. As a result, the financial manager became a "financier," the state or local government a "financial intermediary."

The Risking Scandal

Inevitably, perhaps, scandal followed and has created problems for both capital financing and cash management. Overuse (some call it a scandalous misuse) of private purpose financings by some managers has led to curtailment of several types of economic development efforts for lack of adequate financial tools.

The Strategic Thinker

In each case of scandal, however, new products have appeared and roles have changes so that, substantially, the financial manager has become a "strategic manager of risk." This last role promises to alter radically the skill level of those who are presently in the profession and place greater emphasis on sophisticated practice of the financial manager's fiduciary responsibility.

REACTION TO UNCERTAINTY

In this chapter, I discussed the reaction to uncertainty played out by finance officers in the 1975 to 1990 period. The reaction has taken the form of administrative notions called "coping" (Hickson et al., 1971). Based on a theory of power in organizations, coping suggests where power lies. Those who can cope with the critical contingencies facing the organization, so the theory goes, would wield power. During this period, finance officers have apparently coped in direct ways through prevention and absorption and in more fundamental and indirect ways by helping to reset the policy agenda to preserve initiative and to guard the financial resources of government. But the nagging question remains: Did financial managers cope or did they depend on the networks to aid the effort? If the answer is dependence, then the question about power focuses attention on those managers who were central to coping outside of the government—the financial advisors and their ability to help financial managers construct a coping imagery to overcome fiducial values.

The actors themselves deserve attention. In the catalog that follows, I deal with the financial managers' reactions to change over the decade. First, the catalog briefly notes new products and processes. Then, I review legislation affecting changes and sometimes spurring further change. Finally, I attempt to forecast future changes in the roles of the players in capital project financing.

Revolution in Credit Markets and the Death of Intermediation

Changes occurring in the municipal credit market in the 1980s have created forces that may very well remake the complexion of the field of play. These changes affect the three planks of the market: (a) borrowers, states and cities as well as their creations entitled to the tax exemption; (b) lenders, commercial banks, institutions, such as fire, casualty, and life insurance companies, and households; and (c) intermediaries, such as investment banks and their fellow travelers, bank trust departments, bond counsel firms, credit analysis firms, and insurance companies.

Borrowers

Since 1982, tax legislation has created a sharply defined group of borrowers in the tax-exempt market. Eliminating much of the burgeoning private purpose or industrial development bond borrowing demand, the law has created greater use of a number of existing and long used methods of financing public goods. For instance, the nonprofit corporation, explicitly designed to buy and thus provide cash flow to support public goods, exists to a greater extent than ever before. Tax-exempt leases transform what could have been long-term borrowing objects to simple one-year appropriable items. Third party and co-financing, operating under the guise of privatization of production of public goods, could operate to reduce insistence upon public goods produced by governments.

At the same time, insistence by federal policy that major federally backed capital projects in states and municipalities be paid for, at least in part, by these local governments has created a vast new area of demand for credit. In all, tax reform has appeared at a time of extreme reluctance of governments to carry large long-term debt burdens, leaving short-term burdens to be refinanced from year to year. Thus, the demand for long-term funding for direct government-produced public goods has decreased at the same time that tax reform has mandated a decrease in the use of the publicly financed private project as a tool of economic development.

Lenders

Among those buying municipal securities, municipal bond funds for individual households as well as institutions have developed at a rapid pace. Besides the dilution of risk presented by any individual bond issue, the bond funds serve as a new source of capital by remarketing to a larger and relatively less sophisticated group of investors.

The new source of capital compensates for relatively less interest in municipal securities by banks because of federal tax reform and the normal cyclical swings in the earnings of insurance companies and banks. The emergence of new types of securities, which are marketed to individuals, has encouraged the development of a vast deep pocket of capital for municipal securities.

Intermediaries

The changes that affect the borrowers and the lenders pale directly in comparison to those changes affecting intermediaries and their compatriots and indirectly the borrowers and the lenders regardless. Beginning with the least earth-shattering, tax reform has mandated the registration of municipal securities. This registration creates additional tasks for a bank trust department and additional fees for either bondholders or municipal borrowers to pay. However, the advent of the central depository and registration agent and the computerization of record keeping and other housekeeping duties has created the opportunity for municipalities to undertake the registration and paying-agent functions themselves.

Additionally, the creation of the zero coupon municipal security, which, in effect, is sold at a discount to accrete to full value rather than bear interest, eliminates the paying-agent duty and provides instead the borrower's accountant with the job of ensuring the existence of the accreted amount. In such a case, the bank, which is one of the several participants in the bond issuance process, becomes a relatively less important participant and eventually a party not necessary to the process.

The credit-rating agency, always powerful as analyst and handholder for the uniformed bond buyer, may be on the way to extinction. The risk of loss, by which the credit rating agency creates a role by divining, now may be covered in all but the most obviously unrisky situations by bond insurance on the risk of default. Several such agencies now exist and more are sure to follow this group in supporting a lucrative line of business. The insurance agencies receive a gilt-edged rating by the credit-rating agencies and bequeath this rating to the issues their insurance underwriting supports, in exchange for a fee and by following rudimentary analysis of the terms and conditions of the issue and through a superficial analysis of the borrower's financial condition. Thus, credit analysis and the role of the analyst are replaced by the market or by credit analysis of the insurer.

Finally, change has affected the heretofore pivotal player, the fiscal agent/ underwriter. Presently, intense competition and state laws have created a power struggle among firms for traditional lines of business, general obligation, and traditional revenue bonds. In general obligation bond cases, state law often requires the separation of the financial advising or fiscal agency (which prepares an issue for market) from underwriting. In such a case, the competition for financial advising has become intense.

A cycle whereby greater numbers of firms compete, prices for services fall, rates of return to these firms fall, and shakeouts occur becomes increasingly imminent. In many cases, financial advising for general obligation bond work has become a free service provided to a client in exchange for rights to underwrite other issues which the client has the legal authority to award without competitive bidding. In still other cases, state law requires that bond counsel, rather than an investment banker/financial advisor, substantially complete all work on an issue prior to marketing. If the shakeout cycle has substantial validity, the result of the shakeout holds both promise or warnings for borrowers.

Should the shakeout result in only firms with large capital or most talented and thoughtful staff members remaining, perhaps the cycle will produce innovative substitutes for the tax-exempt general obligation bond, such as the greater reliance on co-production and the ultimate—the taxable municipal security. Firms having two staffs, one working the tax-exempt side and the other the taxable side, with both in the fixed-income department, could realize economies, and the municipality could benefit from the breathtaking innovation taking place in corporate securities marketing.

The warning provided by the shakeout cycle theory, however, has equal validity; that is, the shakeout results in fewer firms, all of which do what has been done traditionally—charging higher prices. As always, the wild card in this scenario probably lies in federal income tax law. Present movements to restrict advanced refunding, to further tighten arbitrage regulations which municipalities follow to gain the tax-exemption, and to lower the capital gains tax rates for individuals may result in less use of tax-exempt securities.

The shakeout extends beyond the financial advising role investment banks play to the underwriting role as well. The creation of and greater reliance on bond insurance, particularly for more exotic financings for which investment banks command high prices, also has the effect of contracting spreads on underwritten securities.

Why should a municipality pay a spread and an insurance premium? In such a case, the municipality must decide the price the expertise exotic financings require and what price the risk entails for underwriting. The other risk feature that underwriters traditionally bear relates to interest rate volatility. Will the issue be priced correctly when resold? Again, insurance exists to hedge the risk, nominally at least, in municipal bond index futures contracts.

Underwriters within reasonable tolerances can reduce losses, and even gain, on the purchase of preset prices. In the case of both insurance against outright borrower default and contracts hedging price changes, the underwriter faces less risk than ever before, allowing a contraction of the spread, as never before. The narrowing of the spread reduces the profit for investment bankers and the incentive for brokers and traders, mitigating the potential for talent and insight to gravitate progressively toward either of these jobs.

Is the investment banker doomed? Probably not. Municipalities, in the short run and probably in the long run, will not acquire the expertise to be able to market and sell securities. No one but investment bankers and traders will have the expertise or the gall to devise strategies to profit from confusion and complexity, given the present tools for designing issues and the speed of innovation. Nevertheless, the investment banker as now known and appreciated may soon cease to exist.

This exploration of the future leads one to be able to conclude, as has been done before, that the present intermediaries will one day no longer exist. However, the conclusion will probably fail for two simple reasons. The first is a matter of concern to public administrators: government cannot recruit and retain the talent necessary to reduce the cost of government, at least the cost of government borrowing. Of course, if government borrowing ceases to exist through privatization, the contraction of government functions, or the sale of assets, the expertise has no value anyway. Second, the investment banking function will continue because of the need to produce the innovations that keep borrowing costs low, whether these innovations concern new ways of marketing fixed income securities or new ways to contract government functions.

SUMMARY

In this section of the chapter, I discussed the reaction to ambiguity that finance officers have had in the 1975 to 1990 period. The reaction has taken the form of administrative notions known as *coping*. In that decade, finance officers coped in direct ways, through prevention and absorption.

The nagging question remains, however: Did financial managers cope or did they depend on their network of investment bankers, attorneys, auditors, and other advisors who aided the effort? Coping suggests a more knowledgeable and sophisticated profession than existed before 1975. Coping also implies a deep understanding of the capital-financing process, the political process which underlies it, and the credit markets which support it, subjects about which, most research suggests, finance advisors are somewhat less than completely knowledgeable.

If not coping but the more likely case of dependence, the question focuses attention on those central to coping outside government—the financial advisors. Financial advisors may be leading government financial managers into what amounts to greater ambiguity, to a casino-like world where puts and floaters, hedges and straddles, and arbitrage and speculation contribute to the creation of debt for the sake of creating debt.

This evidence lends credence to the explanation advanced earlier that managers themselves do not decide what reality is; if they did, their values would tend to limit their innovativeness. Instead, managers participate with others in constructing a reality that many find particularly useful. This reality is constructed specifically to cope with an ambiguous environment outside of the organization; the innovations constructed create stability, perhaps in line with the managers' values while still promoting innovation. Despite the fact that managers do not have values that permit innovation easily, innovation does occur and rather comprehensive innovations at that.

COPING WITH UNCERTAINTY IN CAPITAL FINANCING[4]

This section analyzes the ways state and local government financial managers reacted to *uncertainty* in their capital-financing activities over the last fifteen years.[5] The reaction may be described in terms of two coping strategies (Hickson et al., 1971, p. 217)—prevention and absorption.

Coping by Prevention

Prevention efforts have attempted to forestall uncertainty. Generally, managers aim their efforts at reducing the probability of shocks occurring so that resources flowing to the organization do not vary widely. State and local financial managers have followed four basic strategies to prevent excessive variability: diversification, mergers, leveraging, and securitization.

Diversification

In state and local governments, diversification has applied primarily to revenue sources. The search for alternative revenues to the property tax at the local government level and to the income tax at the state level has become one of the clearest trends of the last decade. The results of the search for alternatives have yielded a trend: user fees and other benefit-based revenues have become a major area of growth for local governments. At this level, the trend toward benefit-based revenues has moved from a ratio of charges to taxes of about one-quarter in the early 1970s to one-third to one-half in the late 1980s (U.S. Bureau of the Census, 1989). Predictions based on that rate of growth suggest that the ratio will exceed one-half, or that municipalities will derive about a third of their own-source revenues from user fees by the early 1990s. Others disagree. In fact, some suggest the proportion will actually decline as the growth in expenditures for traditional user fee financed services stabilizes (Academy for State and Local Government, 1984). The atomizing or special district movement, however, may synthesize the two—numbers of activities financed by charges will grow and demand for these activities may grow as well.

States have diversified to a lesser extent than simply raising taxes. Nevertheless, so-called sin taxes have gained intense scrutiny and debate among state level financial managers. Cigarette taxes, especially, have risen in the face of federal tax cutbacks.

Mergers

Two major types of horizontal mergers and a form of vertical merger have provided much preventive potential for financial managers.

Horizontal Mergers. Annexation, the first type of horizontal merger, reports the U.S. Bureau of Census, has fallen but still remains the merger technique of choice in the South and in the West (U.S. Bureau of the Census, 1980). Horizontal mergers with the private sector have gained more notice as well as notoriety. Privatization of public functions has a substantial following and applies to almost any activity in which former public functions are shared with private sector or profit-oriented groups. There are at least seven major forms of horizontal merger through privatization.

1. Equity "kickers" (*Wall Street Journal*, 1982).[6] In several instances, the government has demanded an equity position in the project as well as the yield from the security financing the project. This has been true especially in short-lived industrial development bond financings in which cities have acted as issuers. However, the equity position has also become a negotiating object when cities have formed partnerships with private parties in using federal funds for redevelopment purposes. Chicago, for example, demanded an equity position in a downtown hotel development project, in the form of a share of future earnings attributable to the improvements funded by city participation. Other cities exhibiting Chicago's behavior include (a) Louisville, Kentucky, (b) San Diego, and (c) New Haven, Connecticut.

Louisville will receive 50% of the cash flow (after the developer gets a 15% return on his equity) and 50% of the future appreciation in a hotel project in return for aiding a development company with the financing for a $50 million project.

In a $200 million project in downtown, including retail space, office space and a hotel, San Diego and the developers agreed that the developer would lend the city $4 million, interest free, for four years to assemble a parcel of blighted acreage. The developer would then buy the land for $1 million. In return, the developer will pay the city 10% of rental income in excess of the base rent for 50 years along with 31% of the parking revenue.

New Haven transformed an old brass mill into a research facility. The city created a nonprofit corporation as developer and sold the project's tax breaks to investors through limited partnerships to raise project equity. Construction financing was a no-interest loan from federal community development block grant money. Permanent financing came from construction unions' pension funds. To meet pension law requirements, the city persuaded the state of Connecticut to guarantee the fist mortgage. An urban development action grant helped underwrite a second mortgage.

2. Tax increment financing. Unlike revenue streams that are due to increased sales or rental of facilities, tax increment financing creates a stream of revenue from the increased value of property and from the resulting taxes on that property after development financed by tax increment securities.

The method relies, first, on a calculation of old and new property values. The issuing entity must establish a base year and value property in that base or predevelopment year. The entity must also decide the allocation of base-year valuation and tax among those other entities relying on the property tax, such as school boards. Next, the entity estimates the value of the property during and after construction and redevelopment and through the immediate future. With these estimates, the entity creates a revenue stream from the incremental difference in postdevelopment tax revenues. The stream relies on the difference between redevelopment era property valuation and base-year valuation, multiplied by tax rates and subtracted from base-year allocations that are due other taxing entities.

The financing method has faced much opposition arising from competing taxing jurisdictions. In effect, these jurisdictions face a static tax base for the term of the repayment period. Defenders argue that tax increment financing reduces the likelihood of further tax-base erosion. Moreover, they claim that redevelopment adds jobs and activity which may increase the value of property in other areas, where houses of workers and businesses servicing these workers exist, and which form the property tax base on which all jurisdictions' tax bases rely.

3. Private-public partnerships. With tax-exempt leverage lease financing, private partnerships assure production of capital goods. Using such a financing plan, a taxable third party builds and owns a facility. The third party, acting as lessor, leases the facility to an operator, including in the lease the cost of maintenance, repair, and insurance. The jurisdiction, in turn, enters into a service contract with a lessee/operator. The service contract secures the builder's loan; the loan comes from tax-exempt revenue bonds, but the builder contributes 20 to 40% of the purchase price. Revenues from the facility's customers would service the contract to the city.

4. "On behalf of" issuers. Assuming congenial state and local law, issuers can create nonprofit corporations which act as issuers "on behalf of" the original issuer, usually a state, county, school board, or city. The authority for the creation of an on-behalf-of issuer rests in federal law. Generally, the government entity forms the corporation for the purpose of leasing real property or equipment from the corporation. The corporation issues bonds or other securities. The lease payment stream from the government to the corporation acts as the underlying security.

5. Sale and leaseback. Using an on-behalf-of issuer, a jurisdiction can not only remove certain assets but also liabilities from its books. A city with a facility wholly owned might decide to create a *municipal assistance corporation* (MAC), an on-behalf-of issuer which might buy the facility and lease the facility back over

a period equal to the facility's "useful life." The MAC would then sell securities based on the lease payments the city pledged.

6. Annuities and pension plans (Yacik, 1985). Jurisdictions now shift their pension liability to the private sector through tax-exempt borrowings. For example, Essex County, New Jersey sold general obligation bonds to purchase an annuity contract from Metropolitan Life Insurance Company, which, after Metropolitan invests the bond proceeds, will be obligated to pay out $10 million more in pension benefits. Thus, the county issued bonds totaling $48 million, and will pay, over the life of the bonds, principal and interest of $94.9 million. Metropolitan will fully fund the pension system with $105.8 million.

7. Tax-exempt leasing (Vogt and Cole, 1983) resembles the on-behalf-of issuing corporation technique. In a tax-exempt lease/purchase agreement, the government entity, as *lessee*, signs an agreement with a bank, investment bank, or leasing company, as *lessor*. The lessor raises funds through a lender or investor to pay for the objects covered by the lease. In return, the lender receives a security interest in the equipment, all rights and title under the agreement, and a stream of lease rental payments (principal and interest) of which the interest is tax exempt. Because of the size of the transaction, more than one lender may participate. Certificates of participation can be issued, allowing lenders to share in a proportionate amount of the stream of the rental payments.

Vertical Mergers. Although intergovernmental sharing of responsibility, especially that involving federal aid, continues to diminish, state aid to local governments in all forms actually may have increased. Most important are new structures, such as (a) equipment loan funds, (b) bond banks, and (c) other forms of state assistance.

Several states and counties have issued bonds to fund equipment loan pools for hospitals or other nonprofit departments within local governments (*The Bond Buyer*, 1983). These programs loan funds on an intermediate-term basis, but the value lies in spreading the financing costs of the bonds over a number of equipment users. Credit-enhancement techniques allow merger of smaller or weaker credits to stronger ones.

The larger, unlimited object version of equipment loan funds is the bond bank (Forbes and Petersen, 1983). Public financing authorities, which pool capital financing for government entities into single, large bond issues, came into being around 1970 in the state of Vermont. By pooling obligations, the issue attracts more interest, spreads underwriting costs, and lowers rates. However, evidence exists to show, at least superficially, that the cost of the bond bank is more than made up by reduced interest costs and earnings from bond proceeds investment.

States also provide assistance to communities in marketing bonds (Forbes and Petersen, 1983). California's Health Facilities Construction Loan Insurance Program insures local revenue and general obligation bonds that finance health facilities' construction and comply with state health plans. In addition, the

Michigan Qualified School Bond Fund operates a revolving loan fund to provide emergency assistance to school districts in meeting debt service. Texas commits royalties from oil extraction sales to secure local school board bonds. The royalties suffice to back up the credit-worthiness of large bond issues from all areas of the state, yielding a AAA rating. Minnesota's Bond Guarantee Fund insures any local general obligation bond issue. If default occurs, state law allows the state to levy a special property tax on a locality.

Leveraging

With newer revenue sources based on an income stream, which are similar to annuities, a government can leverage these streams or borrow on them by using them as collateral. Such approaches amount to simple revenue bonds; however, newer methods, in which various revenue streams act together as *leverage*, provide the potential for new and more reliable sources of capital-financing funds.

Cross-source Leveraging. One of the best examples of leveraging various revenue streams occurred in New Jersey recently (Bayless, 1985). Through the New Jersey Turnpike Authority, the state's Transportation Trust Fund will gain $12 million a year to restore transportation infrastructure. The state's three toll roads earmark a portion of revenues for the trust, a combined total of $25 million yearly over a twenty-year period to service and repay the bond issues financing repair work. Those contributions will be highly leveraged: Every dollar contributed by the toll roads could be used to raise another $5, then matched nine times over by the federal government. The legislature appropriates funds and combines them with the annual contributions from the state's toll roads and a portion of the gasoline tax. This revenue stream guarantees the necessary work and provides for debt service on bonds.

Securitization

Traditionally, municipalities have financed limited-benefit capital improvements through pledges of receivables. For example, paving a residential street often has depended upon the willingness of the residents to pledge monthly repayments for the work. When the pledges emerge, the local government issues bonds with that revenue stream securing it. Private-sector borrowers call this procedure *securitization of assets*. Involving an illiquid loan or lease agreement, the securitization process transforms the asset into a liquid security. Virtually any asset with a payment stream and a long-term payment history is an eventual candidate for securitization. State and local government lease agreements, that is, any fee based service, produce such streams and histories. As a result, their capitalization might rest on securitization of the payment stream.

Likewise, capital improvements capable of "exclusion" or unit benefit analysis, might submit to securitization. Capital goods, usually defined as "public goods," such as streets, sidewalks, and even fire stations and police precinct houses (where fire calls and police calls may be defined as exclusive services) could become candidates.

The reverse could work financially. Regulatory fees for pollution control, where the entity pays regularly based on its emission level, could act as securitization for the capital facilities that might ameliorate the problem. In addition, cities might benefit by private corporations' greater liquidity. A vendor using receivables-backed securities might offer better than the usual trade terms. Liquidity would not be affected because the receivables would be sold. Cities would get better terms because repayment forms a receivable of a given length susceptible to securitization. A city's cash flow could improve, providing it with the foundation for cash management and investment.

According to some sources (Shapiro, 1985; Sloane, 1985), bankers have begun to look at securitizing other kinds of assets. Beyond assets with a payment stream and a payment history, which can be tracked over a sufficient period of time, the next generation is an asset that doesn't have a predictable cash flow associated with it. And it might not have any cash flow associated with it except when it's sold. Commodity-backed agreements could be pledged or a group of assets could be sold to back securities: for instance, natural resources, site improvement incentives, zoning abatements, and more abstract forms of assets, such as the aesthetics of the community or the quality of the school system as they affect business location.

Summary

The prevention of uncertainty through design of systems that increase the potential pool of resources and the willingness to use the resources has marked state and local government finance. Diversification and merger have gained new life. New techniques, such as leveraging and securitizing, have future value. Yet present needs require a great deal of absorption of uncertainty.

Coping by Absorption

Action during a period of uncertainty often occurs as absorption activities. Absorbing uncertainty means adjusting to it by making a given financial system operate within new and changing confines. Offsetting the effects of variations in resources, particularly the ravages of inflation and interest rate increases, uncertainty absorption tactics and strategies used by state and local government financial managers come in several forms. At least four groups of shock absorbers exist: (a) hedging techniques to insure against inflation; (b) new inflation and interest rate sensitive debt products; (c) new advance refunding routines for adjusting existing debt to the variations in interest rates; and (d) leveling demand efforts by which issuers find new bondholders.

Hedging to Absorb Uncertainty

Hedging involves the use of futures or options contracts (or both) to anticipate movements in interest rates. Futures contracts are agreements to deliver or receive cash or securities at a specified time or place.[7] Options give investors the right, but not the obligation, to buy or sell something, such as futures contract or a security, at a specified time or place. Hedging strategies have developed as futures and options markets have offered new products. Basic hedging involves the purchase of a futures contract, or an option on a physical or futures contract, to guard or "lock in" an interest rate.

The fastest growing and the most often used method of absorbing uncertainty today has emerged as "creative capital finance" activities. The nature and type of these creative techniques has changed as quickly as has the volatile trends affecting both borrowers/issuers and lenders/securities holders. These techniques span all dimensions that exist to describe capital financing: short- and long-term, interest sensitive and insensitive, borrower tilted and lender tilted, general and specific use oriented, and relatively more tax weighted versus less.

Over the past fifteen years, six techniques have attained widespread use: (a) stage financing, (b) commercial paper, (c) floating-rate bonds, (d) put option bonds, (e) third-party financial guarantees, and (f) stepped coupons.

Stage Financing.   To respond to an expected population growth and service the demand life cycle of a growth area, stage financing creates a fixed amount of debt service capacity which a governmental unit can maintain over a period of time. For example, a unit may decide to set its tax stream at a fixed mill levy for debt service purposes. In many cases, this will be an average rate, seemingly high in the initial stages of growth, but low in the later ones. This millage which is devoted to debt service permits the unit a borrowing capacity great enough in the early stages to anticipate growth and service demand. The millage devoted to debt service in the later stages is not so great that undue burdens are placed on a stagnant or even declining revenue base.

Commercial Paper.   Tax exempt commercial paper, an unsecured, tax-exempt loan with a shorter than one year maturity, offers another opportunity to limit exposure in a period of volatility (Klapper, 1980). Interest rates on commercial paper follow the short-term debt market and, generally, fall below taxable Treasury bill rates. A commercial paper program requires refinancing of existing issues upon maturity. Because paper is unsecured, a letter of credit from a bank normally backs the program.

Floating-rate Bonds.   Floating or variable rate financing has emerged because chaotic conditions in the municipal bond market reduced reliance on traditional, long-term, fixed-rate issues. Investors who witnessed bond interest rates fluctuate between 5 1/2% and 14 1/2% over the five-year period from September 1977 to

January 1982 had little demand for a bond bearing a fixed rate for 20 to 30 years. Yet the majority of city issuers prefer to finance for as long a term as possible.

The interest rate on variable rate bonds for each interest payment period is not fixed at the time of issuance but instead will "float" or adjust as market conditions change. As such, the rate is tied to an index or a market indicator reasonably sensitive to market conditions.

Pricing strategy is by far the most important factor in structuring and marketing variable rate securities. The strategy relies heavily on some index which is thought to mirror trends in competing investments of similar risk and maturity. The index provides a time-series that can be compared to the interest rates of existing short- and long-term, tax-exempt and taxable securities over a relatively long period of time. The interest rate indices run the gamut from London Interbank Offered Rates (LIBOR) to federal securities rates to indices set by banks for their own customers. The variable rate has an obvious attraction. The issuer borrows in the short-term market at a rate generally 2 to 4% lower than the traditional, long-term market rate.

Put Option Bonds.   A bond carrying a put option allows the bondholder to sell the bond back to the issuer on a given number of days notice. Superficially, the *put* evens the sides, giving the bondholder a method of seeking the advantage the issuer always has had with a *call* feature.

The put option allows the holder of any bond to demand that the bond be purchased by a remarketing agent on a given day by presenting the bond to the remarketing agent on that day or upon a notice specified on the bond. The bondholder receives the principal amount (par value) plus the accrued interest, if any, to the date of the purchase. The remarketing agent finds a new buyer for the bond sold back by the old buyer exercising the put.

If the remarketing agent cannot remarket a bond, a trustee draws on a "liquidity facility," a letter of credit or other liquid financial guarantee of payment usually provided by a bank, to pay the principal and accrued interest. Generally, put options carry with them the need for further guarantees of payments, generally a letter of credit.

The put feature allows issuers to sell long-term bonds with yields close to those on short-term issues, because in effect, the notice period required before the bond is put, acts as the bond's maturity. The put feature first appeared on issues in 1980 and has gained popularity as interest rates have become volatile.

Third-Party Financial Guarantees.   Default by the Washington Public Power Supply System in 1983 has created a desire by borrowers and lenders to "guarantee" the payment of principal and interest on bonds (Forbes and Petersen, 1983). Essentially, borrowers buy an insurance policy to guarantee payment to bondholders in case of default. Along with the guarantee comes the insurer's AAA credit rating that acts to lower the borrower's cost.

Bond guarantees come in several different forms. First, there are strictly defined insurance policies covering the principal and interest on long-term, fixed-rate issues, such as general obligation and revenue bond issues. Second, surety bonds are used when the guarantor has no license for municipal bond credit insurance or for other legal reasons, such as when state regulations cannot issue insurance outright. For all practical purposes, surety bonds differ very little from insurance. Third, banks issue letters and lines of credit. Letters of credit generally fit new types of financings that carry put features. Fourth, layered guarantees provide a mix of security features which no bank can provide alone. Industrial development bonds (IDBs), issued by a tax-exempt entity on behalf of a private company, may be small and the issue relatively unknown outside its locality. The anonymity and accompanying fear of default on the part of bond buyers may be alleviated somewhat by a letter of credit.

The size of the issue may be less of a problem if the issues are combined. A first layer of security provided by a multitude of unknown issuers, companies, and banks can get added security by another layer of security; for instance, a large regional bank's letter of credit. A third layer of security may be needed, however, if the regional bank has no credit rating which the individual investor can rely upon. Therefore, a rated bank, of which there are only a handful in the United States, may provide another letter of credit, relying on the financial well-being of the regional bank. With the third letter of credit, the issues receive a AAA rating, and the letter of credit issuers share the risk of default. Lastly, a variety of interest rate swaps, segmented market penetrations, interest rate caps and floors, and secondary market deals have appeared.

Stepped Coupons.   A stepped coupon bond uses maturities in which the coupons are "stepped" upward to increase yields over the life of the issue (Forbes and Petersen, 1983). All of the bonds may yield 7% in one year, for example, and 10% the next. The security looks like both a short- and a long-term issue; moreover, the investor has some protection from interest-rate volatility.

ABSORBING UNCERTAINTY THROUGH ADVANCED REFUNDING

The rate-sensitive debt instruments and financing techniques, which I discussed, were developed in direct response to the volatile interest rates encountered throughout the last ten years. When rates fall and stabilize, however, governments take advantage of the condition by "locking in" the lower rates through an advance refunding.

The concept of refinancing an existing indebtedness is a long-established practice utilized not only by state and local governments but also by corporations and individuals to reduce interest costs. New, relatively lower interest rate debt replaces the debt issued at relatively higher interest rates.

Most frequently, advance refunding programs are used to reduce debt service costs, with the most common refunding process involving issuing the *refunding* bonds at an interest rate which is lower than the rate of the *refunded* bonds. However, an advance refunding may also be employed to restructure debt payments or to update overly restrictive bond-indenture covenants. Therefore, refunding has several characteristics: (a) it is a "clean" swap of the outstanding bonds with the refunding bonds; (b) outstanding bonds would immediately cease to have any pledge of revenues; (c) the yearly debt service reduction may, if desired, begin immediately; and (d) the holders of the outstanding bonds would have, as security for the outstanding bonds, a portfolio of qualifying securities.

Arbitrage and Escrowed Municipal Bonds

A new, and potentially more useful advance refunding technique developed in the early 1980s has increased the savings and uncertainty absorption potential available to state and local governments. The method employs the floating rate and put option debt features already discussed, but also includes investment in municipal bonds. The new technique requires two innovations. First, the refunding bonds are sold at floating rates with put features. Then the bond proceeds are invested in fixed rate, tax-exempt municipal bonds, which in the late 1970s had reached unusually high levels.

Although a variable rate refunding bond reduces debt service, an escrow of fixed rate municipal securities can multiply these savings. For example, assume that a refunded bond at 8.5% is matched against a refunding bond with a variable rate averaging 6.5%. Future debt service is reduced by the difference. Next, since the old, refunded bond may not be able to be called until a first-call option point, for instance 5 years from now, the refunding bond proceeds can be invested. An investment in municipal bonds at about 8.5% could yield substantial savings. The 2% savings on debt service would be added to the 2% earnings on the municipal bond investment. Therefore, escrowed municipal bonds and variable rate refunding bonds with put option accrue considerable savings in a volatile market. Moreover, no restrictions exist to prevent an issuer from borrowing at a tax-exempt floating rate and investing the proceeds at a tax-exempt fixed rate.

The use of rate-sensitive instruments in general obligation and in advance refunding situations provided governments with a way to absorb the uncertainty (even shock) of interest rate increases to unusually high levels. However, giving debt instruments rate-sensitivity also made them more competitive and helped attract new bondbuyers. Increasing the demand for debt instruments, moreover, had the unique potential to absorb uncertainty by leveling or stabilizing demand.

LEVELING DEMAND THROUGH NEW BOND BUYERS

One major variation that state and local governments had to absorb in the last decade lay in changes in demand that were due to changes in types of bondholders. In fact, as banks and insurance companies stopped buying bonds because of tax law changes and their own low profits (U.S. General Accounting Office, 1983), individuals and households started. Significant new forms of securities have emerged to take advantage of these new buyers, such as unit trusts, zero-coupon bonds, bonds with warrants, and the book-entry of bond certificates. These account for bond interest and principal payments as well as ownership.

Unit Trusts

Fixed, diversified portfolios of long-term municipal bonds have entered the market to appeal to individual investors and households. One marketer describes their appeal as aimed to "income oriented people in their mid-50s or older. They fall into the 40 or 50 percent top income tax brackets. They want a tax-free stream of income, and a packaged product appeals to them" (Vartan, 1985). Unit trusts come in several forms and may carry insurance. They may allow a double (or even triple) tax exemption because the trusts hold same-state securities and sell them to investors in that state.

Zero-Coupon Bonds

Zero-coupon bonds are debt instruments sold at significant discounts from their face values with no annual interest payments. Over the life of the bond, the increased value is the original discount offering price is compounded semi-annually at the original yield. The "zeros" are aimed at individual investors who might be facing volatility in the economy. Specifically, the investor can lock-in the yield desired with a zero-coupon bond, is ultimately benefitting if prevailing interest rates fall. The investor, nevertheless, gambles. If prevailing interest rates rise above the zero's yield, the zero-coupon bond falls in price.

Bonds with Warrants

A bond with a warrant attached allows the purchase of additional bonds. The entitlement to purchase additional bonds carries what amounts to a "reverse call" option on the security. If prices on bonds rise (when interest rates fall), the reverse call would have a high value, and this potential is enticing to bondbuyers.

Book-entry of Bond Certificates

Like the Federal Reserve System's electronic book-entry system for the U.S. Treasury and other federal agency securities, federal law[8] now allows municipal issuers to alleviate the paperwork that is involved in offering genuine engraved bond certificates to bondholders. The paperless system registers all long-term securities, and utilizes electronic transfer of funds (Petersen and Buckley, 1983). Such a book-entry system, which is offered by many bank trust departments, establishes the ownership and records the trades in new issues. An audit trail for tax purposes, as well as a record of interest coupon and principal payment, now exists.

The initial test and evidence of bond-buyer enthusiasm for book entry (and lack of resistance to having anything other than the genuine article in hand) came with Utah's successful sale of a $10 million general obligation issues in July 1984. Using a similar book-entry system, Massachusetts sold $140 million a month later.

SUMMARY

The uncertainty of absorption activities of state and local government financial managers have led to the use of hedging programs to deal with interest rate risk exposure. New financial instruments that move with the changes in interest rates also allow bondholders the opportunity to sell the security if necessary. Advance refunding programs convert relatively high interest rate debt service to lower rates when interest rates fall. Lastly, programs entice an ever larger group of investors into the market to maintain demand.

NOTES

1. The material in this section is based in part on Miller, Rabin, and Hildreth (1987).
2. This section is based on my paper with W. Bartley Hildreth that was delivered by at the annual meeting of the American Political Science Association, Washington, D.C., September 2, 1988.
3. For the difference in banks and investment banks, see the discussion of the distinctions in the Glass-Steagall Banking Reform Act of 1933 in Horvitz (1981) and the distinctions related specifically to present underwriting opportunities in Dale (1988).
4. The material in this section is based in part on Miller (1985).
5. This period dates roughly from the publication of the U. S. Advisory Commission on Intergovernmental Relations, Patton and Hempel (1975), and covers about fifteen years, from 1975 to 1990. During this time a breathtaking volatility occurred when viewed currently. Merely reciting the financial condition of New York City—near default in 1975, embarking on major service increases and capital improvements with large surpluses in 1985, experiencing fiscal stress in 1990—portrays the bust to boom to bust character of many, if not all, state and local governments during these years. The rest covers all bases: boom to bust (Phoenix), still busted (Detroit), and bust to boom (Dallas).

    No longer a matter of surprise, the period witnessed great instability among prices, interest rates, and markets. For example, prices increased to double digits for the first time since the end of World War II. Interest rates on long municipal bonds leaped to double digits for the first time since *The Bond Buyer* began keeping records. As both cause and effect, the distinction among credit market participants, especially the issuer and the intermediary, became obscure (Petersen, 1981). Since the rate instability period, the market has had instability, especially in 1987 and in 1989. Yet the 1980s have witnessed remarkable stability.

6. Equity "kickers" is one of several unpublished, in-house briefing papers from Rauscher Pierce Refsnes, Inc., a Phoenix, Arizona regional investment bank. It forms the survey of financing tools reviewed in this chapter.

7. See Chapter 8, in this volume, for a further discussion of these techniques. See also Fabozzi and Zarb (1981).

9. The Tax Equity and Fiscal Responsibility Act of 1982 (P.L. 97-248, 96 Stat. 595).

8

Investment Managers and Innovation

Governments collect revenues at irregular intervals and, as a result, large amounts of cash not needed immediately accumulate for investment. In no other branch of government financial management is there such an obvious place for rational techniques. The calculation of available funds requires analysis, using the most reliable techniques, to determine the amounts needed for liquidity and for investment.

The managers of these cash balances, in the research that I report here, follow widely varying cash-management practices that resemble *not a science* but a culture—a set of values that are in accord with the role of a fiduciary expected in a government organization.

In this chapter,[1] I compare the prevailing "scientific" theory of cash management with actual practice and suggest an alternate route to understanding the investment prong of government financial management.

PREVAILING THEORY

In cash management and in procurement managers deal in stocks of one sort or another. If revenues poured into the treasury on demand or if the items needed to support activities—from paint to computer tapes—were available readily and reliably, those who manage these stocks would not need an inventory, a cash balance, or a stock of paint and computer tapes. Yet the investment of idle funds now provides substantial additional revenue in times of fiscal stress. Also, the risk

149

of a large inventory may require greater amounts of insurance at greater cost, both of which motivate managers to work with less inventory of cash and other items so that there is more cash available to invest and less exposure to risk.

In both cases, the question becomes how much is too little and how much is too much? Both questions may be answered by using financial-management technology. The question of how much is too much or the optimum cash balance is answered by using one of two models: an economic lot size approach or a related approach which assumes random rather than regular demand for cash or other supplies.[2] The question of how to avoid shortages—how to have enough cash on hand to pay the bills—is a matter of employing a "safety stock model."[3]

Optimum Supply Balances

Two pieces of data are required to compute optimum cash balances. The first is the cost of carrying the item. In regards to cash, carrying costs are usually thought of as interest earnings foregone. The second piece of data needed for computing optimum balances is acquisition cost. A transaction cost for cash is the cost of exchanging cash for a marketable security or the security for cash. Finding the optimum balance requires finding the point where both carrying costs and transaction costs are lowered. Figure 1 shows, in graphic form, these relationships. The equation, however, is somewhat more impenetrable:

$$\text{Optimum balance} = \sqrt{2bT/i}$$

where b is the fixed cost of the transaction (a purchase of a security or some other article of the inventory), T is the amount of cash needed to pay routine expenses, and i is the interest rate available on cash investments.

To illustrate,[4] consider a municipal government with estimated total cash payments (T) of \$6 million for a three-month period. These payments are expected to be at a steady rate over the period. The cost per transaction (b) is \$50, and the interest rate on marketable securities (i) is approximately 12% per annum or 3% for the quarter. Therefore,

$$\text{Optimum balance} = \sqrt{2bT/i}$$

$$= \sqrt{[2(50)\,(6,000,000)]/.03}$$

$$= \$141,421$$

Thus, the optimal initial cash balance and transfer size is \$141,421, and the average cash balance is one-half of \$141,421 or \$70,170. This means that the municipality should make approximately forty-two transfers from marketable securities to cash for the period (6,000,000/141,421 = 42+).

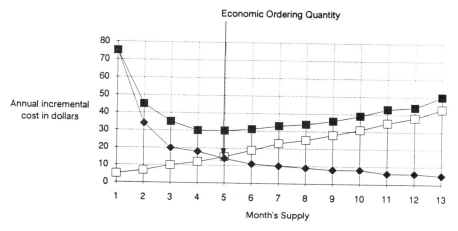

Figure 1   The safety stock model: ■ = total cost, ☐ = carrying cost, and ◆ = incremental order cost.

The optimum number of transactions will be larger if transfer costs are relatively low and interest rates relatively high. On the other hand, the higher the cost per transfer and the lower the interest rate, the higher the starting cash balance for each period and the smaller the number of transfer transactions.

Avoiding Shortages

Since one never knows with absolute assurance when erratic and unpatterned demands for inventory will occur, the most obvious solution to shortages is to stock almost every conceivable item in the largest quantity. This simple solution may create a lost opportunity in not having available all of the cash for short-term investment one might otherwise have. The problem, then, is a tradeoff: How to have enough inventory so that shortages are not commonplace. The problem may be solved with the same formulas used before, substituting a new variable for the old. Thus, we balance the cost of not investing cash (the carrying costs) against the cost that would be incurred if the cash were not on hand. The latter cost is called a "stockout" cost. In the case of cash, it is the amount the bank would charge for not keeping a compensating balance as well as the amount vendors would penalize if they were paid after the due date.

More important than the dollar value, however, is the subjective assessment made by the finance officer. The calculation of the safety factor for inventory involves separating different parts of it into critical and not so critical need. Those that are critical—the unavailability of which would bring the operations of the government to a halt—should be examined for rate of usage and sources of alternate supply. These critical items should be kept on hand especially if their value is great and the availability of substitutes or the source of alternate supply is small.

Having these data, a reorder point is established, which is the monthly usage multiplied by the delivery time (in months) plus the safety factor. At the reorder point, the optimum balance that was calculated earlier is restored.

PRACTICE OF CASH MANAGEMENT

Cash managers in state and local governments lag behind their counterparts in the private sector. Government treasurers have not employed new financial technologies like that described as prevailing theory. Even more, they have not accepted new products, especially financial futures, options, and futures options which deal with the opportunity costs of idle cash. The reasons why may tell more about the differences in public and private sector cultures than the failure to be technically rational. Exploring the failure of innovation in this area can reveal the actual technical theory employed by public financial managers. Knowing how they think, we can describe more faithfully the patterns underlying their activities.

Consider the products end of the argument. This typical cash manager's hoary skepticism toward financial futures products has certainly played its part. No doubt, scandal has lent an unconvincing cast to arguments that new products carry no unnecessary or unforeseen risks. In most cases, however, the language and symbolism attached to financial innovations pose the biggest problem: Should managers who think of themselves as fiduciaries be speculating or, even worse, gambling with taxpayers' money?

Nevertheless, increasing uncertainty exists in what returns on the investment of idle funds might be expected, for short as well as long periods of time. If volatile interest rates bedevil all investors, including those in governments, what then should cash managers do?

Cash managers should heed the strategies used in other financial management activities and should cope with uncertainty in *all* possible ways. Coping with uncertainty in cash management often means hedging investments in the futures or options markets.

Coping with Uncertainty with Financial Innovations

Financial marketeers (see Powers and Vogel, 1984 and Fabrozzi and Zarb, 1981) have created new tools and techniques to aid government cash managers in insulating idle funds investments from interest rate risks. Two major groups of new products have emerged, futures and options contracts, as well as combinations of the two, options on futures or futures options. Before discussing the utility and disutility of these contracts, I will briefly explain what cash managers may actually find in the market.

Futures Contracts

Contracts with which buyers and sellers agree to transfer a government security or another financial instrument at some later time are called *futures*. The contract specifies the amount, the day and place of transfer, and the price of the contract. The agreement about what will transpire at some future time marks the futures contract and its ability to create more certainty for the parties involved.

Three types of futures contracts now exist: the contracts based on U.S. government securities, those on certificates of deposits of major banks, and one contract based on an index of prices heavily traded state and local government bonds.

Treasury and Agency Futures

Treasury and agency futures contracts cover one of five debt instruments sold by the U. S. government.

1. Three-month U. S. Treasury bills. Each contract represents $1,000,000 face value of U. S. Treasury bills with a three-month (13 week) maturity.
2. One-year U. S. Treasury bills. Each contract represents $250,000 face values of U. S. Treasury bills with one-year maturity.
3. U. S. Treasury notes. Each contract represents $100,000 face value maturing in 6 1/2 to 10 years and carrying an 8% coupon.
4. U. S. Treasury bonds. Each contract represents $100,000 face value of bonds with a coupon rate of 8% and maturity in 15 years or more.
5. Government National Mortgage Association (Ginnie Mae) Certificates. Each Ginnie Mae pass-through certificate contract represents $100,000 principal value of a package of Veterans Administration and Federal Housing Administration guaranteed 30-year mortgages with a stated interest rate of 8%.

The yield on a Ginnie Mae collateralized depository receipt contract is called a GNMA or pass-through yield. For further discussion, see Powers and Vogel (1984, pp. 166-172).

Certificate of Deposit (CD) Futures

The CD futures contract rests on a 90-day CD issued by one of a group of selected major banks with a face value of $100,000 and prices quoted at various rates as an add-on yield.

Municipal Futures

The municipal futures contract is pegged to the Bond Buyer Municipal Bond Index[5] and has a face value of $100,000.

Traditionally (and theoretically) cash and futures prices move in similar directions so that the gains or losses in the futures market will be offset by the gains or losses in the cash market, which is the market place for buyers and sellers of Treasury bills. The concept of "basis" defines the difference between futures prices and cash prices, measuring the variance between the price of a treasury bill, for example, and a futures contract on that same treasury bill. Zero basis constitutes a perfect hedge.

Options Contracts

Options provide investors with the right, but not the obligation, to buy or sell something, such as a security or a futures contract at a specified time or place. Two options contracts exist for financial futures: U. S. Treasury notes and U. S. Treasury bonds (Goodman, 1983).

In the case of options, the holder of underlying securities or cash purchases the right, but not the obligation, to sell or buy the asset until the end of the expiration date. The buyer or seller merely reserves the right to offset moves in the interest rates. Compared to futures, options limit the liability of the purchaser to the amount paid for the option. As with an insurance policy premium, a loss may never occur and the money for that premium is, in an absolute sense, lost.

The put or call option on a futures contract is only slightly more complicated. The call (right to buy) option on a futures contract bought by a city treasurer holding or expecting cash provides insurance against losing money on price changes. Should the futures contract guarantee a price of x but the market a price of $x-1$, the call option would remove the obligation on the futures contract and let the treasurer buy at the more favorable cash market price. Similar strategy would work on the put (or sell) side.

Having securities to liquidate in the future, the finance officer can exercise the option to buy (or sell) a futures contract when market movement becomes clearer. The option serves primarily as a backup in case the rate direction changes.

Hedging with Financial Futures

Hedging involves the use of futures or options to anticipate and offset movements in interest rates and remains the primary reason for considering them in governmental or in nonprofit organizational managerial finance (Table 1). Hedging strategies have developed as the futures and options markets have offered new products (Drabenstott and McDonley, 1984; Koppenhaver, 1984; Dew, 1981). Basic hedging involves the purchase of a futures contract (or an option on a futures contract) to guard or "lock in" an interest rate (Kaufman, 1984; Brewer, 1985).

Hedgers take futures positions exactly equal and opposite their position in the cash market. For example, holders of $10 million in Treasury bills, such as city treasurers, would protect themselves against a decline in price by being "short" (selling a contract promising to deliver) or selling $10 million of Treasury bill futures contracts. The treasurer liquidates the inventory of Treasury bills to pay

Table 1 Hedging Strategies with Futures Contracts

Strategy	Process	Purpose
1. Long hedge	Buy futures	Lock in future yields to protect against falling yields of existing investments
2. Short hedge	Sell futures	Lock in current yields against the chance of a rise in rates of funds to be borrowed later
3. Arbitrage	Buy cash investment contract; sell or short a futures contract	Increase yields
4. Spread	Buy one futures contract; sell a different but related contract	Increase yields

city bills, for example, by delivering the bills to the buyer of the futures contracts, thereby canceling the short position.

Hedging with Options on Futures

Using an option on a cash instrument, such as a Treasury note or on a futures contract can limit the loss on investments and give one even greater control over hedging. The options contract gives an investor (a city treasurer, for example) the ability to lock in yields as does the futures contract. The treasurer, expecting some large revenue collection at a future date, can purchase an option to buy (call) treasury notes (see Table 2). The call option secures the price of treasury notes and protects the treasurer's plans to purchase securities against price rises. If prices fall, the treasurer will choose not to exercise the option to buy, but will instead take advantage of cheaper bills and lose only the cost of the call option.

The put or sell option would work in similar ways. Having notes on hand, the treasurer would be protected against having the prices of these notes fall before they could be liquidated by purchasing the option (as shown in Table 2).

Problems with Futures and Options

Using futures has become a sign of speculation by those involved in the market, although the basic futures hedging strategies in use tend toward conservatism—of insuring against calamity. Nevertheless, the notion of speculation, or gambling

Table 2 Hedging Strategies with Options Contracts

Process	Purpose
1. Buying calls	Buyers of calls hold cash and hope prices rise; if they do, they will buy bonds at a bargain price since they are able to buy more bonds for same amount of cash
2. Buying puts	Buyers of puts hold cash or bonds and hope prices fall. If they do, they will sell bonds and get more from them than current market or cash price.
3. Writing calls	Writers (sellers) of calls hope prices fall because they can sell at prices higher than the cash market
4. Writing puts	Writers (sellers) of puts hope prices rise because they can buy at prices lower than the market

through arbitrage and spread, fueled by scandal in financial markets involving public figures has recast the symbols affixed to management decisions to create barriers to the quick acceptance of futures as orthodox financial techniques.

Speculation

The speculation involved in the futures market provides market participants with opportune ways of increasing their yield on portfolios, but that speculation also counters the basic notion of futures use as an aid to reducing the effects of uncertainty. Speculation differs from hedging in that a speculator takes a position in the futures market without having an offsetting interest in the actual commodity. Hedgers take positions exactly equal and opposite their position in the actual commodity.

Speculation entails either arbitrage or spreading or both. Arbitrage, which is a simple operation, aims to take advantage of price disparities that occur between the various markets or the different segments of the same market—between different securities that have the same yield curve—such as Treasury bills and Ginnie Mae's. For example, if an arbitrageur saw U. S. Treasury bills futures *offered* in one place at one price and CD futures *sought* for at another price, buy and sell activity could simultaneously take place to create profit or arbitrage on the transaction (minus, of course, expenses).

Spreading operates in the same market place—for Treasury note futures, for example—or between different settlement months of similar securities. Because futures prices reflect expectations about what will happen to the price of the underlying cash instrument in the future, the risks that emerge depend on any conceivable event which might affect these expectations. The futures market is extremely sensitive with both arbitrage and spread risks.

Arbitrage Risks

The basic arbitrage risk involves changes in one market or one security so great as to create direct or unexpected losses. Market movements (of securities) in relationship to the other can create this risk, a risk that will result in either windfall profits, or financial calamity, or relative amounts of one or the other or even neither.

Spread Risks

Basic spread risks involve the change in the relative value of contracts that are offered in the same market, such as a March Treasury bond futures contract and a September Treasury bond futures contract. Also arbitrage and spreading require the trader to take risks. Using these strategies, the trader takes the buy-and-sell sides (long and short positions) on contracts that, *by definition*, are unequal. The net position is risky but has an ultimate goal of profit-taking equal to the risk. On the other hand, h edging requires that the risk be transferred to an arbitrageur. The hedger takes a position equal but opposite to the position held in the cash market. The net position of transfer is a reduction of risk.

Government and Nonprofit Losses

Recent scandals have illustrated the arbitrage/spread strategies rather than the hedging strategies that are useful to public financial managers. Speculative ventures have involved managers in San Jose, California, Toledo, Ohio, Beaumont, Texas, and in West Virginia, as well as the manager of the Council of Social Work Education. No matter how dissimilar these typical professional officials are, these incidents portray an overarching image which evokes ineptness. The lesson preached is risk aversion. Thus, if one attempts to increase yields on investments of idle funds by playing the casino with public resources, certainly fiduciary responsibility is violated.

The facts do not support such an extreme position, however. In the San Jose and West Virginia cases, cash managers bought long-term bonds as short-term investments; the council's financial manager attempted hedging with stock (not interest rate) options. In both cases, managers violated that most basic of operating rules: Never risk more than you are prepared to lose. The San Jose losses amounted to several tens of millions dollars; the West Virginia case to over $100 million of taxpayer funds. The council's losses delayed the organization's buying a new mansion, which was a practical matter of symbolic importance to the group.

Language and Symbol Inappropriateness

Beyond all the talk of speculation, which could be controlled, and scandal, which has occurred in only isolated incidents, there lies an even more important barrier to financial products' public-sector acceptance. The fiduciary background influencing public cash managers tends to bring together word associations that blur useful distinctions. This "ideological" element in financial practice evidently leads some, if not many, in the profession to view all but the safest investments for idle funds as "speculation." Thus, state legislatures and city councils and commissions often refuse to give cash managers the leeway to be able to avoid loss, much less actually allow them to produce investment earnings or gain. Therefore, the use of financial futures in local government finance, while opportunely affording the cash manager a method of safeguarding potential gain through a very conservative, traditional method of reducing potential losses of principal, finds rare acceptance. Neither does the popular literature help, because lurid stories on financial futures portray such activity as the stuff of gamblers (Bianco, 1985).

Nevertheless, at least three language and symbol problems stand in the way of acceptance of financial futures: (a) public financial-management's emphasis on safety rather than value, (b) the limited elaboration of "risk" and "loss" in public financial-management's language, and (c) the inappropriate and limited guardianship symbol which public financial-management upholds.

Problem of Ultimate Goals. A major conceptual goal disparity or, at least, fuzziness surrounds the very basic notion of what it is that a cash manager should do. Obviously, the goal definition that managers use will affect their receptivity to innovative financial products. Two basic conceptual views prevail. Van Horne (1981) gave the orthodox private sector financial-management definition of the purpose of cash management:

> A number of studies have shown that many local governments carry cash balances in excess of those necessary for immediate transactions. There is a cost involved in carrying excess cash funds: the loss of earnings forgone on the investment of idle funds in marketable securities. (p. 328)

The cash manager, therefore, protects against lost opportunities or threats to the value of investments.

In contrast, speaking for the more conservative, fiduciary-oriented government financial officers actually involved in the practice of cash management, Boldt (1984) stated that "the duty of all financial officers, particularly those responsible for the public's money, is to safeguard the principal first, and to maximize income second" (p. 19). According to Boldt, the cash manager, in all cases, guards the safety of principal.

Many less than naive observers confide the possible reasons for the "safety not value" emphasis. For some, including theorists, one truism runs that, in bureaucracy, rules serve as points of comparison, so that variance, measured as "error," leads to punishment. In less bureaucratically inclined organizations, rules serve to inspire performance (Gouldner, 1954; Golembiewski, 1965). For the investment manager of a bureaucratic or control-oriented public system, highly structured, less discretionary statutory investment authority increases the specificity of rules, reduces the chance of miscalculation, variance, and error, and, therefore, decreases the chance of political repercussions for poor performance (Bleakney, 1980, p. 719).

The high-structure approach values most highly the short-term investment performance by treasury managers. According to Bleakney (1980) public-sector cash managers

> must constantly be looking over their shoulders at what the public may say
> about a market decline that temporarily drives down the value of the funds they
> are managing. . . . In the private sector, aggressive investment managers will
> generally have the opportunity to explain the dips and valleys in their invest-
> ment results. If they are doing a good job in the long run, they need not be
> concerned about short term deficiencies. (p. 719)

Although accountability prompts short-investment time frames, it also dampens the emphasis on value. Accountability imposes an artificial restriction on investments: "Managers influenced by the prospect of adverse publicity and public criticism tend to opt for the same route" (Bleakney, 1980, p. 720). They disregard ventures which tend toward shorter term volatility.

Language Problem.   The professional language used by financial managers and decision-makers, reflecting inbred attitudes deeply and genuinely felt and thought useful, has led those who are involved in public financial affairs to greet financial product innovation with a wary eye. The public and private sectors, despite the efforts of many public administration theorists (Methe et al., 1983), differ in their definitions of key terms in cash management. Two particularly important words, *loss* and *risk*, can have altogether different meanings within a context.

1. Defining loss. First, one view of *loss*, which we argue as *the* public and only one part of the private-sector definition, rests on the notion that something is no longer possessed or is parted with. The other aspect, and a more important part of the private-sector definition, refers to a failure to take advantage of a potential gain or optimizing situation. The notion of opportunities lost has never gained a hold among public decision-makers.

2. Defining risk. Likewise, *risk* in corporate financial theory (Copeland and Weston, 1979) is conceived as that opportunity which, when exploited, defines gain; the risk one assumes affords a corresponding gain. In the bureaucratic literature, which informs both public and private sectors, risk refers to the chance of mishap, the avoidance or prevention of which has primacy (Schwartz, 1981, pp. 401–402). In public administration theory, risk carries ethical connotations, one of the most traditional of which regards risk-taking as a violation of a fiduciary relationship to the polity (Lovrich, 1981).

Public sector/bureaucratic definitions limit the scope of cash management. The language, therefore, breeds a passive response to chance and opportunity. Hedging with futures, an active rather than a passive response, never appears reasonable to these financial managers simply because language places blinders to recognition.

Problem of Conflicting Roles and Symbols.   Carrying language baggage, public financial managers also find themselves mired in role conflict and afflicted with the task of manipulating symbols that constrain their acts. Three of these clashing sets of roles and symbols illustrate the point.

1. Guardian of the treasury versus gambler. The most obvious clash is that between the vision of the financial manager as a wise and careful (and conservative) steward of government finances and the view of many that financial innovations, such as futures and options contracts, amount to nothing more than institutionalized gambling.

2. Hedger versus speculator. Related to the traditional role of "guardian of the treasury" played by most financial managers is that of the hedger. In a sense, the hedging strategy is one in which a manager uses some form of insurance to offset possible losses from catastrophe. Financial products offer this hedging service, but they also offer the chance of vast financial windfalls through arbitrage and spreading. The chance of a windfall besmirches the hedging image and substitutes the image of the riverboat gambler, of the ubiquitous trader waiting for the next hot tip. Ironically, proponents of financial innovation view public managers who do not hedge as "speculators" because these managers simple gamble with the future.

3. Minimizing loss or maximizing gain. In many ways, the traditional role of a government financial manager and any fiduciary is guarding the principal or at least paying careful attention to its safety. In many other ways, the modern financial manager plays the role of squeaking out scarce revenues in a period of fiscal stress. With financial products, the choice made by the manager gets a tough test. Should managers choose not to use futures/options, they run afoul of those who guarantee that additional money must be gained by taxation to replace that ravaged by interest rate volatility and time. At any rate, should managers choose to use futures, they are thought of as "gambling" and not being very careful.

THE STUDY

How do those financial managers in a position of hedging actually reason their way through the choices? Does their decision square with the values they espouse? Are they really any different from their private-sector counterparts?

From late 1987 to early 1989, as part of the continuing United States Cash Management Survey, we asked cash managers about their decisions. I report here a subset of this sample to shed light on what policies and values cash managers must attend to in their work.

Questions

The public sector has unique rules by which to guard against loss in investments. The first series of questions we asked related to how loss was measured. In other words, what did the cash manager understand loss to be? This question seems to be at the heart of what a cash manager does and suggests the basis for accepting or rejecting innovations.

The second series of questions dealt with the balancing of many different but equally valuable goals in cash management. We wanted to know how the cash manager dealt with the return on investment goal as well as the prevention of loss goal, for example.

The third series of questions was meant to determine public-sector managers' perception of risk among investments compared to the so-called experts. In this area, much is made of the unique public-sector cash manager perspective, usually including the fact that there is less knowledge of risk over the broad range of investments, since the public-sector manager has fewer choices to start with.

Methods

In the United States Cash Management survey, city treasurers, investment officers, comptrollers and cash managers were asked to express their views of organizational policies and goals. They were also asked about the riskiness of various financial instruments that are used in private-sector organizations for short-term interest earnings. Questionnaires were mailed to all members of the National League of Cities (NLC). Out of a total NLC survey population of 2,208, 568 responses were received, representing a 25.7% return rate.

The sample, however, has important biases that may add value to this size of a group. Following the University of Chicago's National Opinion Research Center (NORC) methods (Clark and Ferguson, 1983, Appendix 1), we ensured that a 100% sample of all cities over 250,000 population and received sufficient numbers of responses from each of the other population categories to approximate the dimensions of NORC's Permanent Community Sample. Therefore, we have over-represented the groups that would be expected to have cash management and investment policies, to say nothing of highly developed ones. Since these cities tend to lead other cities in policy development, we would expect that what these cities now do, other, smaller cities will do later.

For this discussion, I concentrated on those members of the sample who would know about investment and hedging. After I drew a random sample of city populations in the United States over 250,000, my sample of 29 cities gives me confidence that the answers from this group differed from those of the 51 city populations by no more than 10% most of the time. This level of error is reasonable, given the six-point Likert-type scales to which cash managers responded.

Findings

The three series of questions dealt with rules of thumb, tradeoffs among goals, and similarities of insight with professional investment advisors (the best of the private sector). On rules of thumb, Table 3 shows select statements which appeared on the questionnaire. Those questions with relatively large numbers drew more disagreement; the low numbers attracted relatively less agreement.

Since most of the statements at the top of the list were those with which respondents disagreed, it proved instructive to follow respondents' reasoning. Thus, many ploys were used by a fiduciary even when the ploy might ordinarily imply a loss. Selling ahead of maturity if the market warrants, using repurchase agreements that are adequately collateralized, and taking a loss now and then all suggest experience and tactical sophistication.

Greater insulation and more receptivity to innovation may exist than is commonly thought. Managers believe that with delegated authority, most would

Table 3 Agreed-Upon Activities of Cash Managers

Statement[a]	Mean	Ideal mean	Difference
Selling before maturity results in loss	5.85	3.00	2.85
Repurchase agreements are risky	5.46	3.00	2.46
Law should require no losses ever	5.07	3.00	2.07
Invest with local institutions only	4.78	3.00	1.78
Invest for interest earnings in fiscally stressful times	4.64	3.00	1.64
Primary goal is to maximize yield	4.53	3.00	1.53
Delegate with prudence and diligence	1.64	3.00	1.35
Not an interest of elected officials	4.25	3.00	1.25
Primary goal is to preserve amount invested	1.75	3.00	1.25
Hedging is gambling	2.21	3.00	0.78
Primary goal is to meet cash needs	2.42	3.00	0.57
Cash managers know best	2.60	3.00	0.39
Hedging protects against volatile market changes	2.75	3.00	0.25

[a]Respondents were asked whether they strongly agreed (value of 1), agreed (2), disagreed (5), or strongly disagreed (6) with the paraphrased statement.

act with prudence, diligence, and knowledge. Although to many hedging may appear as a form of gambling, it still seems to these cash managers primarily to be an acceptable strategy.

Looking at the similarities and differences in judgment and insight in relation to investment risk, we can see in Table 4 the comparison of public- and private-sector responses to how risky an investment appeared to be. With the value of one being the least risky and five the most risky, we can follow judgments of both the sectors. In only two of the eight groups, did public-sector managers feel an investment to be less risky than did the professionals, and one of these was in the area of innovation in futures and options. On the whole, the other six groups were riskier to public managers. More to the point, in the areas most familiar to public-sector cash managers (i.e., treasuries and municipals), these managers found them less risky than did the professionals.

Finally, we look at the goals of cash management. Is there a goal structure held in common by cash managers that signals their choices? Does this goal structure reflect the beliefs discussed earlier?

In Table 5 the rankings of goals of sample respondents are depicted. Each cash manager in the sample was asked to rank the six goals, with the most important goal having a rank of one (1) and the least important, relatively, a six (6). Thus, Table 5 shows that the conservative strategy of preserving capital is most often the prime consideration in investing. According to the sample, investing at the convenience of the cash manager and investing to boost interest earnings are the least important goals.

Such results are in accordance with the expectations developed in the earlier parts of this chapter. Public-sector cash managers have a more fiduciary-related socialization, leaving them less likely to favor the maximization of income. The fiduciary frame of reference also makes interest futures and options look speculative (Are interest earnings maximizers?) and far removed from the set of investments which will preserve capital.

Being a means of calculation on a small sample, the ranking of goals raises the question of the statistical independence of these means. Does the sample of cash managers as a whole believe them to be independent of each other, with some more important than others? Or, does the extremely different ranking of some members of the sample make the means that were presented in Table 5 less different than they appear?

Testing for *independence* in a convenient way in such situations as this sample involves the use of a nonparametric statistic—the Friedman two-way analysis of variance (Dinham, 1976, pp. 146–148) (see Table 6). Since the statistic indicates independence, we can assert that six different goals are ranked.

Finally, we deal with the *concordance* of the rank orders across respondents. Although the means give the appearance of a rank ordering, we need to know if there is a statistical relationship (like a correlation coefficient) among the different

Table 4 Investment Risks Assessed by Cash Managers and Investment Advisors

Investment		Public sector	Private sector
A. Bonds	1. U.S. Treasury Bonds	1.5	1.7
	2. Municipal Bonds, AA rated	2.2	2.4
	3. Corporate Bonds, AA rated	2.7	2.6
B. Futures	4. Sell 60-day put option, Exxon at 5% below		
and options	current price	3.8	3.8
	5. Purchase 60-day call option, Exxon at 5%		
	above current price	3.8	4.1
	6. Financial futures, S&P 500 (60-day)	3.7	4.3
	7. Wheat futures (#2 hard Kansas City 60		
	days to delivery)	4.1	4.6
C. Mutual funds	8. GNMA bond fund	2.8	2.4
	9. Corporate bond fund	3.3	2.5
	10. Growth & income mutual fund	3.6	2.5
	11. International mutual fund	3.9	3.2
D. Partnerships	12. Oil and gas partnership (income		
	oriented)	4.8	3.9
	13. Cable TV partnership	4.4	4.0
E. Personal	14. House you live in	2.2	1.6
real estate	15. Vacation cottage (established resort		
	area)	2.9	2.6
F. Short-term	16. Treasury bill (6-month)	1.1	1.1
investments	17. Bank CD ($10,000 6-month)	1.4	1.2
	18. Money market fund	2.2	1.2
	19. Commercial paper (90-day)	2.5	1.4
G. Stocks	20. 100 shares, utility stock (e.g., Duke or		
	Idaho Power)	2.9	2.6
	21. 100 shares, blue-chip stock (e.g., IBM or		
	Pepsico)	2.8	2.7
	22. 100 shares, major European company stock		
	(e.g., NV Philips)	3.4	3.2
	23. 100 shares, major Japanese company stock		
	(e.g., Toyota)	3.4	3.8
	24. 100 shares, small growth company stock		
	(e.g., Tandon)	4.1	4.0
H. Tangible	25. 18th Century American table	3.4	3.1
investments	26. French Impressionist painting	3.1	3.1
	27. Gold bullion (20 ounces)	3.2	3.3
	28. 2-carat diamond (investment grade)	3.3	3.4
	29. Silver bullion (100 ounces)	3.2	3.5
	30. 1956 baseball cards (complete set)	3.7	3.7
	31. Race horse (25% ownership)	4.4	4.9

Table 5 Cash Management Goal Priorities

Goal	Mean rank
Preservation of capital (Vault)	1.36
Legal compliance (Lcomp)	2.08
Liquidity (Lqdty)	3.09
Rate of return on investment (Retrn)	3.44
Budget expectations for interest earnings (Expct)	4.64
Convenience (Convn)	5.73

cash managers' rankings. If the rankings are statistically *dis*cordant, we would assume that there was no agreement (among this sample) as to which goals were the more important. However, if there were some statistical *con*cordance, I would assert, with a great deal more assurance, that the sample of respondents agreed about their preferences for cash management investment.

The statistical test for agreement among the cash managers is the *Kendall coefficient of concordance* (W) (Siegel, 1956, pp. 229–238) (see Table 7). Given the strength of the concordance, we can assert that the sample members are in substantial agreement with each other about the rank order of the goals. Therefore, the means of the ranks indicate the order of the goals. The concordance statistic does not suggest any interval between the goals or the strength of the difference in means as an interval.

Discussion

The last comparison provides a portrait of cash managers that we have learned to expect. The more they know from experience with a product, the less risk averse they become. Yet this willingness to take risks is based on the firm conviction that they must act to preserve capital even when legal dictates might force them to do otherwise. Having little to work with, because of legal limits on investments, they have become tactically adroit at preserving capital in the face of a volatile economy and market.

SUMMARY

The controversy over acceptance of financial innovations will continue to rage at two levels. At the ideological level, acceptance of futures and options depends as much on the role and size of government in society as the inherent productivity potential of the techniques. A government that does little more than what is absolutely necessary may regard these innovations as highly irrelevant. A govern-

Table 6 Testing the Statistical Independence of Means

Obs	Vault	Lcomp	Lqdty	Retrn	Expct	Convn
1	1	3	2	4	5	6
2	1	4	4	4	4	4
3	2.5	2.5	2.5	2.5	5	6
4	1	4	2	3	5	6
5	Invalid response					
6	3	1	2	4	5	6
7	1	2	4	3	5	6
8	2	1	3	4	5	6
9	4	4	4	1	4	4
10	1	4	2	3	5	6
11	1	2	5	3	4	6
12	2	1	3	4	5	6
13	1	4	3	2	5	6
14	1	3	2	4	6	5
15	1	2	3	4	5	6
16	2	1	3	4	5	6
17	1	2	3	4	5	6
18	1	2	5	4	3	6
19	1	2	3	4	5	6
20	1	2	5	3	4	6
21	1	4	2	3	5	6
22	1	2	4	3	5	6
23	1	4	4	4	4	4
24	2	1	3	4	5	6
25	1	3	2	4	5	6
26	2	1	3	4	5	6
27	2	1	3	5	4	6
28	2	1	4	3	5	6
29	5.5	1	5.5	2	3	4

Research hypothesis: The six goals differ.

Statistical hypotheses:
   H_0: Distributions Vault, Lcomp, Lqdty, Retrn, Expct, and Convn are identical.
   H_1: Distributions Vault, Lcomp, Lqdty, Retrn, Expct, and Convn are not identical.

Test statistic: Friedman's two-way analysis of variance by ranks (Dinham, 1976)

$$T = \frac{12}{rk\,(k+1)} \sum_{}^{k} \left[R - \frac{r\,(k+1)}{2} \right]^2$$

where r = number of observers (cities), k = number of conditions (goals of cash management), R = sum of ranks for column k, and T is distributed as χ^2 with $df = k\text{-}1$.

Decision rule: For $p \leq 0.001$, H_0 may be rejected if $p \geq 20.517$ ($df = 5$).
Computation:
   $T = (12/1176)*[(46\text{–}98)^2 + (64.5\text{–}98)^2 + (91\text{–}98)^2 + (96.5\text{–}98)^2 + (135\text{–}99)^2 + (159\text{–}98)^2]$
   $= 0.0102 * [8687]$
   $= 88.61$
Decision: H_0 may be rejected.
Conclusion: There are differences among the six goals of cash management.

Table 7 Concordance of Rankings among Respondents

Obs	Vault	Lcomp	Lqdty	Retrn	Expct	Convn
1	1	3	2	4	5	6
2	1	4	4	4	4	4
3	2.5	2.5	2.5	2.5	5	6
4	1	4	2	3	5	6
5	Invalid response					
6	3	1	2	4	5	6
7	1	2	4	3	5	6
8	2	1	3	4	5	6
9	4	4	4	1	4	4
10	1	4	2	3	5	6
11	1	2	5	3	4	6
12	2	1	3	4	5	6
13	1	4	3	2	5	6
14	1	3	2	4	6	5
15	1	2	3	4	5	6
16	2	1	3	4	5	6
17	1	2	3	4	5	6
18	1	2	5	4	3	6
19	1	2	3	4	5	6
20	1	2	5	3	4	6
21	1	4	2	3	5	6
22	1	2	4	3	5	6
23	1	4	4	4	4	4
24	2	1	3	4	5	6
25	1	3	2	4	5	6
26	2	1	3	4	5	6
27	2	1	3	5	4	6
28	2	1	4	3	5	6
29	5.5	1	5.5	2	3	4

Research hypothesis: The respondents' ranks of the six goals are alike.

Statistical hypotheses: H_0: Respondents do not agree. H_1: Respondents do agree.
Test Statistic: Kendall's coefficient of concordance (Siegel, 1956)

$$W = \frac{s}{[\frac{1}{12} k^2(N^3 - N)] - [k(\sum T)]}$$

where s = sum of squares of observed deviations from the mean of each goal R_j, that is, $s = \sum (Rj - \frac{\sum Rj}{N})^2$, k = number of judges (city cash managers), N = number of entities (goals) ranked, t = number of tied ranks on each goal, $T = k\sum (\frac{\sum(t^3 - t)}{12})$ and $1/12k^2(N^3 - N)$ = maximum possible sum of the squared deviations, i.e., the sum s which would occur with perfect agreement among k rankings.

Decision rule: For $p \le 0.01$, H_0 may be rejected if $s \ge 2148.2$.
Computation: $s = 8687.5$

$$W = 8687.5/[1/12(28)^2(6^3 - 6)] - [3266.67]$$
$$= 0.8311$$

Decision: H_0 may be rejected.
Conclusion: There is significant agreement about the rank order of goals.

ment that does everything may not need financial management, let alone futures and options, since it faces no scarcity (Wildavsky, 1975).

NOTES

1. The material in this chapter extends the argument that originally was made in Miller (1988).
2. The economic lot model was developed for cash management by Baumol (1951). The other model, which assumes a random demand function, was developed by Miller and Orr (1966).
3. The safety stock model is a derivative of the Baumol model (1951) and incorporates as well the collective wisdom of many purchasing officers.
4. See Schwartz (1981) and Van Horne (1981).
5. The Bond Buyer Municipal Bond Index was designed by the Chicago Board of Trade to serve as the basis for trading the Long-Term Municipal Bond futures contract. The Index is based on a list of 40 bonds. The bonds priced are the most recent term issues meeting the following criteria: The principal amount must equal $50 million or more, except for housing bonds for which a minimum of $75 million applies. The issue must be rated A or better by either Moody's Investors Service or Standard & Poor's. Each bond must mature in no less than 19 years, have a first call in no less than 7 and no more than 16 years, and be callable at par. A bond's initial reoffering price must be between 95 and 105. Only two bonds from a single issuer are permitted. Data supplied by the National Securities Clearing Commission are used to drop less actively traded bonds. The Index pricing list now comprises the most current issues along with the more active issues that have come to market in the last 18 months.

Appendix (Chapter 8)

Cash Management Survey

THE STATE UNIVERSITY OF NEW JERSEY

RUTGERS

Graduate Department of Public Administration • Graduate School-Newark
Hill Hall • Newark • New Jersey 07102 • 201/648-5093/5199

May 1, 1988

Dear Colleague,

Considerable attention to investment policy has hallmarked the 1970s (during a period of high inflation) and the 1980s (perhaps due to smarter and more perceptive cash managers).   Cash management's time has come, especially in government.

Since you practice cash management in your government, we want to find out the principles you use in putting idle funds to their best use.

Please take a moment and help us by answering the questions on the enclosed response form. We've designed the form to use your time as efficiently as possible; the form will take no more than a short period of your work day.

The United States Cash Management Survey results from my work with Dr. W. Bartley Hildreth (Louisiana State University). We will use the responses to this survey to inform our teaching and research, and we hope to contribute to the development of generally agreed upon standards for the practice of this professional activity. Your participation will assist in these ways, in all of which we share a mutual interest.

Please return the questionnaire as quickly as possible; a postage-paid envelope is enclosed. Thank you.

Sincerely,

Gerald J. Miller
Co-investigator, United States Cash Management Survey

GJM/gd

Attachments

United States CASH MANAGEMENT Survey

Please circle the number on the scale which represents your views.   The higher the value you give, the stronger the disagreement with the statement you suggest.   Circle the question mark if you do not know. Thank you.

	Strongly Agree				Strongly Disagree		

1. The primary goal of investing idle public funds is to maximize yield.   1 2 3 4 5 6 ?
2. The intention on making an investment is to hold it to maturity.   1 2 3 4 5 6 ?
3. Investment policy should delegate significant authority but requires the exercise of prudence and diligence.   1 2 3 4 5 6 ?
4. Elected officials have little interest in investment   results.   1 2 3 4 5 6 ?
5. The primary goal of investing idle public funds is to preserve the amount invested.   1 2 3 4 5 6 ?
6. To use hedging techniques (such as futures and options) is to gamble with public funds.   1 2 3 4 5 6 ?
7. Repurchase agreements are inherently risky investments.   1 2 3 4 5 6 ?
8. Investment law should require that there never be any loss of money on any investment, no matter how small.   1 2 3 4 5 6 ?
9. Investments should be made only with local financial institutions.   1 2 3 4 5 6 ?
10. Investments should be made only after checking competitive rates.   1 2 3 4 5 6 ?
11. Investment results should be equal to or better than what other governments achieve with their investments.   1 2 3 4 5 6 ?
12. It is important to avoid the loss of value on idle funds which might result from inflation.   1 2 3 4 5 6 ?
13. All investments should be fully insured, guaranteed or collateralized.   1 2 3 4 5 6 ?
14. To sell an investment security prior to maturity always results in a loss.   1 2 3 4 5 6 ?
15. Good investment results will enhance my career.   1 2 3 4 5 6 ?
16. The legal provisions affecting the investment of public funds are about right in balancing all competing views.   1 2 3 4 5 6 ?
17. The primary goal of investing idle public funds is to insure that cash needs are met on a timely basis.   1 2 3 4 5 6 ?
18. Investment decisions are made to meet budgetary expectations on investment earnings.   1 2 3 4 5 6 ?
19. Legal hedging techniques help protect against interest rate changes which can hurt budgeted earnings projections.   1 2 3 4 5 6 ?
20. I am the most knowledgeable person on cash management in my government unit.   1 2 3 4 5 6 ?

21. How many years of public sector cash management experience do you have? _____ years.

22. What is the job title of the person to whom you formally report? _____
What is *your* job title: _____

23. Is the person to whom you formally report the employing organization's chief financial officer?
____ Yes ____ No

24. If the answer to #23 is No, are you the Chief Financial Officer? ____ Yes ____ No

25. If the answers to #23 and #24 are NO, are you the person to whom the Chief Financial Officer reports?
____ Yes ____ No

26. Would you say that you have primary responsibility for making daily investment decisions in your organization?
____ Yes ____ No

27. Would you say that you have primary responsibility for making investment policy in your organization?
____ Yes ____ No

28. Is your job (Please check one):
____a. Merit system classified (Permanent)
____b. Temporary position
____c. Politically appointed position
____d. Appointed by a non-elected official but not merit system classified
____e. Elected position
____f. Other (Please explain: _____)

29. Other than your current position:
a. Have you held a publically-elected office at any time?   ___Yes ___No
b. Have you held a politically-appointed position at any time?   ___Yes ___No

30. **The foremost responsibility of a public investment officer is to:**
(Please circle ONLY ONE response)

1. invest cash to maximize yield.
2. guard the principal of invested public funds against loss.
3. insure that cash needs are met on a timely basis.
4. meet legal standards of investment practice.
5. achieve budgeted interest earnings projections.
6. other (please describe:_____)
7. do not know.

31. Please rank the answers to the following question by giving the most important a value of one (1).

The investment of idle public funds should be done to achieve:

_____ budget expectations
_____ convenience
_____ legal compliance
_____ liquidity
_____ preservation of capital
_____ rate of return
_____ other (please name: _____)

32. In your cash management practice, do you hedge interest rate risk?

____Yes, with   _____ No
____ interest rate futures contracts
____ interest rate options
____other _____

33. As a person with knowledge of financial markets, you can assess risk. Assess the long- or short-term risk, as appropriate, of the following investments. On the following page, place an X on the line after the investment in the position on the scale which best indicates your assessment. If you are unfamiliar with the investment and cannot assess its risk, please place a question mark (?) anywhere on the appropriate scale.

Example: Consider the following question of risk, one in which a person might feel squeamish about investing public funds or one's own funds, as you assume the constant advance of information technology:

	Very Safe	Relatively Safe	Medium Risk	Relatively Risky	Very Risky
30 year bonds of company specializing in reconditioning IBM personal computers (original PC version):				X	

Please indicate your assessment of the level of risk by placing an X on the line corresponding to one of the values:

	Very Safe	Relatively Safe	Medium Risk	Relatively Risky	Very Risky

a. Bonds
    1)   U. S. Treasury Bonds
    2)   Municipal bonds, AA rated
    3)   Corporate bonds, AA rated

b. Futures and options
    4)   Sell 60-day put option, Exxon at 5% below current price
    5)   Purchase 60-day call option, Exxon, at 5% above current price
    6)   Financial futures, S&P 500 (60-day)
    7)   Wheat futures (#2 hard Kansas City 60 days to delivery)

c. Mutual funds
    8)   GNMA bond fund
    9)   Corporate bond fund
    10) Growth and income mutual fund
    11) International mutual fund

d. Partnerships
    12) Oil and gas partnership (income oriented)
    13) Cable TV partnership

e. Personal real estate
    14) House you live in
    15) Vacation cottage (established resort area)

f. Short-term investments
    16) Treasury bill (six-month)
    17) Bank CD ($10,000, six month)
    18) Money market fund
    19) Commercial paper (90-day)

g. Stocks
    20) 100 shares, utility stock (e.g. Duke Power or Idaho Power)
    21) 100 shares, blue chip stock (e.g. IBM or Pepsico)
    22) 100 shares, major European company stock (e.g., N.V. Philips)
    23) 100 shares, major Japanese company stock (e.g., Toyota)
    24) 100 shares, small growth company stock (e.g., Tandon or Teradyne)

h. Tangible investments
    25) 18th century American table
    26) French impressionist painting
    27) Gold bullion (20 ounces)
    28) 2-carat diamond (investment grade)
    29) Silver bullion (100 ounces)
    30) 1956 baseball cards (complete set)
    31) Race horse (25% ownership)

THANK YOU FOR PARTICIPATING IN THE SURVEY OF PUBLIC CASH MANAGERS IN THE UNITED STATES. PLEASE RETURN THE QUESTIONNAIRE IN THE ATTACHED STAMPED, SELF-ADDRESSED ENVELOPE or mail your response to   Dr. Gerald J. Miller, Department of Public Administration, Rutgers University, Newark, NJ 07102

9

Command and Control in
Management Information Systems

In this chapter, I present a study of a typical intergovernmental financial-management information system—the grant review and status notification process. I argue that such systems are intended by their designs to be cybernetic, a conceptual feature they share with all financial accounting and auditing systems in government. The various uses of these systems, as well as their results, do not accord with cybernetics, however. In fact, their results and uses might make better sense if placed in a somewhat broader framework (Feldman and March, 1981).

This chapter ought to provide a more durable conceptual base for financial-management information systems in government by proposing that we discard cybernetics as a central concept and, instead, place it on the periphery to explain only special cases. Instead, the idea of ritualistic manipulation of symbols and signals may provide a broader, more revealing central concept.

The chapter is organized as a documented argument. First, prevailing theory in the form of the science of cybernetics and its basic concepts and components will be described. Second, the review process will be examined as it is set up in circulars and manuals published by the Office of Management and Budget (OMB) and the reviewing agencies.

With this case study, I will construct a model to connect, superficially, the basic cybernetic components and the corresponding or similar components of the system created by OMB Circulars A-95 and A-98. As a result, the implications of a system of communications and control in government may be analyzed. Third, I provide an alternative paradigm; once again, it is ambiguity theory. Finally, I discuss the implications of the differences in approach the two models—prevailing and alternative—provide.

CYBERNETICS

By subjecting heretofore inaccessible systems of communications and control to direct observation and analysis, *cybernetics*, is beneficial in examining systems of decisions and information. There are many ways of conceptualizing cybernetic models, and the models themselves can be uni- or multidimensional. A unidimensional model, however, is simpler and will be used here because it seems to have the explanatory power to better understand the A-95/A-98 System.

The development of cybernetics as a "new science" can be traced by definition to early philosophy and is closely related to the more recently developed concepts of information processing. The derivation of the term *cybernetics* is traced to the Greek *kybenetes*, which meant "steersman." The Latin term, taken from the Greek, means "governor." In English, the "governor" connotation of cybernetics denotes a mechanism (on a steam engine, perhaps) which keeps the system of which it is a part at a constant state under varying conditions. Thus, the concept of control is the connotation often given governor, and ultimately by definition, cybernetics.

During the 1940s, new developments in communications engineering made possible the construction of machines with self-monitoring, self-controlling, and self-steering properties. Deutsch (1961) observed that by "making equipment that fulfills the functions of communications, organization, and control, significant opportunities were gained for a clearer understanding of the functions themselves" (p. 75). Given a "laboratory" on which to theorize, scientists began this study of the functions of control and communications under the principles they called *cybernetics*.

Major Definitions

Norbert Weiner, the first major proponent of the concepts of cybernetics, conceptualized the method used to control systems—biological, mathematical, or social—as signals or messages. In fact, from his study (Weiner, 1948), he defined cybernetics as the theory of messages:

> When I control the actions of another person, I communicate a message to him, and although this message is in the imperative mood, the technique does not differ from that of a message of fact. . . . [Messages from him] . . . indicate that the order is understood and has been obeyed. (p. 20)

Stafford Beer (1959) defined cybernetics more generally as "the science that studies the flow of information around a system and the way in which that information is used by the system as a means of controlling itself" (p. 5). Beer emphasized the study of information flows rather than the actual connection between communication and control as did Weiner. Hence, Beer's definition seems to lend itself more readily as a basis for describing the general components of an information-processing system.

Components

The major components of a message or information-processing system are: (1) the information itself, (2) channels through which it passes, (3) patterns through which a part of the original information returns as a sort of "progress report" on how well the system is doing (feedback), and (4) points at which stored information is inserted or piped into the communications channel.

Information

Information is the basic commodity within any communications system. Generally, it is as Weiner stated (1948) "a name for the content of what is exchanged with the outer world as we adjust to it, and make our adjustment felt upon it" (p. 21). Any communication system is concerned with transferring information. Information can therefore be termed a *physical commodity* and handled as such in a physical process. Furthermore, information can be defined in terms of the state in which it is found: either active, that is, moving between points, or idle, as found in storage or memory.

Information Channels

The channels within a communications system can be conceptualized as the paths the commodity (e.g., information) follows. Deutsch (1961) referred to an information channel as a mechanism through which information is transferred. He later stated that information channels are the major parts of any communications network because the information never changes. Only the channel changes, whether it be a radio wave or electrical impulse, and its usefulness can be measured in the amount of information distorted or lost.

Feedback

In a self-regulating system, the unique feature allowing this self-regulation is its ability to receive feedback. As Deutsch explained (1961),

> by feedback is meant a communication network that produces action in response to an input of information, and includes the results of its own action in the new information by which it modifies its subsequent behavior. (p. 88).

This feature—a servomechanism or self-correcting device—is common to all self-monitoring systems whether it is an electronic control device or a social organization. Feedback, simply put, is the method of controlling a system by reinserting into it the results of its past performance.

Furthermore, feedback can be classified as either negative or positive. Negative feedback results in a modification of performance, whereas positive feedback is a reinforcement of the system's performance level. In addition to feedback based on present performance, there are feedback loops or patterns that recall information from the system's past or from its memory. Thus, feedback permits the system to share two flows of data: "one from the system's performance in the present and in its environment, the other from the system's past . . . from its memory" (Deutsch, 1961, p. 90).

Insertion of Information into the System

There are points on a feedback loop where stored information is "fed back" into the system. They are strategic and are termed *decision points*. These points are the positions where decisions are actually made. As Beer stated (1959): "Decisions . . . are not made at the top (of an organization structure). Rather, in any system, decisions are taken at the node or plexus of nodes in a network which has the most information" (p. 28).

Conceptualizing Cybernetic Systems.   These components, interacting with each other in a total system, conform to the basic components of a cybernetic model of any communications system.

Cybernetic models can be built for any level of complexity and dimension. They can be seen as one system among many systems that interact with each other and as systems within systems in a multidimensional scheme. A unidimensional model (Figure 1), however, can easily explain the way the concepts of cybernetics apply to almost any system of communication and self-regulation and will be adopted here.

Within this model, the basic components of cybernetics can be seen. First, the communications channel is represented by the inner star. This is the actual path through which information passes. Feedback, as shown in the loops, is the way in which the communications system interacts with its environment and brings information from its storage or memory into the system. The point at which the feedback loops meet the communications channel is the decision point.

Information, therefore, moves along the communications channel and into each feedback loop. Within these loops it is processed or refined through the addition of information from other sources outside the system and from the memory of the system itself. Thus, information coming into the loop is reshaped and assumes the form of a decision. It is then permitted to flow back into the communications channel at the decision point and on to the next feedback loop.

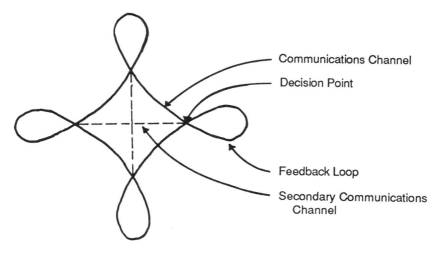

Figure 1 A unidimensional cybernetic model.

Summary. Cybernetics studies the methods any system uses to communicate and control itself by the way information flows through that system. A cybernetic model of a system includes channels along which this information flows and feedback loops that allow some return of information to aid in self-regulation. The unidimensional model (Figure 1) illustrates the dynamics of these components and makes possible the application to an otherwise inaccessible communications system (particularly the A-95/A-98 system) to help better understand those systems.

CASE STUDY OF THE USE OF PREVAILING THEORY: THE A-95/A-98 SYSTEM

In October, 1969, the Office of Management and Budget published a set of guidelines entitled "Circular A-95: Evaluation, Review, and Coordination of Federal Assistance Programs and Projects." Essentially, these guidelines created a process by which agencies at *all* levels of government were brought into the grant-in-aid review process before the grant proposal was funded. This review consisted of examination and comment on the consistency of any proposed project with projects already in existence and those planned for the future. Moreover, Circular A-95 covered projects that were funded under nine cabinet departments and five independent agencies.

Later, in June, 1970, OMB published another circular—A-98—that went beyond A-95 and required federal agencies, for the first time, to inform the grant applicant *and* the state and local agencies which originally reviewed the application of its decision on funding.

Thus, Circulars A-95 and A-98 designed a complete grant information system. A-95, by the systematic review it prescribed, allowed agencies at lower levels of government to evaluate and coordinate requests for assistance on the basis of what had been done or was planned. But A-98 went one step further and required that agencies be kept informed of the status of proposals they reviewed.

Because of its circular flow or "messages," the A-95/A-98 grant information system is an example of communications and control in government and may be understood best by employing a cybernetic model.

The central purpose of the A-95/A-98 review and notification system was to coordinate policy-making and the administration of domestic development programs[1] among agencies at all levels of government. The coordination concept was set forth by Congress and implemented by the Office of Management and Budget in the form of a "communications" system for grant applications to involve not only federal agencies but also state and local agencies in grant-in-aid decision-making cycle.

The theme of intergovernmental grant coordination through a communications system may be traced from its legal background to its practical application in rules and regulations. Additionally, the flow of a grant under this system illustrates the apparent communications and control intention of the A-95/A-98 system designers.

The basic concept of coordination was set forth by Congress in law and translated into rules and regulations by OMB in its circulars. The Demonstration Cities and Metropolitan Development Act of 1966[2] was the first law to require any review of federally funded project applications at a government level other than the federal level. It stated that

> all applications . . . for Federal loans or grants to assist in carrying out projects . . . shall be submitted for review to any areawide agency which is designated to perform metropolitan or regional planning for the area within which the assistance is to be used.

These review agencies, the law stated, were to comment on the application's consistency with current comprehensive planning or the extent to which the application fulfilled the objectives of that planning. For the first time, therefore, development project applications were to include more than the grant applicant's comments. The federal agency, as a result, had more information on which to base its decision.

Later, the Intergovernmental Cooperation Act of 1968[3] declared or "editorialized" development assistance or grant policy. After elaborating the need nationwide for appropriate use of land and for wise development, the law required that

> All viewpoints—national, state and local—... to the extent possible, be fully considered and taken into account in planning federal or federally assisted development programs and projects. State and local government objectives, together with the objectives of regional organizations, shall be considered and evaluated within a framework of national objectives.

Again, Congress legislated coordination of domestic planning by requiring that state and local planning objectives be communicated and understood by the federal agencies granting assistance.

The objectives and requirements of these two laws were implemented in Circular A-95. The requirement of coordination of planning and the use of grants-in-aid became practice in the Project Notification and Review System (PNRS) the circular prescribed. The PNRS was designed to be a communications system composed of state, metropolitan, and regional clearinghouses[4] through which all applications for domestic development assistance would pass for comment.

The comments made by these clearinghouses reflected first, the objectives outlined to implement state and local comprehensive plans and second, the proposed project's ability to fulfill the plans. Thus, the application sent to a particular federal agency had to include the applicant's plans and the opinion of state and local governments as to how well that proposal conformed with their programs. Therefore, in an evolutionary way, the A-95 preliminary review system became a blueprint, or map, for charting the flow of information—the needs of state and local areas and how well any proposed program might meet that need—from the local to the federal level of government.

The basis for constructing the other half of a total communications system of informing clearinghouses of what funding decisions were made on which projects at the federal agency level, was also included in the Intergovernmental Coordination Act of 1968, which required that the state and local governments be notified of "the purpose and amounts of actual grants-in-aid" to their areas. Complying with the Act, OMB published Circular A-98, requiring federal offices and agencies to notify state, metropolitan, and regional clearinghouses of *all* grant-in-aid actions.

State and local governments, under A-98, would receive the exact status of the grant-in-aid proposals they had reviewed. The state, counties, and cities were also to be given information enabling them to monitor the grant from application stage (A-95) through the status notification stage (A-98).

Given the chain of events which first created the A-95 review system and then the A-98 notification system, a working model may now be constructed. First, A-95 review is an "early warning system" that facilitates the coordination of grant applications with existing state, metropolitan, and regional plans. Also, the final application or proposal resulting from this coordination communicates state and local program priorities to federal agencies administering grant funds. Consequently, by coordinating requests for federal assistance with local plans and spending priorities, the A-95 preliminary review system becomes basically the means for bringing the management machinery of state and local government into the grant-in-aid system. This forward flow of information, then, is designed to coordinate, communicate, and manage.

Supplementing A-95, the A-98 process adds a notification requirement or a return flow of information. This return flow allows state and local governments to know how much grant money will go where and assists in coordination, communication, and management. By linking the A-95 review to the A-98 notification, state and local governments gain a major management tool. Because they can track the timing, the amount, and the point of impact of federal grant-in-aid awards, state and local governments can determine the funding levels and geographic priorities of their own program expenditures.

Thus, our working model of the total A-95/A-98 system performs as a *circular flow of grant information.* Information flows forward when state and local governments classify the priority of a grant application within their plans and programs and communicate this priority through clearinghouse comments to federal funding agencies. Information moves back down to the state and local governments when the federal agency decides on the grant proposal and communicates this decision to these government units.

This model can be illustrated by tracing the grant or the basic piece of information through the cycle. The grant application is first sent from the applicant to the metropolitan or regional (urban or rural) clearinghouse under whose jurisdiction the project falls. The clearinghouse receives it and sends it to *other* local government level agencies who might also be affected. Both the clearinghouse, if it is also a planning agency, and other local agencies may comment on the project's effect on their plans or programs. Next, the state clearinghouse receives the application and proceeds, as did the metropolitan or regional clearinghouses, by gathering comments from concerned agencies at the state level. After reviews at both the state and local levels, the project application is sent to the federal funding agency which considers the application together with the comments. A decision is then reached and the state and local clearinghouses, as well as the grantee, are notified of the project application's status.

The system of review and notification, therefore, is a complete cycle of information, one major purpose of which is to enable state and local agencies to monitor grant proposals and awards in their localities. In addition to the monitoring capability the system allows, several other purposes are served which cannot be seen in the cycle of information flow.

First, the object of the review at the local level is to encourage consultation between applicant and planner and to develop the best possible solution to problems the proposed project is designed to alleviate. The idea is to assure that any proposed project or activity is of the highest quality in terms of the applicant's needs and the needs of the area as a whole. Also, the review can identify possible project improvements and save costs by identifying savings.

Another purpose of the review at the local and state level is to resolve conflicts in the *method* used to solve the problem before the proposal is funded. By consulting the local and state agencies, the applicant may explain the project and its future impact and prevent conflict and misunderstanding among agencies affected after the application is sent to the federal agency and the project machinery is set in motion.

Most important, however, among the A-95/A-98 system's purposes is the coordination it encourages and the channels it opens to communication among all levels of government—between local governments and regional clearinghouses, and also among state agencies themselves. In fact, this purpose of the system is its fundamental contribution.

SUMMARY

The A-95/A-98 grant information system is a means of opening or establishing a circular flow of grant information. The use of the grant information system is also a method of managing the funds available at each level of government, since state and local agencies know what federal grants will go where. Through this system, furthermore, channels of communication are opened between levels of government and among agencies at each level. Basically, therefore, A-95/A-98 is a method of *communicating* the plans and programs of state and local governments to federal agencies together with the amount and type of assistance needed from these federal agencies to implement them. As a result of knowing what grants will go where within this framework of plans and programs, state and local governments are able to manage and *control* the amount and impact of their own funds.

The A-95/A-98 system can be understood by using any one of a number of approaches. Here, I have viewed the A-95/A-98 process as an information process in which the communications within the review system might be understood in the context of the principles and concepts of cybernetic modeling. This approach yields insight and could well be the simplest means of understanding the process of A-95/A-98 review and notification.

THE A-95/A-98 SYSTEM AS A CYBERNETIC MODEL

The similarity between the components of the A-95/A-98 system and the components in cybernetic modeling makes it possible now to relate these components to each other. There is no attempt to infer that this particular cybernetic model is universal, nor is there any attempt to tailor this model to the A-95/A-98 system. Rather, this model is constructed to assist in understanding the A-95/A-998 system and to relate its basic components to the fundamental concepts and components of cybernetic modeling.

Because the components of the cybernetic model are general, the model constructed earlier will serve as the base over which the components of the A-95/A-998 system may be placed (see Figure 2).

In the basic model, the figure described by *ABCD* is the communications channel. L_1 to L_4 are the feedback loops, and each "corner" of the communications channel (letters *A, B, C,* and *D*) is a decision point at the confluence of feedback loop and communications channel. Communications channels are not meant to be rigid paths of communication; therefore, lines *a* and *b* are added as secondary or informal communications channels.

On this basic model, the A-95/A-98 system can be overlaid (see Figure 3). First, the communications channel can be defined as the flow of grant applications. Each of the feedback loops is a level of review of these applications, including local and state agencies, the federal-funding agency, and the grant applicant.

Since one purpose of a clearinghouse is solicitation of reviews and comments from other agencies at the particular government level, these comments must flow back into the channel. This happens at point *B* or *C* or the decision points. With both sets of components in place, we may now view how the system operates as a grant flows from applicant to federal agency.

First, the applicant sends the proposed project to the regional clearinghouse for comments. In Figure 3, the initial review takes place from L_1 to L_2 along *AB*.

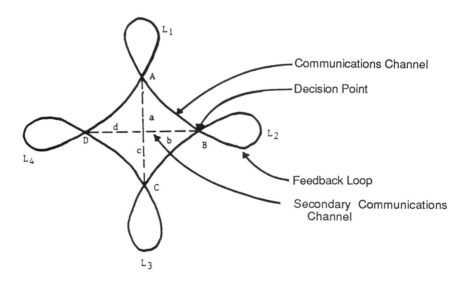

Figure 2   A cybernetic model in a communications system.

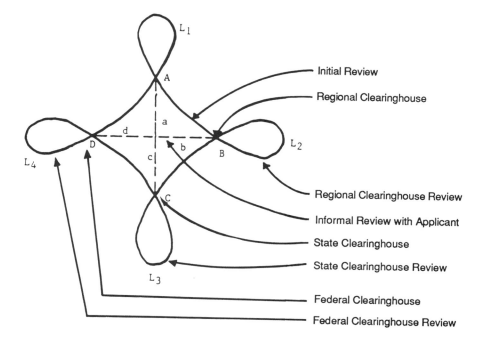

Initial Review

Regional Clearinghouse

Regional Clearinghouse Review

Informal Review with Applicant

State Clearinghouse

State Clearinghouse Review

Federal Clearinghouse

Federal Clearinghouse Review

Figure 3   The cybernetic model of the project notification and review system.

The application has now entered the communications channel from its first feedback loop (the decision to propose the project) to its second (the clearinghouse and other agency review). In the second feedback loop, the clearinghouse secures comments from other agencies on the grant application's consistency with its plans and programs. Also, the application is reviewed by the planning agency (sometimes, also, the clearinghouse) on its ability to fulfill present needs or plans.

Thus, the comments represent feedback on the application's present performance (its conformance with present plans and programs) as well as the infusion of memory (how well the proposed project fulfills present needs and plans). These comments are then written into the application, and the application is sent back into the communications system on its way to the third feedback loop.

The state clearinghouse can be this third feedback loop. A similar review procedure is used here a was used at the regional or metropolitan clearinghouse, except that the application is judged against the state's plans and programs. Again, comments are solicited and become part of the application. Suppose, however, that there were conflicts in programs at either feedback loops L_2 or L_3 (local or state clearinghouses). The secondary communications channels (*c* or *b* to *a*) might then be used as a way of consulting with the applicant to clarify or change the program proposal to conform to already established programs. There would be no need to use the primary channel, although it could be utilized. The clearinghouse could consult directly with the applicant; *b* connecting L_2 with L_1, represents this possible consultation.

If the conflict is resolved, the application again flows into the channel to the federal funding agency at L_4. Again, review takes place but within the scope of national objectives. When the federal review is completed, its comments (the decision, actually) becomes the status notification of the grant and flows back into the system to the applicant at L_1 and to the clearinghouses at L_2 and L_3.

Thus, the process has come full turn. The review prescribed in Circular A-95 takes place from points *A* to *B* to *C* to *D* involving L_1 to L_4. Notification of the decision prescribed in Circular A-98 begins at point *D* and goes to point *A* and to points *B* and *C*.

The A-95/A-98 system was designed to improve intergovernmental communication, coordination, and management of grant funds. This enabled state and local government decision-makers to know the timing and impact of federal funds, especially when state and local governments could develop and execute the concept further by adding resources of their own.[5]

SUMMARY

Cybernetics is one key to understanding systems of communications and control in any discipline or area. By understanding the concepts of cybernetics and applying these concepts to the A-95/A-98 process, the dynamics of A-95/A-98 may be conceived as a general system of communications and control.

The A-95/A-98 system is similar to a cybernetic system, in that it can be studied as "a flow of information" on grants, a self-regulatory device which keeps the plans and programs of governmental agencies in force by "controlling" grant applications so that the objectives of these plans and programs may best be fulfilled.

On the basis of the application of cybernetic principles to the components of the A-95/A-98 system, we arrive at these conclusions:

1. Grant applications flow through a communication channel between clearinghouses and federal funding agencies.
2. Clearinghouses function as feedback loops and reinforce or modify the action of the grant application system as a result.

In conceptualizing the A-95/A-98 process as a cybernetic model by showing similar processes and components of each, the intent of the system of review and status notification of grant applications may be better understood as a decentralized, intergovernmental management information system.

THE PROPOSITIONS

What would we expect a true A-95/A-98 system to produce? Using a cybernetic framework, theoretical results should "prove" the validity of command and control concepts *even* in a federalist system.

Let us consider four propositions that we could infer from cybernetics about PNRS. First, information gathered should have a direct bearing on decision outcomes. In the PNRS case, agencies negotiate in order to shape community development decisions and the information that the negotiations produce should directly affect community development. Second, the more participation, the better the decision outcome. In the case of PNRS, the participation and decision outcomes, if they are to be thought of as superior, must convince decision-makers to bind themselves to the outcome. Third, the more timely the information, the more relevance it will have for decision-making. In other words, information and negotiation occur before a development decision takes place. Fourth, the more stable the information system over time, the more likely the participation of affected parties in the process and in the outcome.

INVESTIGATION METHODS AND EVIDENCE

Successive efforts to substantiate the results of the PNRS have been made over the last 25 years. Four studies stand out as comprehensive attempts to determine the effectiveness of the A-95/A-98 process: those by the Advisory Commission on Intergovernmental Relations (1973) and the Council of State Governments (1971) completed early in the development of PNRS, two by the U. S. Department of Housing and Urban Development (1973, 1974) somewhat later, and one by the U. S. General Accounting Office (1975) at a mature stage of development.

The first study by the Advisory Commission on Intergovernmental Relations (ACIR) suggested that the formal A-95 process had not caused substantive changes in, or withdrawal or consolidations of applications. Speculation focused on a number of variables: the absence of areawide plans, policies or other criteria for evaluating proposals; the tendency to rubber stamp projects due to limited agency staff, funds, and time; and the tendency for projects to be modified before they entered the formal review process (ACIR, 1977, pp. 218–219). According to the report, "A-95 agencies have [sometimes] been unwilling or unable to make the necessary staff, time, and financial commitments to the review process, and have done little more than rubber stamp applications" (p. 153).

The second study by the Council of State Governments (CSG) suggested that, overall, the PNRS and clearinghouses had been well received and were operating effectively on promoting project-by-project planning and coordination. The early warning features were the single most effective element in the system (ACIR, 1977, p. 219). The CSG also concluded that the PNRS had not reached the point of being used as a major vehicle for implementing statewide and areawide policies and priorities. This was due to the fact that most clearinghouses had not developed sophisticated policy and coordination processes and, at the state level, had not received the necessary recognition and support of the governors.

Among the problems CSG found with PNRS implementation was (a) inadequate applicant understanding of the process, (b) failure of Federal agencies to inform their personnel of A-95 requirements (although this was a diminishing criticism), and (c) their failure to provide feedback to clearinghouses on the disposition of project applications, the timing of notification of intent to apply, and the cost of conducting reviews and the lack of additional funding to pay for it. CSG found among state officials that the most common complaint was directed at the inadequacy of the review process because of limited program coverage by PNRS/A-95.

The third major set of studies of PNRS effectiveness came from the U. S. Department of Housing and Urban Development (HUD) whose study of PNRS in 1973 and of coordinating mechanisms among levels of government in 1974 included assessments of A-95. The first study, which concentrated on A-95 alone, found that

> most OMB effort was devoted to developing procedures and conducting orientation, so that there was no systematic monitoring and enforcement of Federal agency participation. Federal agencies responded to the letter of PNRS requirements at their own pace and with no major efforts to emphasize use of PNRS comments in funding procedures. Despite this limited Federal commitment, PNRS had support from states, areawide councils, and public interest groups. This encouraged OMB to expand the program coverage substantially. (ACIR, 1977, p. 221)

The report found that state governments had moved with relish and dispatch to form state and areawide clearinghouses. Yet such enthusiasm did nothing to encourage active local government participation in the PNRS process, leaving local government involvement very limited.

The study also pinpointed more deep-seated local problems. Local officials had too narrow a view of the responsibilities of their governments, the study said. In addition, HUD found that local governments had fragmented and uncoordinated objectives, were short of staff, failed to exploit already existing opportunities for review and policy influence, and were unaware of the independent local role available in the PNRS process. These were the major problems countering the positive, intended effect of PNRS (ACIR, 1977, p. 221).

In the second study, which coordinated all the mechanisms including PNRS, HUD concluded that A-95 made a contribution to coordination. Yet the study also cited instances in which PNRS failed to live up to expectations because of

> (1) lack of local staff capacity to provide . . . comments on applications submitted to the areawide clearinghouses for review, (2) lack of substantial Federal commitment (*i.e.*, Federal Regional Council support, Federal agency

accountability to local comments, and direct contact between the local chief executive and Federal agencies), and (3) limited program coverage." (ACIR, 1977, p. 221)

The fourth study by the GAO found fault with the federal agencies. Because they had significant impact on local planning and development these agencies were not subject to PNRS; the circular overlooked their funding programs, and frequent changes in the number and nature of the federal program that was covered led many agencies to disregard the review process. GAO concluded that "participants in the PNRS were uncertain as to what programs were covered, clearinghouses were hampered in determining whether proposed projects had potential impact, and state and areawide planning activities were handicapped by incomplete data" (ACIR, 1977, p. 223).

GAO could find little of the certainty, much less command and control that process intended. The study observed that

> the several parties in the PNRS process were not fully complying with the circular, mostly because of confusion and misunderstanding as to the requirements and procedures. Applicants were not entering proposals consistently, not giving clearinghouses enough time to review project proposals, contacting either the areawide or state clearinghouse but not both, and not transmitting review comments with the applications to funding agencies. Clearinghouses were uncertain about the time allowed to review applications, and generally not working with applicants and commentators to resolve conflicts. For their part, federal agencies often reviewed and approved application without evidence that applicants had complied with the PNRS requirements, did not adequately instruct applicants in those requirements, and failed to inform clearinghouses of the disposition of applications subject to PNRS. A result of these Federal agency failures was that state and local governments did not consistently have a chance to review proposed projects. (GAO, 1975, p. 12)

OMB administered the circular with very limited staff, GAO found, with the result that there were wide variations among Federal agencies' implementing regulations, and the office relied on complaints rather than a positive approach for monitoring compliance. Policy interpretations were issued to individual parties rather than to the entire audience that was affected.

SUMMARY OF EVIDENCE

The evidence from the three studies revealed that first, areawide plans were inadequate with which to compare new projects, instead providing incentives to use randomly selected criteria for judging or not judging grant applications. Second, there was little staff commitment, in either interest or resources (time, money, staff) to devote to clearinghouse activity, which may have led to a random selection of participants to enter or not enter the review process. Finally, personnel involved in the federal departments lacked interest or were not forced by OMB to include clearinghouse comments in their decisions, providing another random process of solution-provider selection.

OTHER STUDIES AND OTHER CONCLUSIONS

The evidence from the three studies can be summarized and related to evidence compiled from other studies of information use (Feldman and March, 1981, p. 174, footnote 1):

> (1) Much of the information that is gathered and communicated by individuals and organizations has little decision relevance. (2) Much of the information that is used to justify a decision is collected and interpreted after the decision has been made, or substantially made. (3) Much of the information gathered in response to requests for information is not considered in the making of decisions for which it was requested. (4) Regardless of the information available at the time a decision is first considered, more information is requested. (5) Complaints that an organization does not have enough information to make a decision occur while available information is ignored. (6) The relevance of the information provided in the decision-making process to the decision being made is less conspicuous than is the insistence on information.

ACCOUNTING FOR THE EVIDENCE

Above all, the findings suggest that a decision outcome in the PNRS process did not necessarily relate to information gathered in that process. Why then were information, participants, and decision so disconnected? First, the clearinghouses had no direct incentive to curb or align information gathering in light of what is needed by decision-makers. Clearinghouses were paid, often by decision-makers themselves or the governments they head, to gather information, but not to use it. Moreover, the criticism of clearinghouses was likely to come from those who overestimated what they knew about events (i.e., were surprised by what they did not expect) and actually could have used more information, than from those who underestimated what they knew and got more information than they could use.

Second, not knowing the exact shape community development should take, decision-makers could not use information clearinghouse procedures that were provided to guide them to the best alternative. For one thing, economic change forced decision-makers to contemplate new urban and rural development forms and goals, even as clearinghouses told them the best way to what were now relatively obsolete development forms and goals. Often the question to ask, and not the alternative answers, were needed.

Third, the information provided by participants in a clearinghouse process often had strategic importance for more than one participant in more than one way. Conflicts of interest were often apparent as one community might compete with another, with each's review of the other's projects becoming jaundiced as a result. Strategic misrepresentation could be commonplace. Without trustworthiness, the information fell in value and consequently all information became suspect.

Nevertheless, the clearinghouse process had legitimacy, especially for its symbolic attention to the rational decision process, if not for PNRS's adherence to the substance of the rational decision process. In government, legitimacy attached to decisions that were made in apparently rational ways; that is, made in accordance with long-standing norms about appropriate procedures (Olsen, 1970; March and Sevon, 1984; March and Weissinger-Baylon, 1986). Whether the clearinghouse procedure actually led to good or better decisions or whether the procedures even had a relation to decision-making, nonetheless the clearinghouse process itself led participants to believe in the appropriateness of grant decisions and sometimes even the development of plans and decisions related to them, all of which led to support for clearinghouses and their ongoing development.

ALTERNATIVE THEORY: AMBIGUITY

The PNRS has been called an effort involving the "politics of negotiation" (ACIR, 1973, p. 143). That is, PNRS attempted to bring many parties, through advanced notification and review, into negotiation over grant-funded projects, given their impact on community development. No one agency would be given the sole power to decide a particular project, thereby imposing one view on the community or on others.

The "politics of negotiation" may fall somewhat short of describing the actual situation with PNRS, however. Almost a dozen evaluations over the life of the process[6] concluded that community development problems, project solutions, clearinghouse and agency participation, and sign-offs were haphazardly connected with each other (ACIR, 1977). The nature of a process in which everyone could join at will, despite the gravity of some of the decisions produced, led to a rather random association among problems, solutions, participants, and their choice opportunities. Such a random association characterizes Cohen and March's "organized anarchy" (1974, 1986). This type of structure can be characterized by independent flows of problems, solutions, participants, and choice situations. No consistent shared goals guided the members participating in PNRS activity. No clear stimulus forced or even encouraged the different members to participate. In both cases, the control and coordination that are necessary to a cybernetic system were not present.

What did exist in PNRS was a stream of different problems or goals served by different participants, different projects offered as solutions, and a sign-off opportunity. The problems were varied, from local planning agencies with a sense of priorities for development to developers with an urgency for a particular project. The federal agencies provided solutions to problems through the grant funds they could provide. Over the wider number of projects submitted for review, federal and state agencies sometimes participated in PNRS and sometimes did not. Local planning staffs were sometimes fully involved with funding to support clearing-house review, sometimes not. Through all of this, however, choice opportunities appeared—through A-95 notification and review.

Instead of a cybernetic process, the PNRS looked to evaluators much like organized haphazardness. Less like traditional views of management information systems, including accounting and auditing procedures, this system incorporated randomness. Instead of a command and control system that required discipline, above all, this system resembled a political-administrative process involv-ing independent and only loosely-coupled organizations. It presented, as do all organized anarchies, novel management problems, but none nevertheless as dire as *discipline*.

INTERPRETING PNRS AS A GARBAGE CAN MODEL OF ORGANIZATION CHOICE

As it actually existed, the process resembled a garbage can in which various combinations of problems, solutions, participants, and choice opportunities became attached to each other. The streams of each of the four elements were independent and exogenous to the system.

The garbage can choice process, according to Cohen, March, and Olsen (1972), results in an interpretive system. Since much of the problem-solving in the PNRS may be random associations of problems and solutions, few conclusions may be made about the outcomes without elaborating some existing scheme of reference. Lacking definitive results, agencies, such as the ACIR (1977), call for more federal funding and report the general satisfaction government jurisdictions have with the system.

The important differences between a system that relies on cybernetics and much of the rest of the world inhabited by real people is the degree of ambiguity with which decision-makers contend. Cybernetics requires that the question be known, the goal be shared widely among organization members. But seldom does this degree of certainty or agreement actually exist. Such is more likely the case in a federalist system where federal funding agencies may have far more concrete ideas about community development and where local governments are far more predatory in seeking these funds than a cybernetic system might allow. Combin-ing three different sets of participants in a choice structure in which funding solutions may have little relation to problems as they are comprehended by any or all of the participants prompts what we know as an *organized anarchy*.

Such a system relies on symbolic moves for creating "progress." Thus, creating a PNRS may have little direct technological relevance to decision-makers. Whatever technological relevance the process has lies in its random juxtaposition of problems, solutions, and participants. By random mating, some problems get solved, some solutions get used and some participants feel they have actually created an outcome.

However, the PNRS has remarkable salience in legitimizing or even justifying decisions *after* they are made. In whatever way a decision was reached, a decision-maker has incredible amounts of information on which to build a case for a decision already made.

Even in going through the process, moreover, the decision-makers achieve legitimacy for action. Following what is widely believed by voters to be a good decision-making process in which competing alternatives are weighed against each other in terms of contributing to a goal, the decision-maker creates the potential for attachment and commitment by those who will carry it out as well as those who will live with the result.

NOTES

1. Programs included open space land projects or planning and construction projects for hospitals, airports, libraries, water supply and distribution facilities, sewerage facilities and waste treatment works, highways, transportation facilities, law-enforcement facilities, water development and land conservation projects. Housing facilities were added in 1971.
2. 80 Stat. 1255, 42 U.S.C. Sect. 3301–314 (1966).
3. 82 Stat. 1103, 42 U.S.C. Sect. 4201–243 (1970).
4. Metropolitan clearinghouses were located in Primary Metropolitan Statistical Area (PMSA) size urban areas while regional clearinghouses serve mostly rural areas.
5. Exemplifying this concept of an A-95/A-98 cybernetic model is the development in West Virginia of an information system designed to meet the needs of that state in view of the expanding federal grant program. The FAIR program of West Virginia is designed to monitor grants-in-aid and manage program administration. Using the A-95/A-98 System, the state set up its own computer-based information system which effectively tracks all grant proposals and monitors the status (review and notification) of all grants in the state. At any one time, the exact location and stage of any application is known. In addition, the management capability the FAIR program added enables the state to use its program funding more effectively by knowing the time and point of impact of federal grant projects.
6. Advisory Commission on Intergovernmental Relations (1973); the Council of State Governments (1971); Wilson and Watkins (1975); National Service to Regional Councils 91971); Urban Data Service (1972); U. S. Department of Housing and Urban Development (1974); Morris (1974); U. S. House of Representatives (1974); U. S. General Accounting Office (1975); and U. S. Office of Management and Budget (1975).

10

Government Revenue Forecasts

Recently, the *New York Times* reported that the early skirmishing over budgets at the federal government level involved the revenue forecasts. Not surprising, this skirmishing took on added significance because legislation passed by Congress dictating automatic cuts made legislative action dependent on forecasts of revenues and expenditures. Should there be a mismatch, the forecast would actually create the need for automatic cuts. Thus, Congress became especially aware of the potential that forecasts had for eliminating legislative discretion in spending—the very essence of constitutional and political power vested in this branch of government.

The policy problems and consequences of forecasting are not based on political differences alone. Since no revenue forecaster can know the future and, instead, must monitor various data sets, judgments must be made about what to consider important enough to follow closely, what is novel, and what is a trend. One's assumptions, built not only through political views but also through organizational and professional effort, guide one to search to all three questions (Pierce, 1971, p. 53). Thus, forecasting, the only major administrative action in revenue management (besides policing and recordkeeping), has the greatest interpretive potential. Likewise one can influence the course of events. If one's view is substantially influential, the guidance this forecast provides can influence the course of events (Pierce, 1971, p. 41). As Klay (1985) has pointed out, however, what one wants to see can happen. Views do become self-fulfilling prophecies.

In this chapter, I describe the technical aspects of forecasting revenues and then place the technology in the larger management framework that issues from the interpretive approach used throughout this book. This discussion depicts forecasting as a diverse set of methods that have an appropriate but limited use until joined with management and purpose. Therefore, forecasts may help decide policy and budget, but one often finds a drastic need for a management approach to structuring and using forecasts.

FORECASTING AS A RATIONAL EXERCISE

Many different classifications schemes exist to understand forecasting as a rational exercise. Quantitative methods are those depending on empirical data and in which theories play a central role. Such is often the case in revenue forecasting, where a normative position taken by the forecaster allows use of these methods. For example, many, if not most, practicing property tax forecasters take the position that demand for housing will continue to rise, that market values will rise, and that property tax rates will have no more than a marginal effect on demand and values so that revenue will rise as well.[1] Of course, others, especially those viewing the federal income tax from the "supply-side" perspective, tend to assume that, at some rate level, the value of work diminishes, thus leading to less revenue (Fullerton, 1982).

Qualitative methods also may come into play. Forecasters may have only a fuzzy understanding of their production theories under various conditions. Finally, as I illustrate in the Troika case (see Appendix), forecasters may combine both forms, implicitly a reflection of organization biases, or the forecaster may reason backward from a desirable conjectured state of affairs to data and assumptions necessary to support the conjecture (see Dunn, 1981, p. 195).

Before looking at the latter complex situation, I review and evaluate quantitative methods, then look at the qualitative methods that are commonly used.

Quantitative Methods

Quantitative methods are those forecasting methods involving data and mathematical analysis. These quantitative methods fall into two basic categories: *time-series analytical methods* and *causal models*.

Time-Series Analysis

A time series is a sequence of observations of phenomena of interest. Usually, these observations are spaced at specific and constant intervals. For example, the expenditures of a state government would form a time series when these expenditures, or a specific class of expenditures (the variable), were measured over a period of years. Analysis of a time series involves describing the source of the sequence of realizations, the factor generating the time series.

Forecasting experts have classified characteristic patterns of time series in at least six (see Figure 1). First, a process may remain constant over time, with variations from time to time because of some random influence. A second pattern, a trend, reveals a constant rate of change in addition to random influences. Third, patterns emerge as cycles, sequences that repeat over time.

Three additional patterns vary from the basic types. An impulse pattern develops when a temporary influence causes the variation. A step change results when, instead of a temporary influence, one observes a permanent influence. Finally, a changing (increasing or decreasing) rate of change in the variable observed creates a ramp pattern.

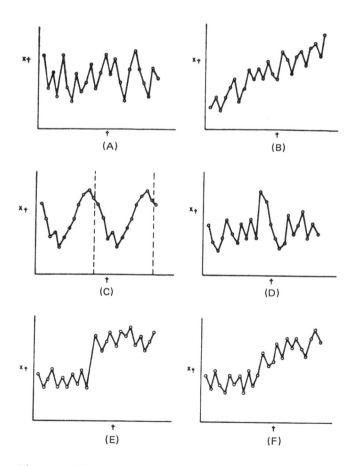

Figure 1   Time-series characteristics. (A) Constant process; (B) linear trend; (C) cyclic variation; (D) impulse; (E) step function; (F) ramp. Source: Montgomery and Johnson, 1976, p. 10.

Methods of Forecasting Time Series

The simplest method of forecasting time series assumes that present trends may be extrapolated. The basic methods used for extrapolation are least squares and other forms of regression analysis.

Least Squares and Regression

Simple regression requires that a relationship between two variables exist and that enough history describing this relationship be accessible to determine quantitatively the degree to which movement in one variable may be predicted by movement in the other. Yet decision makers doubt that what lies ahead will have been repeated in the past. Many discredit regression techniques which try to find linearity where none exists.

Causal Models

A model consists of explicitly stated relationships among variables that portray an abstraction of some phenomenon, such as taxes and economic growth. Most models build on history but, in addition, elaborate theoretical relationships, such as that involving the curvilinear relationship among productivity, tax rates, and revenue yields illustrated earlier. Forecasting models range from relatively simple judgmental models to highly complex econometric models.

Judgmental Models. A judgmental model is a method of economic analysis that is relatively unstructured and informal. Generally, the forecaster does not use mathematical equations to represent the economy but relies instead on any information that seems useful—information about future investment intentions and upcoming political events, judgments and hunches of people familiar with economic events, and other considerations not explicitly a part of the national income accounts framework.

Econometric and Mathematical Models. At the other extreme, an econometric model is a system of analysis in which the economic systems of a unit is represented by a complex system of statistically estimated mathematical equations. The number of equations that are needed to adequately represent the economy depends on the number of actors that are to be considered. The larger the number of equations, the greater the number of subtle economic variations that can be accounted for by the model.

In the equations that follow, taken from the econometric forecasting literature (Pierce, 1971), econometric models are used for forecasting and policy analysis. The model begins by assuming that the following economic relationships exist in the nation's economy:

$$C = 210 + 0.7 \, (Y - T) \tag{1}$$

$$I = 20 + 0.1 \, (Y_{-1}) \tag{2}$$

$$T = 0.2Y \tag{3}$$

$$Y = C + I + G \tag{4}$$

According to Equation 1, consumption C depends on disposable income $Y - T$. Investment I from Equation 2 depends on the income received in the previous period Y_{-1}. Taxes T from Equation 3 depend on current income Y. And the last equation defines current income Y as the sum of consumption, investment, and government expenditures G.

These equations consist of four unknown variables—consumption, investment, taxes, and national income—each of which is to be predicted or analyzed for some future period by the model. It also contains two known variables—government expenditures and income received in the previous period Y_{-1}.

Once the forecasters find out what government expenditures are expected to be in the period to be forecasted, and have a figure for the previous period's income, they can then determine what the unknowns will be by solving the four equations. For instance, if government expenditures are expected to be 20, and (say) this year's national income is 100, then substituting $G = 20$ and $Y_{-1} = 100$ into the equations and solving gives $C = 540.9$, $I = 30$, $T = 118.2$, $Y = 590.9$. Of course, this is a highly simplified example of an econometric model, but it illustrates the procedures that are used to make a forecast.

Policy Analysis with Models

The same model can be used for policy analysis as well as for forecasting. To investigate any specific set of possible government actions, the policy-makers simply insert the change into the model and solve to find out what the impact of the action is likely to be. In periods of inflation, the figure for taxes might be raised and expenditures lowered. In periods of depression, the opposite actions might be taken.

An econometric model allows the government to predict the effects of a policy action before enacting it. The quality of the model depends on the accuracy with which it can predict these values. In summary, the distinguishing feature of econometric models is an attempt to depict the economy by a set of statistically estimated mathematical equations. Particular emphasis is placed on having as many variables as possible explained within the system of equations, on the use of hard economic data, and on the simultaneous solutions of the model without the introduction of other considerations.

Qualitative Approaches

Qualitative forecasting methods are those in which subjective estimation predominates. Such methods have greatest utility in murky or confusing areas of activity, those areas where our knowledge of the relevant variables and the patterns of interaction among these variables may not be well developed. Often the loudest partisans of qualitative methods are those who reject *a priori* reasoning or positive theory.

The most basic qualitative forecasting technique is the judgmental forecast. Using judgment, individuals create a relatively unstructured and informal process. Those people with information relevant to the phenomena being considered essentially pool that knowledge and make educated guesses about the future. Hunches and intuition play a large role in the outcome of a judgmental forecasting process.

Delphi Technique

A well-known form of judgmental forecasting is termed the *Delphi technique* (Brown and Helmer, 1962). To employ this method, one empanels a group of experts who respond to a sequence of interrogations in which their responses are communicated to each other. Specifically, their responses to one questionnaire are used to produce a subsequent questionnaire. Any set of information available to some experts and not to others is passed on to the others through this sharing process. This information, the method envisions, sharpens judgment among experts and focuses attention and forecasts.

Brainstorming

Another information-gathering technology that is useful in aiding judgment and forecasting future events is brainstorming (Osborn, 1953). This method follows a very disciplined format. Criticism of any source of information or of the information provided is banned. In fact, farfetched ideas are encouraged as an aid to eliciting a large number of practical ideas. The quantity of data is emphasized. The first step in the process—the generating phase—rests primarily on creativity. The second phase is a winnowing out phase in which individuals evaluate ideas generated earlier. The third phase builds on the best ideas surviving the second phase by focusing attention on synthesizing these best ideas. Finally, the evaluation phase forces the elimination of all but the best idea or forecast.

Many organizations employ the *nominal group technique* (Delbecq, Van de Ven, and Gustafson, 1975) to forecast future events. A nominal group is composed of the pooled outputs of randomly chosen individuals who have worked alone.

THE INTERPRETIVE APPROACH TO FORECASTING

Revenue forecasting in government is hardly ever the prerogative of only one group. In fact, intergroup effort describes what takes place when both legislative and executive bodies cooperate (Kamlet, Mowery and Su, 1987), but such effort is also required among different offices within the executive (Pierce, 1971), and, at the local level, among the different activities within the finance department (Meltsner, 1971).

Common to all whose task is forecasting is ambiguity. Seldom is there a clear definition of cause-effect relationships. Seldom less is there agreement about what one wants to happen. Thus, forecasting is often a judgmental process, especially influenced by the social construction of reality by forecasters.

To understand the judgmental process and revenue forecasting, it is necessary to understand the elements that interact to construct cause-effect relationships and desired outcomes. The interaction among actors in forecasting, as in all other organizational and judgmental exercises, assumes that all want stability; all participants interact and confine behavior in ways to trade stable expectations about behavior.

Explaining reality construction solely as an economy of social interactions is incomplete. March and Olsen (1989: 62) suggested that the market centers on bias:

> Although there seems to be ample evidence that when performance fails to meet aspirations, institutions search for new solutions . . . , changes often seem to be driven less by problems than by solutions. . . . When causality and technology are ambiguous, the motivation to have particular solutions adopted is likely to be as powerful as the motivation to have particular problems solved, and changes can be more easily induced by a focus on solutions than by a focus on problems. Solutions and opportunities stimulate awareness of previously unsalient or unnoticed problems or preferences.

All parties to making judgments have a solution in mind. Judgment in a collective choice situation is a matter of convincing other parties of the connection between a preferred solution and the problem at hand.

The argument about one's preferred solution may be easier to make when the party realizes the importance of sequential attention. Parties to the making of judgment have limited time and limited willingness to devote more than a fair share of that time to a given judgment call. Any party realizing the limited time problem can choose (or not choose) to focus attention on a given solution.

One's ploy may well be to focus on the aspect of the problem which a given solution seems most capable of resolving. Or one's time may best be spent in characterizing a problem as one which a favorite solution has always been chosen by the group to use. In fact, Brunsson (1989) has argued that it is possible to sustain a coalition among members who have what appear to be strictly inconsistent objectives because of sequential attention.

The ploys can be illustrated with the Troika (cf. Appendix), which is a federal executive branch forecasting group consisting of representatives of the U. S. Department of the Treasury, the Council of Economic Advisors, and the Office of Management and Budget. According to the research by Pierce (1971), the favorite solutions to budget and economic problems stand behind the Troika members' contributions and thus can influence forecasts. Through the use of econometric models in policy analyses, members of the Troika can run any policy solution through the econometric model, varying the assumptions built into the model. Solutions, in the form of policies, often drive Troika forecasting.

The members of the Troika also have their unique biases. According to Pierce (1971, p. 49), "Treasury technicians tend to place a higher priority on the goal of price level stability than on unemployment or growth," whereas the Council of Economic Advisors, with the exception of recent past periods,[2] usually places greater emphasis on full employment and economic expansion.

The Office of Management and Budget (OMB) is responsible to Presidential norms. The norms command that no action may lead to a depression or recession, at least not in an election year, and that no forecast should create conditions for a self-fulfilling prophecy.

Also, OMB must reflect the policy thinking of the Chairman of the Committee on Ways and Means in the House of Representatives. Since a proposal based on a forecast by the Troika, but not liked by the chairman, can doom the proposal, such a forecast is viewed as presumptuous, because it can lead to opposition and ultimately reduce public confidence in the President's ability to manage the national economy. Such threats must be avoided; therefore, OMB indirectly reflects the chair's views as well as those of the President.

According to observers (Kettl, 1986; Greider, 1987; Pierce, 1971), the procedure used by the Troika is one of sequential attention. First, Treasury forecasts revenue. Then, OMB forecasts expenditure. Finally, the Council forecasts the economic outlook.

The procedure can be iterative as it includes computing a "bench-mark model" and alterations called *add-ons*. More importantly, the economic outlook has a subsequent effect on revenue and expenditure estimates, since the economic outlook directly affects expectations about employment and interest rates which, in turn, affect revenue and expenditure.

According to Pierce (1971) in manipulating sequential attention in the process, the Council seems to have an advantage that is due to technology and expertise:

> Because the council technicians determine what goes into the forecasting model, actually do the arithmetic, and make most of the judgmental computations, they are in a very good position to influence, if not control, the troika proceedings. The preeminence of the council members in the technology of the forecasting exercise gives them considerably more weight in the forecasting exercise. . . . The council is also able, because of its immense prestige among economists, to attract some of the most outstanding young forecasters in the

economics profession. Each year, two or three academic economists who are specialists in forecasting join the council staff for one-year assignments, bring new ideas and the most up-to-date techniques to the council's forecasting effort. (p. 50)

By adroitly applying technology and expertise, council members can manage the assumptions and judgments which must be made to combine revenue and expenditure forecasts in some reasonable way and predict economic change.

The recognition of biases, and the understanding that differences may be useful, underscores much research in judgment making (Wright and Ayton, 1987). Differences can thus create a healthy skepticism about the views and assumptions of others, bringing them out in the open (Golembiewski and Miller, 1981). Research by Klay (1985, 1983) and Ascher (1978) suggested that the airing of such differences can reduce over-reliance on outdated core assumptions, or "assumption drag," in forecasts to improve their accuracy.

The structuring of forecasters to exploit their differences may not depend on simply adding more forecasters who distrust the work of others. Subtly nudging forecasts in other ways may require more attention but may have substantially larger payoffs.

The sequential attention factor may have the most potential for improving or changing forecasting practice. Varying the sequence of attention may lead those who want to control attention to focus it on important matters. Such seemed to be the case in studies by both Crecine (1969) and Meltsner (1971).

Crecine's work in local government budgeting confirmed the idea that there exists a sequence of budget decisions, each of which has an influence on the next one and which, as the sequence unfolds, influences the entire budget's final shape and substance. The decision process conforms to a hierarchy, each level of which provides constraints for that which follows.

Meltsner's work on local government revenue systems notes the same structure for decision-making, especially when applied to forecasting. His model (see Figure 2) implies a sequencing of work (separate sequences for large and small "other" revenue sources and then, property taxes) and a hierarchy of steps within these sequences.

From this emerges a set of potential roles through which individuals assume responsibility for parts of an idealized process. A recordkeeper/data driver finds the average rate of change over previous years, various observers determine why the average rate might be different in the future and offer another, higher rate of change with these potential events in mind. Another, more cautious officer might recommend that the two be averaged and rounded down.

This view corresponds to Wildavsky's view of budget deliberations (1988; see also Schick, 1988, p. 64). An advocate recommends more money for programs, and a guardian recommends less, but more than the previous year. The decision may be somewhere in between.

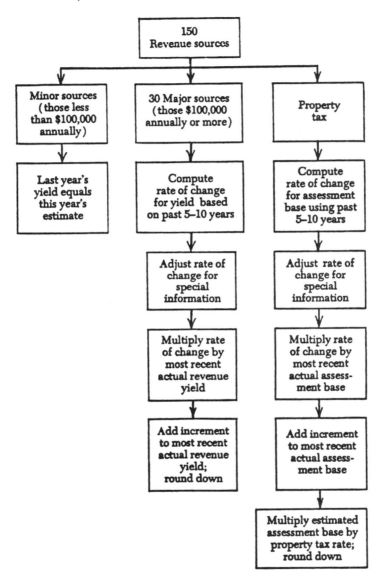

Figure 2   Oakland's revenue estimating procedures. Source: Meltsner, 1971.

The question, of course, is always what was last year's appropriation. In cases where programs remain as they were, are not formula driven, and are related to some batch of linear, independent variables (such as time) the calculation is straightforward.

In cases where this is not so, Wildavsky and others (Gist, 1982; Wanat, 1974) have shown the base to be somewhat difficult to construe. The outcomes reached through base-advocate-guardian "negotiation" in such cases are far from predictable.

Such may as easily be the case in forecasting. One would assume that forecasts are computational exercises for the most part. If they are not completely computational, we would expect them to be a combination of interpretation and computation, using the full range of methods outlined earlier.

If this is more reasonable as a surmise, truly interesting questions emerge. First, whose interpretations guide forecasts? In cases where there are different interpretations, how does a group of forecasters decide which one to use?

Second, is there an inherent bias in the forecasting process? Is such a bias toward high numbers in someone's political interest, or toward low ones?

Theory

In ambiguous circumstances, who rules assumptions and guides forecasting? Two competing explanations seem to draw agreement: sequence and institutional bias.

Sequence

The sequential attention partisans (Hammond, 1986; Plott, 1976) explained assumption rules in terms of structure. Sequential attention finds support in agenda research on legislatures and in hierarchy research in bureaucracies. First, agendas dictate what is considered first and so on through legislative work sessions. Plott (1976) modeled the agenda of a decision process and showed how the agenda may force decisions in certain ways (see Figure 3). When, for example, three different preference orderings existed, each possible agenda yielded a different outcome. Whoever controls the agenda controls the outcome.

Second, in more ambiguous circumstances where preferences are not known, agenda strategy can still have importance. For instance, March and Olsen (1986) argued that there was practical value in tactically loading agendas. Loading some agendas rather than others (such as college self-studies and budget deliberations rather than investment committee meetings) took high pressure issues away from other agendas and permitted work to get done. Moreover, they pointed out, loading meeting agendas at the front end with controversial items may work in favor of actually gaining acceptance (or encouraging ignorance) of other issues that are more serious and that are placed in a less vulnerable position later in the agenda. Such front loading provides garbage cans in which all parties can put solutions, problems, and other such.

Person 1's Preference Ordering	Person 2's Preference Ordering	Person 3's Preference Ordering	Committee's Preferences
x	y	z	x
y	z	x	y
z	x	y	z
			x

Three different binary agendas are possible here:

(1) Compare *x* and *y*, and then pit the majority winner against *z;*

(2) Compare *x* and *z*, and then pit the majority winner against *y;* and

(3) Compare *y* and *z*, and then pit the majority winner against *x*.

Diagrammatically, we have:

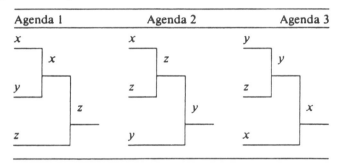

Figure 3 Agenda control based on known preference ordering. Source: Plott, 1976, pp. 513–515.

Compelling arguments have also been made by Padgett (1980) in bureaucracy studies. He showed that altering subordinates' attention rules—through variants of agendas such as structural stratagems—actually reduced the amount of close control and scrutiny required of the chief executive and, by sequencing attention, increased the amount of unclouded information the chief executive gets.

Institutional Bias

The second role-bias explanation (Wildavsky, 1988; Schick, 1988), held that forecasting was inherently conservative, with all extreme positions moderated by the need for compromise. This view held that institutions that have a stake in the outcome of a forecast must compel representatives to "vote" this bias in strategically important ways in interorganizational confrontations or cooperative ventures. Without staking out initial positions at the extreme, these institutions found that later decisions or compromises did not incorporate the points of view of the institutions.

Troika: Site for Competing Explanations

From those who have studied the way the Troika functions, we can infer that roles provide a way to test sequential attention against institutional bias. The data driver is obviously the Council of Economic Advisors since the chair directs the manipulation of data provided by the Federal Reserve using whatever the staff thinks advisable as technique.

In the second role of environmental scanner, the Office of Management and Budget and the Office of the Treasury participate. OMB staff looked at the consequences of past, present, and future policies and the political negotiations and outcomes that occurred over special budget amounts. Treasury took a more cautious view of trends, typically, in the staff members monitoring of market reaction to budget assumptions.

Finally, as guardian of the treasury, the staff members in the Department of Treasury also played the most cautious role. Treasury staff, ever conservative, took part as the "round down" advocate.

Moreover, the Troika literature (Pierce, 1971), explained preferences: no single set of preferences has guided forecasters. Rather, roles are played and the Troika forecast has depended on numbers generated through these roles.

Second, the forecast is derived from negotiation rather than computation. The properties of a forecasting process include negotiation over the limits and middle ground. This negotiation guides and dictates the outcome of that process. In the case of the Troika, we would expect that whoever controls the agenda has a greater say in the outcome than those who are at the outer limits, which corresponds to the sequential attention position.

In the second finding of the Troika literature, the neutrality of the agenda-setter is examined. If we assume that all parties consider CEA as primarily neutral and its chairing the Troika as merely a way to open discussion on a neutral note, we could discard the idea of agenda setting. Instead, assuming that the CEA forecasts rest on random values of a few variables, we could determine that forecasts that are near the CEA forecast to a greater extent than the other parties' forecasts suggest a random influence in the process. This point of view still supports sequential attention.

In the third finding of the Troika literature, the effect of extreme positions is explained and resembles the institutional bias position. The more extreme the initial position the more likely the position will have some influence on the outcome.

Hypotheses

Now, I want to test the sequence of the decision-making position against the institutional bias view. I studied the proposition in two ways. First, as a function of agenda-setting, the sequence in which the steps in a decision take place has gained general confirmation in the literature, especially in the economics of collective behavior (Plott, 1976). Following Plott (1976) and Hammond (1986), I have modeled the process that is shown in Figure 4.

Since the preference orderings of the members of the Troika are known, I can place them in the same agenda ordering as Plott (1976) did in discussing agenda control. The surprising result is that the group's decision ends in the same place

CEA_{OMB} :   Same --> More --> Less

CEA_{TRS} :   Same --> Less --> More

TRS: Less --> Same --> More

OMB: More --> Same --> Less

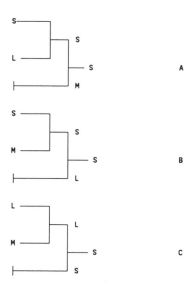

Figure 4   Troika decision-making following the Hammond/Plott variation.

each time, *no matter who controls the agenda*. The status quo is the proverbial second best when all cannot agree on what is preferred. Since all of the members except the CEA have linear preference orderings, the CEA controls the middle ground by specifying the status quo.

Does the same situation hold when we place positions (Figure 5) with numbers? In the latter case, the person who holds the key middle ground position or step in a negotiation can dictate the outcome to the other more extreme conditions. The position on the agenda does not matter. For example, consider preferences of 10, 20, and 30. When the opening position is 10 and the next is 30, the negotiated position is 20. If the bargain is struck between that position, 20, and the only remaining preference, also 20, the result will not have depended on an agenda position.

In all cases, the middle position ended closer to the group decision than either of the other two positions. Why? If the chair of the group makes the first move by suggesting the first forecast or even providing assumptions that the group will use in its forecast, the chair will tend to dominate the outcomes, since the Treasury and the OMB are assumed to be the extreme low and high forecasters, respectively.

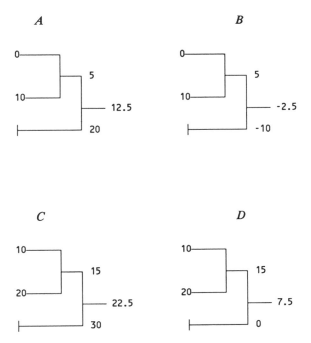

Figure 5 Troika compromises following the Hammond/Plott variation.

Thus, our first hypothesis,[3] from the institutional view, states:

> *H1a*: The average of the initial positions of a three-person group will relate to the final position of the group.

In this case, extreme positions would have an effect.

However, because the middle position might, by chance, hit the middle point, I test for the middle position. Thus:

> *H1b*: The position of the middle person will relate to the final position of the group.

From the sequential attention view, I test the effect of position in decision-making. This view is expressed in a related hypothesis:

> *H1c*: When the chair sets the initial position, the three-person group choice will end in a position closer to this initial position, than to either of the other positions or to the average of these positions.

Being a relatively permanent fixture in fiscal policy making, the Troika process probably has many of the features of other bureaucratic structures. Among these is learning to expect what others want and do. In fact, fear of reprisal may convince parties in permanent relationships to avoid violating those expectations, so strong do they become.

The accountability in these permanent government structures plays a part as well. The agencies involved are responsible for reading the indicators, interpreting them, and applying unique, expert interpretation to these data as their contribution to the policy-making process (March and Simon, 1958). The sequence of decision may play a part, but the interpretation placed on events becomes the central point around which bargaining takes place.

My second hypothesis, therefore, urges recognition of the fact that the process does resemble a more random set of events in which bargaining may occur over the amount of movement from an initial positions (Miller, 1987), a position which itself may be randomly associated with the past or present policy position of any bargainer. Such a condition resembles, in part, the backward voting process described and explored by Wilson (1986).[4] Thus:

> *H2*: When random events create the initial position, the group choice will tend to follow the same pattern, even though random.

Methods

I used a simulation, involving three-person groups, entitled *Troika*, and based on Pierce's work (1971).[5] Asked to forecast the budget deficit of the U. S. government for the coming fiscal year, undergraduate students in introductory public administration classes assumed one of three roles in each of eleven groups: head of the Council of Economic Advisors, Office of Management and Budget, or Department of Treasury.

Each participant had role instructions guiding the choice of forecasts. These role instructions[6] provided positions that each member had to use convincingly to persuade the others to believe and accept. The OMB director role commanded increasing the deficit, thus representing supply-side economics' focus on tax reduction at the expense of the deficit. The Treasury secretary role occupant was instructed to reduce the deficit drastically. The CEA director's instruction varied. In one condition, the CEA director was told to be neutral and defend a forecast derived by a quantitative method (moving average, least-squares trend) or one derived by listening to the other members of the group. In another condition, the director was told a rate of change in the deficit number to defend.

As I stated, two conditions were used: one relating to each major hypothesis. In the first condition, I systematically varied the chair among the three parties and further tested the strength of the chair's initial position for the group by designating, in each case, a voting ally for the chair to cultivate. The variation of the chair enabled me to test the strength of the chair's role and allowed the conditions to determine if the "agenda" dictated the decision.

The chair of the game was allowed to move from the person who was given the role of OMB head to the one who acted as Treasury secretary to the one acting as CEA director. In each of the six variations of the first condition, the chair was told to cultivate one other group member who was named specifically. The variations are arranged as follows:

Group	1	2	3	4	5	11
Chair	TRS	OMB	TRS	CEA	CEA	OMB
Ally	OMB	TRS	CEA	OMB	TRS	CEA
Other	CEA	CEA	OMB	TRS	OMB	TRS

In the second condition, the CEA director remained the chair in every variation of the game. However, the assumption about budget deficit growth was changed to approach randomness; each CEA/chair was given an assumption $(-4\%, -2\%, 0\%, +2\%, \text{or} +4\%)$[7] around which to engineer agreement. However, this assumption became the chair's forecast and, in the sequence of proposals, was announced first. The other members were not told of this assumption in preparing their own forecasts, which were still OMB/high deficit and Treasury/low deficit. The variations are:

Group Assumption about about change in deficit from FY 5 to FY 6	6	7	8	9	10
	-4%	-2%	0%	+2%	+4%

Findings

Tables 1 and 2 provide the results of the first and second conditions. My original, first hypothesis (*H1a*) specified that the group's decision would be very close to that of average of the initial positions of all three roles. This was an indication that the group would have a conserving effect in pulling extreme positions to a middle ground. But the data do not bear this out. Of the four possibilities, the group decisions are closer to the chair's initial position than to the average initial position of the group or to any other position.

The second hypothesis (*H1b*) stated that the middle-ground forecaster's position would relate to the group decision. The deliberation, therefore, would

Table 1 Hammond-Binary Selection Condition

Group	1	2	3	4	5	11	
Chair	TRS	OMB	TRS	CEA	CEA	OMB	
	220	352	207	212	206	186	
Ally	300	208	210	212	206	212	
Other	212	212	260	212	206	181	
Group	220	260	281	212	206	183	

Group	1	2	3	4	5	11	Strength (R^2)
Average Initial v. Chair	24	−95	19	0	0	7	0.79178
Group v. Chair	0	−92	74	0	0	−3	0.92503*
Group v. Ally	−80	52	71	0	0	−29	0.03478
Group v. Other	8	48	21	0	0	2	0.36868
Group v. Average Initial	−24	3	55	0	0	−10	0.91901**
Group v. Average of Chair and Ally	−40	−20	72.5	0	0	−16	0.83848*
Group v. Middle Position	0	−46	−71	0	0	3	0.2851

*$p < .05$ (one-tailed test).
**$p < .01$ (one-tailed test).

Table 2   Random Selection and Agenda-Setting Condition

Group	10	9	8	7	6	Strength (R^2)
%	4	2	0	-2	-4	
CEA	220	230	212	240	205	
OMB	220	212	220	300	225	
TRS	217	210	210	181	181	
Group	220	230	216	240	203	
Group-CEA	0	0	3	0	-2	0.99072**
Group-OMB	0	18	-5	-60	-22	0.63295
Group-TRS	2.8	20	6	59	22	0.00327
Group-Average Initial	0.9	13	1	0	-1	0.91939*

*p < .05.
**p < .01.

gravitate toward moderation. This did not occur either. Where the average of initial positions of the group do not relate strongly to any member's position, the group decisions do relate strongly to that of the chair.

I explored the chair's influence in the third of these hypotheses (*H1c*) because I wanted to find whether the chair's influence exists independently of some middle ground. It does. As already stated, the group decisions are closer to the chair's initial position than to the average initial position of the group or to any other position.

The second hypothesis (*H2*) sought to confirm the chair/sequential attention hypothesis. As the CEA/chair's assumption varied (from -4% to +4%) so did that of the group. The effect of the chair was stronger after the deliberation than before, because the CEA-group relationship became statistically stronger than the CEA-average of initial positions relationship.

Discussion

My discussion began by advocating means other than adding distrustful managers to a forecasting effort in order to improve revenue and expenditure forecasts. Specifically, the literature seemed to suggest that by sequencing the attention of the forecasters, we might have substantially larger payoffs. The research by Meltsner (1971) seemed to relate this view. I then studied two competing positions: the sequential attention factor which represented the view that whoever controls the agenda controls the outcome and the institutional bias view, which supported the notion that representation of important biases contributed to extreme forecasts that were moderated, though not overcome, by group effort.

The test of the position suggests that sequential attention seems strongest and most defensible. The chair in both conditions of the research design dominated the outcome. The relationship between the chair and bias seemed weak since the chair was as likely as not to have one of the extreme positions. Moreover, the chair in providing the initial position guided the outcome.

Conclusions

For this research, Pierce (1971) had important observations to make about the assumptions that Troika used in forecasting. He stated that the Federal Reserve Bank provided data as well as assumptions about the data into the Troika effort. From the last set of findings, we can see the power of the Federal Reserve Bank in addition to the power of the CEA in controlling forecasting outcomes. In this last set of findings, I varied the CEA/Chair's deficit assumption. The Troika's decision ended very close to it consistently.

The research shed light on the Federal Reserve Bank and the data used in their forecast. Is the bank the provider of information that other forecasting units outside the executive branch cannot duplicate? Are these units—like the Congressional Budget Office—held hostage with the same data?

NOTES

1. This is known as the *user fee approach* to measuring incidence and effect. The two other views are traditional—land values decrease by the amount of the tax paid—and the new view—tax rates lower the return on capital used in housing production but may actually lead to increased revenues based on higher values that result from scarcity (see Aaron, 1975; Mieszkowski, 1972).
2. Only when Murray Weidenbaum and Martin Feldstein successively chaired the group, from 1981 to 1986, did the emphasis change to price stability.
3. The null hypothesis states that there will be no relationship among the averages of the initial positions of a three-person group, the middle estimate of a range of estimates, the initial position of the chair, and the group's final decision.
4. The null hypothesis is as follows: When random events create the initial position, the group choice will tend to randomness.
5. See the Appendix to this chapter for a copy of the game.
6. The roles are included with the copy of the simulation in the Appendix to this chapter.
7. The groups in the second variation were given five years of budget figures and asked to compute the fiscal year 6 budget deficit of the U. S. government. The student who played the CEA role and chaired the forecasting group had to compute the deficit that was proposed based on the particular special role assumptions.

APPENDIX

Troika

The "Troika" simulation places you in a role as a member of the U. S. Treasury Department, the Office of Management and Budget, or the Council of Economic Advisors. Your task is *to forecast revenue collections* for the U. S. Government's consolidated budget for the next fiscal year.

Schedule of Work

1. Assemble in the main meeting room;
2. Receive general instructions from the simulation director and special role instructions. Review as needed with the instructor. DO NOT REVEAL THE CONTENT OF YOUR SPECIAL ROLE INSTRUCTIONS.
3. Divide into conferences and adjourn to conference rooms where the following occur:
   a. The chairperson of the conference will briefly review the conference's task;
   b. The members of the conference will break for the first strategy session (10 minutes) during which time each individual conference member will map his or her strategy, in accordance with the special role instructions given each conference member to use during the balance of the conference meeting;
   c. The members will reconvene for a proposal session (15 minutes) during which each conference member will state his or her suggestion;

d. After the conclusion of the proposal session, conference members will adjourn for a second strategy session (10 minutes) during which conference members may meet privately with other members to form a working coalition to be used in the voting-deliberation session;

e. After the second strategy session has concluded, conference members will again be called back to order by the chairperson; the chairperson will then lead the conference into the voting-deliberation session (25 minutes) during which time committee members discuss the proposals before them and take a vote; a three-fourths vote (5 members out of 7; 6 out of 8; and so on) is necessary for any proposal to carry;

f. After the conference has reached a decision or if it has become deadlocked, the chairperson informs the simulation director and leads the committee back to the main meeting room.

4. Feedback session.

Your Troika Exercise

In this brief period, you will work with a group in a troika exercise very similar to that which occurs regularly in Washington. However, you will not have the use of computers or the counsel of econometricians or of government forecasting technicians. You will have simplifying assumptions to speed your work which is to forecast the government's revenues for the coming fiscal year.

The first set of assumptions you will use are the sets of data that will underlie whatever manipulations you decide to use. These data are provided in the next section.

The second set of assumptions you will use are those dealing with your view of the world or your relationships to policy makers and the policy-making process which allows you to select the data assumptions. This second set of assumptions, which we will call *behavioral assumptions*, are your *special role instructions* which are attached to this essay. The behavioral assumptions, unlike the data or technical assumptions, are *confidential* and must not be revealed in any literal way until the stimulation is concluded and the facilitators have asked you to reveal this special role.

Special Role Instructions

Director, Office of Management and Budget

You are one of the President's most trusted advisors and so you should be since you are the *only* member of the President's inner circle from the Eastern Republic Establishment or the so-called Rockefeller wing of the party. Your ties with establishment Republicanism are very close. You served as a principal with

Data Set

REMEMBER YOUR TASK:

Forecast the U.S. budget deficit for the next fiscal year (FY 6).

In order to do so, you should employ these data in whatever manner you see fit.

1	2	3	4	5	6	7	8	9
				Variable*				
Year	Government spending	Consumption	Taxes	Investment	GNP	Potential GNP	Percentage of difference between GNP and potential GNP	Deficit**
1	678.20	2,183.48	599.3	329.55	3,191.23	3,183.87	0.2%	78.9
2	745.70	2,165.41	617.8	339.12	3,250.23	3,314.41	-1.9%	127.9
3	808.30	2,037.35	600.6	345.02	3,190.67	3,450.30	-7.5%	207.7
4	851.80	2,319.57	666.5	339.07	3,510.44	3,591.76	-2.3%	185.3
5	946.30	2,266.85	734.1	371.04	3,584.19	3,739.02	-4.1%	212.2

20* All variables (except year and deficit) are expressed in billions of dollars.

22** Deficit equals government spending (Column 2) minus taxes (Column 4).

the American Enterprise Institute, an exemplary supporter of the President's programs before he was elected in a think tank known for its conservatism.

Your background is investment banking. Your firm was Bobbling, Bobeld, Bobert, and Bmith, the largest anywhere in the world. You know what there is to know about government finance and the marketplace.

A deficit forecast really doesn't bother you because it is disposable income (what people have left to spend after taxes) that you harp on. If after-tax income is large, investment will grow and savings can be encouraged. The larger the deficit, as a matter of fact, the more the disposable income (taxes have been held down and the government spending pumps more disposable income into the economy).

As far as technique is concerned, the more sophisticated the better. There's all wrong anyway, since economists know little more about the economy than a witch doctor or a medicine man knows about medicine.

Special Role Instructions

Secretary of the Treasury

You are an attorney by trade, not an economist. Forecasting is a bunch of baloney as accurately accomplished by the man on the street as by an economist.

This deficit, however, scares you. Why can't we have discipline? Why not the gold standard, for crying out loud?

The Fed (as you call the Federal Reserve Bank System) has probably committed every mistake that Milton Friedman claims. How can anyone have any faith in people who are in love with their own mystique. This forecast should serve to crowd the Fed out of decision-making. Assume that a computer will tune the money supply and leave them out of any of the process.

The financial markets, which you represent as chief borrower for the government, are jittery. Better not make them any more rattled by forecasting a bigger deficit. In fact, project the smallest you can find, one no bigger than that two years ago. By holding down the forecast for taxes and expecting that to keep Congress' spending habits in line, the deficit just might come out that way.

Fancy models won't work as well as plain old dime-store calculator driven ones. The simpler the better. That'll show anybody that can add the logic of cutting the budget.

Special Role Instructions

Chair, Council of Economic Advisors

You are a distinguished economist in all counsels but this. Nobody has any respect for your methods. Yet you know your models are biased toward *Truth*!

Your numbers will come out so that policy makers can make decisions without worrying about the data to begin with.

There's really no reason to explain to this bunch how or why your models work in the President's interest.

At all costs, you want to keep the forecast neutral to protect its predictive power. You know this administration will send a budget to Congress assuming all its programs will be enacted. To you that gives Congress all the ammunition in the world to call the budget "dead on arrival." This forecast, by your lights, won't be DOA. You'll fight with anyone to keep policy and so-called judgment (political play) out of the economic forecast. If you didn't, what would they say about at Harvard when you want to go back or at the Brookings seminars.

Economists can fight; you are an economist; you know what to do, and that is to project no change in the deficit from last year.

Special Role Instructions

Chair, Council of Economic Advisors

You are a distinguished economist in all counsels but this. Nobody has any respect for your methods. Yet you know your models are biased toward *Truth*! Your numbers will come out so that policy makers can make decisions without worrying about the data to begin with.

There's really no reason to explain to this bunch how or why your models work in the President's interest.

At all costs, you want to keep the forecast neutral to protect its predictive power. You know this administration will send a budget to Congress assuming all its programs will be enacted. To you that gives Congress all the ammunition in the world to call the budget "dead on arrival." This forecast, by your lights, won't be DOA. You'll fight with anyone to keep policy and so-called judgment (political play) out of the economic forecast. If you didn't, what would they say about you at Harvard when you want to go back or at the Brookings seminars.

Economists can fight; you are an economist; you know what to do, and that is to project no change in the deficit from last year.

A note on your work as Chair:

You will need to keep a firm hand on the meeting to conform to the time limits outlined under Schedule of Work.

Let members of your group calculate as they please; encourage it; give them time to do it. Analyze the numbers rather than the polemics.

Be fairly formal; let everyone identify him or herself at the start; let each person present a proposal; let everybody talk within limits. But be firm about getting to a vote. Remember your task is to Forecast the dollar amount of the next fiscal year's budget deficit.

Cultivate the Secretary of the Treasury.

Special Role Instructions

Syndicated Columnist based at the Washington Post

Often you like to return to the investigative beat and delve into the machinations behind the scene at, of course, the highest levels. You have decided today to visit a meeting of the troika, dealing with forecasting the President's budget deficit. This is not a press-stopping story, but it is big enough for you to get interested and for a number of people to worry that you are.

You are distinguished for a number of different types of stories, but you have always given economics reporting your hobby interest and time because you are the only one who is any good at it or understands the dismal science enough to talk about it in the press. There's Leonard Silk at the *New York Times*, of course, but what does he know?

Since you are famous, feel free to ask anybody any question, especially whether they know what they're doing. (Remember you aren't fainthearted around the inflated egos in this town.)

Try to frame a story from what you've seen.

Special Role Instructions

Director, Office of Management and Budget

You are one of the President's most trusted advisors and so you should be since you are the *only* member of the President's inner circle from the Eastern Republic Establishment or the so-called Rockefeller wing of the party. Your ties with establishment Republicanism are very close. You served as a principal with the American Enterprise Institute, an exemplary supporter of the President's programs before he was elected in a think tank known for its conservatism.

Your background is investment banking. Your firm was Bobbling, Bobeld, Bobert, and Bmith, the largest anywhere in the world. You know what there is to know about government finance and the marketplace.

A deficit forecast really doesn't bother you because it is disposable income (what people have left to spend after taxes) that you harp on. If after tax income is large, investment will grow and savings can be encouraged. The larger the deficit, as a matter of fact, the more the disposable income (taxes have been held down and the government spending pumps more disposable income into the economy).

As far as technique is concerned, the more sophisticated the better. There're all wrong anyway, since economists know little more about the economy than a witch doctor or a medicine man knows about medicine. The only people to beware of are those who harp on technique.

A note on your work as Chair:

You will need to keep a firm hand on the meeting to conform to the time limits outlined under Schedule of Work.

Let members of your group calculate as they please; encourage it; give them time to do it. Analyze the numbers rather than the polemics.

Be fairly formal; let everyone identify him or herself at the start; let each person present a proposal; let everybody talk within limits. But be firm about getting to a vote. Remember your task is to Forecast the dollar amount of the next fiscal year's budget deficit.

Cultivate the Secretary of the Treasury.

Special Role Instructions

Secretary of the Treasury

You are an attorney by trade, not an economist. Forecasting is a bunch of baloney as accurately accomplished by the man on the street as by an economist.

This deficit, however, scares you. Why can't we have discipline? Why not the gold standard, for crying out loud?

The Fed (as you call the Federal Reserve Bank System) has probably committed every mistake that Milton Friedman claims. How can anyone have any faith in people who are in love with their own mystique. This forecast should serve to crowd the Fed out of decision-making. Assume that a computer will tune the money supply and leave them out of any of the process.

The financial markets, which you represent as chief borrower for the government, are jittery. Better not make them any more rattled by forecasting a bigger deficit. In fact, project the smallest you can find, one no bigger than that two years ago. By holding down the forecast for taxes and expecting that to keep Congress' spending habits in line, the deficit just might come out that way.

Fancy models won't work as well as plain old dime-store calculator driven ones. The simpler the better. That'll show anybody that can add the logic of cutting the budget.

Don't trust fancy pants economists who use fancy models.

A note on your work as Chair:

You will need to keep a firm hand on the meeting to conform to the time limits outlined under Schedule of Work.

Let members of your group calculate as they please; encourage it; give them time to do it. Analyze the numbers rather than the polemics.

Be fairly formal; let everyone identify him or herself at the start; let each person present a proposal; let everybody talk within limits. But be firm about getting to a vote. Remember your task is to forecast the dollar amount of the next fiscal year's budget deficit.

Cultivate the Director of the Office of Management and Budget.

Special Role Instructions

Chair, Council of Economic Advisors

You are a distinguished economist in all counsels but this. Nobody has any respect for your methods. Yet you know your models are biased toward *Truth*! Your numbers will come out so that policy makers can make decisions without worrying about the data to begin with.

There's really no reason to explain to this bunch how or why your models work in the President's interest.

At all costs, you want to keep the forecast neutral to protect its predictive power. You know this administration will send a budget to Congress assuming all its programs will be enacted. To you that gives Congress all the ammunition in the world to call the budget "dead on arrival." This forecast, by your lights, won't be DOA. You'll fight with anyone to keep policy and so-called judgment (political play) out of the economic forecast. If you didn't, what would they say about you at Harvard when you want to go back or at the Brookings seminars.

Economists can fight; you are an economist; you know what to do, and that is to project no change in the deficit from last year.

A note on your work as Chair:

You will need to keep a firm hand on the meeting to conform to the time limits outlined under Schedule of Work.

Let members of your group calculate as they please; encourage it; give them time to do it. Analyze the numbers rather than the polemics.

Be fairly formal; let everyone identify him or herself at the start; let each person present a proposal; let everybody talk within limits. But be firm about getting to a vote. Remember your task is to forecast the dollar amount of the next fiscal year's budget deficit.

Cultivate the Director of the Office of Management and Budget.

Special Role Instructions

Secretary of the Treasury

You are an attorney by trade, not an economist. Forecasting is a bunch of baloney as accurately accomplished by the man on the street as by an economist.

This deficit, however, scares you. Why can't we have discipline? Why not the gold standard, for crying out loud?

The Fed (as you call the Federal Reserve Bank System) has probably committed every mistake that Milton Friedman claims. How can anyone have any faith in people who are in love with their own mystique. This forecast should serve to crowd the Fed out of decision-making. Assume that a computer will tune the money supply and leave them out of any of the process.

The financial markets, which you represent as chief borrowers for the government, are jittery. Better not make them any more rattled by forecasting a bigger deficit. In fact, project the smallest you can find, one no bigger than that two years ago. By holding down the forecast for taxes and expecting that to keep Congress' spending habits in line, the deficit just might come out that way.

Fancy models won't work as well as plain old dime-store calculator driven ones. The simpler the better. That'll show anybody that can add the logic of cutting the budget.

A note on your work as Chair:

You will need to keep a firm hand on the meeting to conform to the time limits outlined under Schedule of Work.

Let members of your group calculate as they please; encourage it; give them time to do it. Analyze the numbers rather than the polemics.

Be fairly formal; let everyone identify him or herself at the start; let each person present a proposal; let everybody talk within limits. But be firm about getting to a vote. Remember your task is to forecast the dollar amount of the next fiscal year's budget deficit.

Cultivate the Chair of the Council of Economic Advisors.

Special Role Instructions

Director, Office of Management and Budget

You are one of the President's most trusted advisors and so you should be since you are the *only* member of the President's inner circle from the Eastern Republic Establishment or the so-called Rockefeller wing of the party. Your ties with establishment Republicanism are very close. You served as a principal with the American Enterprise Institute, an exemplary supporter of the President's programs, before he was elected in a think tank known for its conservatism.

Your background is investment banking. Your firm was Bobbling, Bobeld, Bobert, and Bmith, the largest anywhere in the world. You know what there is to know about government finance and the marketplace.

A deficit forecast really doesn't bother you because it is disposable income (what people have left to spend after taxes) that you harp on. If after-tax income is large, investment will grow and savings can be encouraged. The larger the deficit, as a matter of fact, the more the disposable income (taxes have been held down and the government spending pumps more disposable income into the economy).

As far as technique is concerned, the more sophisticated the better. There're all wrong anyway, since economists know little more about the economy than a witch doctor or a medicine man knows about medicine.

A note on your work as Chair:

You will need to keep a firm hand on the meeting to conform to the time limits outlined under Schedule of Work.

Let members of your group calculate as they please; encourage it; give them time to do it. Analyze the numbers rather than the polemics.

Be fairly formal; let everyone identify him or herself at the start; let each person present a proposal; let everybody talk within limits. But be firm about getting to a vote. Remember your task is to forecast the dollar amount of the next fiscal year's budget deficit.

Cultivate the Chair of the Council of Economic Advisors.

Special Role Instructions

Chair, Council of Economic Advisors

You are a distinguished economist in all counsels but this. Nobody has any respect for your methods. Yet you know your models are biased toward *Truth*! Your numbers will come out so that policy makers can make decisions without worrying about the data to begin with.

There's really no reason to explain to this bunch how or why your models work in the President's interest.

At all costs, you want to keep the forecast neutral to protect its predictive power. You know this administration will send a budget to Congress assuming all its programs will be enacted. To you that gives Congress all the ammunition in the world to call the budget "dead on arrival." This forecast, by your lights, won't be DOA. You'll fight with anyone to keep policy and so-called judgment (political play) out of the economic forecast. If you didn't, what would they say about you at Harvard when you want to go back or at the Brookings seminars.

Economists can fight; you are an economist; you know what to do.

A note on your work as Chair:

You will need to keep a firm hand on the meeting to conform to the time limits outlined under Schedule of Work.

Let members of your group calculate as they please; encourage it; give them time to do it. Analyze the numbers rather than the polemics.

Be fairly formal; let everyone identify him or herself at the start; let each person present a proposal; let everybody talk within limits. But be firm about getting to a vote. Remember your task is to forecast the dollar amount of the next fiscal year's budget deficit.

Nevertheless, estimate the deficit to be –2% over last year, given the factors your models incorporate.

Special Role Instructions

Chair, Council of Economic Advisors

You are a distinguished economist in all counsels but this. Nobody has any respect for your methods. Yet you know your models are biased toward *Truth*! Your numbers will come out so that policy makers can make decisions without worrying about the data to begin with.

There's really no reason to explain to this bunch how or why your models work in the President's interest.

At all costs, you want to keep the forecast neutral to protect its predictive power. You know this administration will send a budget to Congress assuming all its programs will be enacted. To you that gives Congress all the ammunition in the world to call the budget "dead on arrival." This forecast, by your lights, won't be DOA. You'll fight with anyone to keep policy and so-called judgment (political play) out of the economic forecast. If you didn't, what would they say about you at Harvard when you want to go back or at the Brookings seminars.

Economists can fight; you are an economist; you know what to do.

A note on your work as Chair:

You will need to keep a firm hand on the meeting to conform to the time limits outlined under Schedule of Work.

Let members of your group calculate as they please; encourage it; give them time to do it. Analyze the numbers rather than the polemics.

Be fairly formal; let everyone identify him or herself at the start; let each person present a proposal; let everybody talk within limits. But be firm about getting to a vote. Remember your task is to forecast the dollar amount of the next fiscal year's budget deficit.

Nevertheless, estimate the deficit to be –4% over last year, given the factors your models incorporate.

Special Role Instructions

Chair, Council of Economic Advisors

You are a distinguished economist in all counsels but this. Nobody has any respect for your methods. Yet you know your models are biased toward *Truth*! Your numbers will come out so that policy makers can make decisions without worrying about the data to begin with.

There's really no reason to explain to this bunch how or why your models work in the President's interest.

At all costs, you want to keep the forecast neutral to protect its predictive power. You know this administration will send a budget to Congress assuming all its programs will be enacted. To you that gives Congress all the ammunition in the world to call the budget "dead on arrival." This forecast, by your lights, won't be DOA. You'll fight with anyone to keep policy and so-called judgment (political play) out of the economic forest. If you didn't, what would they say about you at Harvard when you want to go back or at the Brookings seminars.

Economists can fight; you are an economist; you now what to do.

A note on your work as Chair:

You will need to keep a firm hand on the meeting to conform to the time limits outlined under Schedule of Work.

Let members of your group calculate as they please; encourage it; give them time to do it. Analyze the numbers rather than the polemics.

Be fairly formal; let everyone identify him or herself at the start; let each person present a proposal; let everybody talk within limits. But be firm about getting to a vote. Remember your task is to forecast the dollar amount of the next fiscal year's budget deficit.

Nevertheless, estimate the deficit to be 0% (the same as last year), given the factors your models incorporate.

Special Role Instructions

Chair, Council of Economic Advisors

You are a distinguished economist in all counsels but this. Nobody has any respect for your methods. Yet you know your models are biased toward *Truth*!

Your numbers will come out so that policy makers can make decisions without worrying about the data to begin with.

There's really no reason to explain to this bunch how or why your models work in the President's interest.

At all costs, you want to keep the forecast neutral to protect its predictive power. You know this administration will send a budget to Congress assuming all its programs will be enacted. To you that gives Congress all the ammunition in the world to call the budget "dead on arrival." This forecast, by your lights, won't be DOA. You'll fight with anyone to keep policy and so-called judgment (political play) out of the economic forest. If you didn't, what would they say about you at Harvard when you want to go back or at the Brookings seminars.

Economists can fight; you are an economist; you know what to do.

A note on your work as Chair:

You will need to keep a firm hand on the meeting to conform to the time limits outlined under Schedule of Work.

Let members of your group calculate as they please; encourage it; give them time to do it. Analyze the numbers rather than the polemics.

Be fairly formal; let everyone identify him or herself at the start; let each person present a proposal; let everybody talk within limits. But be firm about getting to a vote. Remember your task is to forecast the dollar amount of the next fiscal year's budget deficit.

Nevertheless, estimate the deficit to be +2% over last year, given the factors your models incorporate.

Special Role Instructions

Chair, Council of Economic Advisors

You are a distinguished economist in all counsels but this. Nobody has any respect for your methods. Yet you know your models are biased toward *Truth!* Your numbers will come out so that policy makers can make decisions without worrying about the data to begin with.

There's really no reason to explain to this bunch how or why your models work in the President's interest.

At all costs, you want to keep the forecast neutral to protect its predictive power. You know this administration will send a budget to Congress assuming all its programs will be enacted. To you that gives Congress all the ammunition in the world to call the budget "dead on arrival." This forecast, by your lights, won't be DOA. You'll fight with anyone to keep policy and so-called judgment (political play) out of the economic forecast. If you didn't, what would they say about you at Harvard when you want to go back or at the Brookings seminars.

Economists can fight; you are an economist; you know what to do.

A note on your work as Chair:

You will need to keep a firm hand on the meeting to conform to the time limits outlined under Schedule of Work.

Let members of your group calculate as they please; encourage it; give them time to do it. Analyze the numbers rather than the polemics.

Be fairly formal; let everyone identify him or herself at the start; let each person present a proposal; let everybody talk within limits. But be firm about getting to a vote. Remember your task is to forecast the dollar amount of the next fiscal year's budget deficit.

Nevertheless, estimate the deficit to be +4% over the last year, given the factors your models incorporate.

References

Aaron, Henry (1975). *Who Pays the Property Tax? A New View*. Washington, D.C.: Brookings Institution.

Academy of State and Local Government (1984). "Local Alternatives to the Property Tax: User Charges and Nonproperty Taxes, " in Becker, Stephanie, "Local Finance: A Bootstraps Operation" *Intergovernmental Perspective*. 10(2) (Spring): p. 20.

Adams, Carolyn Teich (1988). *The Politics of Capital Investment: The Case of Philadelphia*. Albany, N.Y.: State University of New York Press.

Adrian, Charles R. (1987). *A History of American City Government: The Emergence of the Metropolis, 1920–1945*. New York: Lanham.

Adrian, Charles R. and Ernest S. Griffith (1976). *A History of American City Government: The Formation of Traditions, 1775–1870*. New York: Praeger.

Advisory Commission on Intergovernmental Relations (ACIR), (1961). *Investment of Idle Cash Balances by State and Local Government*. Washington, D.C.: U.S. Government Printing Office.

Advisory Commission on Intergovernmental Relations (ACIR), (1973). *Regional Decision-Making: New Strategies for Substate Districts* (A-43). Washington, D.C.: Superintendent of Documents.

Advisory Commission on Intergovernmental Relations (ACIR), (1977). *Improving Federal Grants Management: The Intergovernmental Grant System: An Assessment and Proposed Policies*. Washington, D.C.: U.S. Government Printing Office.

Aldrich, Howard E. (1979). *Organizations and Environments*. Englewood Cliffs, N.J.: Prentice-Hall.

Aldrich, Howard E. and David A. Whetten (1981). "Organization-Sets, Action-Sets, and Networks: Making the Most of Simplicity," in *Handbook of organizational Design, Vol. 1*. Nystrom, Paul C. and William H. Starbuck, eds., New York: Oxford University Press.

Ansoff, Igor (1965). *Corporate Strategy*. New York: McGraw-Hill.

Anthony, Robert N. (1965). *Planning and Control Systems*. Cambridge: Harvard University Press.

Anton, Thomas J. (1967). "Roles and Symbols in the Determination of State Expenditures." *Midwest Journal of Political Science*. 11: pp. 27–43.

Archer, Stephen H. (1964). "The Structure of Management Decision Theory." *Academy of Management Review*. 7: pp. 269–287.

Aronson, J. Richard (1968). "The Idle Balances of State and Local Governments: An Economic Analysis of National Concern." *Journal of Finance*. 23 (June): pp. 499–508.

Aronson, J. Richard and Eli Schwartz (1987). *Management Policies in Local Government Finance*, 3rd ed. Washington, D.C.: International City Management Association.

Ascher, William (1978). *Forecasting: An Appraisal for Policy-Makers and Planners*. Baltimore, Md.: Johns Hopkins University Press.

Astley, W. Graham (1985). "Administrative Science as Socially Constructed Truth." *Administrative Science Quarterly.*. 30: pp. 497–513.

Bachrach, Samuel B. and Edward J. Lawler (1980). *Power and Politics in Organizations*. San Francisco: Jossey-Bass.

Barber, James David (1966). *Power in Committees*. Chicago: Rand-McNally.

Barker, Lucius J. and Donald Jansiewicz (1970). "Coalitions in the Civil Rights Movement," in *The Study of Coalition Behavior*, Groennings, Sven, E. W. Kelly, and Michael Leiserson, eds., New York: Holt, Rinehart & Winston.

Barnard, Chester, I. (1968). *The Functions of the Executive*, 30th Anniversary Edition. Cambridge, Mass.: Harvard University Press.

Baumol, William J. (1951). "The Transactions Demand for Cash: An Inventory Theoretic Approach." *Quarterly Journal of Economics*. 66 (November): p. 543.

Bayless, Pamela (1985). "A Fast-Lane Financing." *Institutional Investor*. 19:1 (January): pp. 253–254.

Bear, Robert M. (1981). Futures Contracts, in *Handbook of Financial Markets: Securities, Options, Futures*. Fabozzi, Frank J. and Frank G. Zarb, eds., Homewood, Ill., Dow Jones-Irwin, pp. 629–639.

Beer, Stafford (1959). *Cybernetics and Management*. New York: John Wiley & Sons.

Bennett, James T. and Thomas J. DiLorenzo (1983). *Underground Government: The Off-Budget Public Sector*. Washington, D.C.: Cato Institute.

Berelson, Bernard R., Paul F. Lazarsfeld, and William N. McPhee (1954). *Voting.* Chicago: University of Chicago Press.

Berger, Peter L. and Thomas Luckmann (1966). *The Social Construction of Reality: A Treatise in the Sociology of Knowledge.* New York: Doubleday.

Bermany, Larry (1979). *The Office of Management and Budget and the Presidency 1921–1979.* Princeton, N.J.: Princeton University Press.

Berne, Robert and Richard Schramm (1986). *The Financial Analysis of Governments.* Englewood Cliffs, N.J.: Prentice-Hall.

Bettis, Richard (1983). Modern Financial Theory, Corporate Strategy and Public Policy: Three Conundrums. *Academy of Management Review.* 8(3): pp. 406–415.

Bianco, Anthony (1985). Playing with Fire. *Business Week.* (September 16): pp. 78–90.

Bibb, James W. (1984). "A Retrospective Look at State Budgeting." *State and Local Government Review.* 16(3): pp. 123–129.

Black, Fischer and Myron Scholes (1973). "The Pricing of Options and Corporate Liabilities." *Journal of Political Economy.* 81: pp. 637–654.

Bland, Robert L. (1985), "The Interest Cost Savings from Experience in the Municipal Bond Market." *Public Administration Review.* 45: pp. 233–237.

Bleakney, Thomas P. (1980). Municipal and State Pension Plans, in Levine, Sumner N., ed., *Investment Manager's Handbook.* Homewood, Ill.: Dow Jones-Irwin, pp. 709–724.

Blinder, A. S. and R. M. Solow (1973). "Does Fiscal Policy Matter?" *Journal of Public Economics.* (November): pp. 319–337.

Boldt, Harold E. (1984). "Do You Know the Way to San Jose? Or Would You Like to Invest City Funds in Long Term Government Bonds?" *Missouri Municipal League Journal.* (September): pp. 17–19.

Bolles, Albert S. (1869). *The Financial History of the United States*, 3 vols. New York: D. Appleton & Company.

The Bond Buyer (1983). "Innovative Financing." *The Bond Buyer.* (August 1): pp. 11.

Borcherding, Thomas E. (ed.) (1977). *Budgets and Bureaucrats: The Sources of Government Growth.* Durham, N.C.: Duke University Press.

Boss, R. Wayne (1976). "Decision Making: Theories and Applications to the Budgetary Process," in Golembiewski, Robert T., Frank K. Gibson, and Geoffrey Y. Cornog, eds., *Public Administration.* Chicago: Rand McNally.

Bozeman, Barry and Jeffrey D. Straussman (1982). "Shrinking Budgets and the Shrinkage of Budget Theory." *Public Administration Review.* 42 (November/December): pp. 509–515.

Braybrooke, David and Charles E. Lindblom (1963). *A Strategy of Decision: Policy Evaluation as a Social Process.* Glencoe, Il.: Free Press of Glencoe.

Break, George F. (1967). *Intergovernmental Fiscal Relations in the United States.* Washington, D.C., Brookings Institution.

Brewer, Elijah (1985). "Bank Gap Management and the Use of Financial Futures." *Federal Reserve Bank of Chicago: Economic Perspectives.* 9(2) (March/April): pp. 12–22.

Brown, B. and O. Helmer (1962). *Improving the Reliability of Estimates Obtained from a Consensus of Experts.* Santa Monica, Calif.: Rand Corporation.

Brown, Richard E. (1985). "On the State of State Auditing: Analysis, Reflections." *Public Budgeting and Finance.* 4: pp. 85–86.

Brunsson, N. (1989). *The Organization of Hypocrisy.* Chichester, England: John Wiley.

Buchanan, James M. (1987). *Public Finance in Democratic Process: Fiscal Institutions and Individual Choice.* Chapel Hill: University of North Carolina Press.

Buchanan, James M. and Gordon Tullock (1962). *The Calculus of Consent: Logical Foundations of Constitutional Democracy.* Ann Arbor: University of Michigan Press.

Burchell, Stuart, C. Clubb, A. G. Hopwood, J. Hughes and J. Nahapiet (1980). "The Roles of Accounting in Organizations and Society." *Accounting, Organizations and Society.* 5 (June): p. 14.

Burgelman, R. A. (1983). "A Model of the Interaction of Strategic Behavior, Corporate Context, and the Concept of Strategy." *Academy of Management Review.* 8: pp. 61–70.

Burkhead, Jesse (1956). *Government Budgeting.* New York: John Wiley & Sons.

Caiden, N. (1983). "The Politics of Subtraction," in Schick, Allen, ed., *Making Economic Policy in Congress.* Washington, D.C., American Enterprise Institute.

Caiden, Naomi (1988). "Shaping Things to Come: Super-Budgeters as Heroes (and Heroines) in the Late-Twentieth Century, in Rubin, I., ed., *New Directions in Budget Theory.* Albany: State University of New York Press.

Caplan, Edwin H. (1966). "Behavioral Assumptions of Management Accounting." *The Accounting Review.* 16(July): pp. 496–509.

Carter, Lief H. (1985). *Contempory Constitutional Lawmaking: The Supreme Court and the Art of Politics.* New York: Pergamon.

Cartwright, Dorwin (1959). *Studies in Social Power.* Institute for Social Research, Ann Arbor: University of Michigan.

Cater, Douglass (1964). *Power in Washington.* New York: Vintage.

Chandler, Jr., Aldred D. (1962). *Strategy and Structure: Chapters in the History of the American Industrial Enterprise.* Cambridge, MIT Press.

Churchman, C. West (1968). *The Systems Approach.* New York: Dell.

Clark, Terry Nichols and Lorna Crowley Ferguson (1983). *City Money.* New York: Columbia University Press.

Clayton, Ross, Patrick Conklin and Raymond Shapek (eds.). (1975). "Symposium: Policy Management Assistance—A Developing Dialogue." *Public Administration Review.* 35: pp. 693–818.

Cleveland, Frederick, A. (1915). "Evolution of the Budget Idea in the United States." *Annals of the American Academy of Political and Social Science.* 62: pp. 1–23.

Coe, Charles K. (1982). "Structuring the Finance Department in a Time of Uncertainty." *Government Finance.* 11(4): pp. 7–9.

Cohen, Michael D. and James G. March (1974). *Leadership and Ambiguity.* New York: McGraw-Hill.

Cohen, Michael D. and James G. March (1986). *Leadership and Ambiguity: The American College President,* 2nd ed. Cambridge, Harvard Business School Press.

Cohen, Michael D., James G. March and Johan P. Olsen (1972). "A Garbage Can Model of Organizational Choice." *Administrative Science Quarterly.* 17: pp. 1–25.

Collins, Randall (1981). On the Microfoundations of Microsociology. *American Journal of Sociology.* 86: pp. 984–1014.

Comptroller General of the United States (1985). *Managing the Cost of Government: Building an Effective Financial Management Structure.* Vol. 2, Conceptual Framework (GAO/AFMC-85-35-A). Washington, D.C.: U.S. General Accounting Office.

Cope, Glen Hahn (1987). "Local Government Budgeting and Productivity: Friends or Foes?" *Public Productivity Review.* 41: pp. 45–57.

Copeland, Thomas E. and J. Fred Weston (1979). *Financial Theory and Corporate Policy.* Reading, Mass.: Addison-Wesley Publishing Company.

Crecine, John P. (1967). "A Computer Simulation Model of Municipal Budgeting." *Management Science.* 13: pp. 786–815.

Crecine, John P. (1969). *Government Problem Solving.* Chicago: Rand McNally.

Cummings, Larry L. (1982). "Organizational Behavior." *Annual Review of Psychology.* 33: pp. 541–579.

Cyert, Richard M. and James G. March (1963). *A Behavioral Theory of the Firm.* Englewood Cliffs, N.J.: Prentice-Hall.

Daft, R. L. and Karl E. Weick (1984). "Toward a Model of Organizations as Interpretation Systems." *Academy of Management Review* 9(2): pp. 284–295.

Dale, Betsy (1988). "The Grass May Not be Greener: Commercial Banks and Investment Banking." *Economic Perspectives.* 12(6): pp. 3–15.

Dandridge, Thomas C., Ian Mitroff, and William F. Joyce (1980). "Organizational Symbolism: A Topic to Expand Organizational Analysis." *Academy of Management Review.* 5: pp. 77–82.

Davis, Otto A., Michael A. H. Dempster, and Aaron Wildavsky (1966). "A Theory of the Budgetary Process." *American Political Science Review.* 60(3): pp. 529–547.

Delbecq, Andre L., Andrew H. Van de Ven, and David H. Gustafson (1975). *Group Techniques for Program Planning: A Guide to Nominal Group and Delphi Processes.* Glenview, Ill.: Scott, Foresman.

Deutsch, Karl W. (1961). *The Nerves of Government: Models of Political Communication and Control.* New York: Free Press.

Dew, James Kurt (1981). "Financial Futures for State and Local Governments." *Government Finance.* 10 (December): pp. 29–34.

Dewey, Davis Rich (1930). *Financial History of the United States,* 12th ed. New York: Longmans, Green & Co.

Dinham, Sarah M. (1976). *Exploring Statistics.* Monterey, Calif.: Brooks/Cole.

Downs, Anthony (1967). *Inside Bureaucracy.* Boston: Little, Brown.

Downs, Anthony (1957). *An Economic Theory of Democracy.* New York: Harper & Bros.

Drabenstott, Mark and Anne O'Mara McDonley (1984). "Futures Markets: A Primer for Financial Institutions." *Federal Reserve Bank of Kansas City: Economic Review.* 69(9) (November): pp. 17–33.

Dror, Yehezkel (1964). "Muddling Through—"Science" or Inertia?" *Public Administration Review.* 24: pp. 153–157.

Duncan, Harley T. (1980). *Local Government Idle Funds Management in Texas.* Austin, Tex.: Lyndon B. Johnson School of Public Affairs, University of Texas at Austin.

Dunn, William N. (1981). *Public Policy Analysis.* Englewood Cliffs, N.J.: Prentice Hall.

Edelman, Murray (1988). *Constructing the Political Spectacle.* Chicago: University of Chicago Press.

Edelman, Murray (1977). *Political Language: Words that Succeed and Policies That Fail.* New York: Academic Press.

Edelman, Murray (1964). *The Symbolic Uses of Politics.* Urbana, Ill.: University of Illinois Press.

Eghtedari, Ali and Frank Sherwood (1960). "Performance Budgeting in Los Angeles." *Public Administration Review.* 20: pp. 25–33.

Eisner, Robert and Paul J. Pieper (1984). "A New View of the Federal Debt and Budget Deficits." *American Economic Review.* 74: pp. 11–29.

Elder, Charles D. and Roger W. Cobb (1983). *The Political Uses of Symbols.* New York: Longman.

Elkin, Stephen L. (1987). *City and Regime in the American Republic.* Chicago: University of Chicago Press.

Enke, Stephen (1967). *Defense Management.* Englewood Cliffs, N.J.: Prentice-Hall.

Epstein, Paul (1984). "The Value of Measuring and Improving Performance," in Bozeman, Barry and Jeffrey Straussman, eds., *Directions in Public Administration.* Monterey, Calif.: Brooks/Cole, pp. 265–269.

Ernst & Whinney (1979). *How Cities Can Improve Their Financial Reporting.* New York: Ernst & Whinney.

Evan, William M. (1966). "The Organization-Set: Toward a Theory of Inter-organizational Relations," in Thompson, James D., ed., *Approaches to Organizational Design.* Pittsburgh: University of Pittsburgh Press.

Executive Summary (of Volume II of the Study Committee on Policy Management Assistance reports, "Strengthening Public Management in the Intergovernmental System") (1975), *Public Administration Review*. Special Issue: pp. 700–705.

Fabozzi, Frank J., Sylvan G. Feldstein, Irving M. Pollack and Frank G. Zarb (Eds.). (1983). *The Municipal Bond Handbook*, 2 vols. Homewood, Ill.: Dow Jones-Irwin.

Fabozzi, Frank J. and Zarb, Frank G. (1981). *Handbook of Financial Markets*. Homewood, Ill.: Dow Jones-Irwin.

Fama, Eugene F. and Merton H. Miller (1972). *The Theory of Finance*. New York: Holt.

Federalist #51 (n.d.) Modern Library Edition, New York: Random House.

Feldman, Martha S. and James G. March (1981). "Information as Signal and Symbol," *Administrative Science Quarterly*. 26: 171–186.

Fenno, Richard (1966). *The Power of the Purse*. Boston, Mass.: Little, Brown.

Ferguson, Thomas and Joel Rogers 91986). *Right Turn*. New York: Hill & Wang.

Fischer, Frank (1980). *Politics, Values and Public Policy: The Problem of Methodology*. Boulder, Co.: Westview.

Fischer, Gregory W. and Mark S. Kamlet (1984). "Explaining Presidential Priorities: The Competing Aspiration Levels Model of Macro-budgetary Decision Making." *American Political Science Review*. 78: pp. 356–371.

Forbes, Ronald W. and John E. Petersen (1983). "State Credit Assistance to Local Governments," in Petersen, John E. and Wesley C. Hough, eds. *Creative Capital Financing for State and Local Governments*. Chicago: Municipal Finance Officers Association, pp. 225–235.

Fox, Kenneth (1977). *Better City Government: Innovation in American Urban Politics, 1850–1937*. Philadelphia, Penn.: Temple University Press.

Fox, Kenneth (1986). *Metropolitan America: Urban Life and Urban Policy in the United States 1940–1980*. Jackson: University Press of Mississippi.

Freeman, J. H. (1978). "The Unit of Analysis in Organizational Research," in Meyer, Marshall W., John H. Freeman, Michael T. Hannan, John W. Meyer, William G. Ouchi, Jeffrey Pfeffer and W. Richard Scott, eds. *Environments and Organizations*. San Francisco: Jossey-Bass, pp. 335–351.

Freeman, J. Leiper (1965). *The Political Process*. New York: Random House.

Freeman, Robert J., Craig D. Shoulders and Edward S. Lynn (1988). *Governmental and Nonprofit Accounting: Theory and Practice*, 3rd ed. Englewood Cliffs, N.J.: Prentice-Hall.

French, John R. P., Jr. and Bertram Raven (1959). "The Bases of Social Power," in Cartwright, Dorwin, ed. *Studies in Social Power*. Ann Arbor: Institute for Social Research, University of Michigan.

Friedman, Lewis B. (1975). *Budgeting Municipal Expenditures: A Study in Comparative Policy Making*. New York: Praeger.

Friedman, Milton (1953). "The Methodology of Positive Economics," in Friedman, Milton, ed. *Essays in Positive Economics*. Chicago: University of Chicago Press.

Friedman, Milton (1956). *Studies in the Quantity Theory of Money*. Chicago: University of Chicago Press.

Fullerton, Don (1982). "On the Possibility of an Inverse Relationship between Tax Rates and Government Revenues." *Journal of Public Economics*. 19(1): pp. 3–22.

Gergen, K. J. (1978). "Toward Generative Theory." *Journal of Personality and Social Psychology*. 36: pp. 1344–1360.

Gerwin, D. (1969). "A Process Model of Budgeting in a Public School System." *Management Science*. 15: pp. 338–361.

Gist, John R. (1982). "Stability and 'Competition' in Budgetary Theory." *American Political Science Review*. 76: pp. 859–872.

Gist, John R. (1989). "Decision Making in Public Administration," in Rabin, Jack, Gerald J. Miller, and W. Bartley Hildreth, eds. *Handbook of Public Administration*. New York: Marcel Dekker.

Glassman, R. B. (1973). "Persistence and Loose Coupling in Living Systems." *Behavioral Science*. 18: pp. 83–98.

Goffman, Erving (1961). *Asylums*. Garden City, N.Y.: Doubleday.

Goffman, Erving (1974). *Frame Analysis: An Essay on the Organization of Experience*. New York: Harper & Row.

Golembiewski, Robert T. (1964). "Accountancy as a Function of Organization Theory." *Accounting Review*. 39 (April): pp. 333–341.

Golembiewski, Robert T. (1965). *Men, Management and Morality: Toward a New Organizational Ethic*. New York: McGraw-Hill.

Golembiewski, Robert T. (1969). "The Wages of Methodological Inelegance Is Circularity, III: Simon's 'Decision-Making' as Intent and Content," in Golembiewski, Robert T., William A. Welsh, and William J. Crotty, eds. *A Methodological Primer for Political Scientists*. Chicago: Rand-McNally: pp. 191–225.

Golembiewski, Robert T. (1977). *Public Administration as a Developing Discipline, Part 1: Perspectives on Past and Present*. New York: Marcel Dekker.

Golembiewski, Robert T. (1980). "The Near-Future of Graduate Public Administration Programs in the U. S." *Southern Review of Public Administration*. 3: pp. 337–353.

Golembiewski, Robert T. (1989). *Men, Management, and Morality: Toward a New Organizational Ethic*, Piscataway, N.J.: Transaction Books.

Golembiewski, Robert T. and Jack Rabin (1975). *Public Budgeting and Finance*. Itasca, Ill.: Peacock.

Golembiewski, Robert T. and Gerald J. Miller (1981). "Small Groups in Political Science," in Long, Samuel, ed., *Handbook of Political Behavior*, Vol. 2, pp. 1–71. New York: Plenum Press.

Goodman, Laurie S. (1983). "New Options Markets." *Federal Reserve Bank of New York: Quarterly Review.* 8(3) (Autumn): pp. 35–47.

Gouldner, Alvin W. (1954). *Patterns of Industrial Bureaucracy.* New York: Free Press of Glencoe.

Graen, George Bearnard and Terri A. Scandura (1987). "Toward a Psychology of Dyadic Organizing." *Research in Organizational Behavior.* 9: pp. 175–208.

Gregory, K. L. (1983). "Naive-View Paradigms: Multiple Cultures and Culture Conflicts in Organizations." *Administrative Science Quarterly.* 28: pp. 359–376.

Greider, William (1987). *Secrets of the Temple: How the Federal Reserve Runs the Country.* New York: Simon & Schuster.

Greiner, L. E. (1983). "Senior Executives as Strategic Actors." *New Management.* 1(2): pp. 11–15.

Grizzle, Gloria (1986). "Does Budget Format Govern Actions of Budgetmakers?" *Public Budgeting and Finance.* 6(Spring): pp. 60–70.

Gross, Bertram M. (1969). The New Systems Budgeting. *Public Administration Review.* 29: pp. 113–137.

Grossman, David A. and Frederick O'R. Hayes (1981). "Moving Toward Integrated Fiscal Management." *Public Budgeting and Finance.* 1(2): pp. 41–46.

Groves, Sanford and Maureen Godsey (1980). *Evaluating Financial Condition,* 5 vols. Washington, D.C.: International City Management Association.

Groves, Sanford, Maureen Godsey, and Martha Shulman (1981). "Financial Indicators." *Public Budgeting and Finance.* 1(2): pp. 5–19.

Gulick, Luther and L. Urwick (1937). *Papers on the Science of Administration.* New York: Institute of Public Administration.

Hammond, Bray (1970). *Sovereignty and an Empty Purse: Banks and Politics in the Civil War.* Princeton: Princeton University Press.

Hanushek, Eric A. (1986). "Formula Budgeting: The Economics and Analytics of Fiscal Policy Under Rules." *Journal of Policy Analysis and Management.* 6(1): pp. 3–19.

Harman, B. Douglas (1972). "Areawide Review of Federal Land Grant Applications: Implications for Urban Management." *Urban Data Service.* 4(2): pp. 1–8.

Harmon, Michael M. and Richard T. Meyer (1986). *Organization Theory for Public Administration.* Boston: Little, Brown.

Harriman, Linda and Jeffrey D. Straussman (1983). "Do Judges Determine Budget Decisions? Federal Court Decisions in Prison Reform and State Spending for Corrections." *Public Administration Review.* 43: pp. 343–351.

Hayek, Friedrich (1944). *The Road to Serfdom.* Chicago: University of Chicago Press.

Heclo, Hugh (1978). "Issue Networks and the Executive Establishment," in King, Anthony, ed., *The New American Political System*. Washington, D.C.: American Enterprise Institute.

Heilbroner, Robert L. and Lester C. Thurow 91984). *Understanding Microeconomics*, 6th ed. Englewood Cliffs, N.J.: Prentice-Hall.

Hershey, Robert D., Jr. (1989). "New Market is Seen for 'Pollution Rights'." *New York Times*. national ed. (June 14): pp. 29, 32.

Herson, Lawrence (1957). "The Lost World of Municipal Government." *American Political Science Review*. 51: pp. 330–345.

Hicks, J. R. (1940). "The Valuation of the Social Income." *Economica* (May): pp. 105–124.

Hickson, D. J., C. R. Hinings, C. A. Lee, R. E. Schneck, and J. M. Pennings (1971). "A Strategic Contingencies Theory of Intraorganizational Power." *Administrative Science Quarterly*. 16: pp. 216–229.

Hildreth, W. Bartley (1986). "Strategies of Municipal Debt Issuers." Paper presented at the National Conference of the American Society for Public Administration, Anaheim, California (April).

Hildreth, W. Bartley (1987). "The Changing Roles of Municipal Market Participants." *Public Administration Quarterly*. 11(3): pp. 314–341.

Hildreth, W. Bartley (1989). "Financing Strategy." in Rabin, Jack, Gerald J. Miller, and W. Bartley Hildreth, eds., *Handbook of Strategic Management*. New York: Marcel Dekker, pp. 279–300.

Hildreth, W. Bartley and Gerald J. Miller (1983). "Risk Management and Pension Systems," in Rabin, Jack and Thomas D. Lynch, eds., *Handbook of Public Budgeting and Financial Management*. New York: Marcel Dekker, pp. 481–488.

Hildreth, W. Bartley and Gerald J. Miller (1985). "State and Local Officials and Their Personal Liability." in Rabin, J. and D. Dodd, eds., *State and Local Government Administration*. New York: Marcel Dekker.

Hinings, C. R., D. J. Hickson, J. M. Pennings and R. E. Schneck (1974). "Structural Conditions of Interorganizational Power," *Administrative Science Quarterly*. 19(Winter): pp. 22–44.

Hirschman, A. O. (1967). *Development Projects Observed*. Washington, D.C.: Brookings Institution.

Hirshleifer, J. (1964). "Efficient Allocation of Capital in an Uncertain World." *American Economic Review*. 54: pp. 77–85.

Hirshleifer, J. (1970). "Investment Decision Under Uncertainty: Application of the State-Preference Approach," *Quarterly Journal of Economics*. 66: pp. 252–277.

Hirshleifer, J. (1970). *Investment, Interest and Capital*. Englewood Cliffs, N.J.: Prentice-Hall.

Hirshleifer, J. (1965). "Investment Decision Under Uncertainty: Choice-Theoretic Approaches." *Quarterly Journal of Economics*. 65: pp. 509–536.

Hitch, Charles J. (1960). *On The Choice of Objectives in Systems Studies.* RAND Corporation, Santa Monica, Ca. Quoted in Wildavsky, Aaron (1966), "The Political Economy of Efficiency: Cost Benefit Analysis Systems Analysis, and Program Budgeting." *Public Administration Review.* 26(292): p. 310.

Hofstadter, Richard (1955). *The Age of Reform.* New York: Vintage Books.

Horvitz, Paul M. (1981). "Commercial Banks," in Fabozzi, Frank J. and Frank G. Zarb, eds., *Handbook of Financial Markets.* Homewood, Ill.: Dow Jones-Irwin.

Hyde, Albert C. (1978). "A Review of the Theory of Budget Reform, in Hyde, Albert C. and Jay M. Shafritz, eds., *Government Budgeting.* Oak Park, Ill.: Moore Publishing Co.

Hyneman, Charles S. (1950). *Bureaucracy in a Democracy.* New York: Harper & Bros.

Ippolito, Dennis S. (1984). *Hidden Spending: The Politics of Federal Credit Programs.* Chapel Hill, N.C.: University of North Carolina Press.

Jay, Edward J. (1964). "The Concepts of 'Field' and 'Network' in Anthropological Research." *Man.* 64: pp. 137–139.

Jernberg, James (1969). "Information Exchange and Congressional Behavior: A Caveat for PPB Reformers." *Journal of Politics.* 33(August): pp. 722–740.

Johnson, Richard A., Fremont E. Kast, and James E. Rosenzweig (1953). *Organization and Management: A Systems and Contingency Approach.* New York: McGraw-Hill.

Joint Financial Management Improvement Program (1988). *Federal Financial Management Systems: Core Financial System Requirements.* Washington, D.C.: Joint Financial Management Improvement Program.

Jones, William A. and C. Bradley Doss (1978). "Local Officials' Reaction to Federal 'Capacity'-Building." *Public Administration Review,* 38: pp. 64–69.

Jump, William (1946). "Testimony." *Hearings Before the Subcommittee of the Committee of Appropriations,* 2nd session on the Agriculture Department Appropriation Bill for 1947. Washington: U.S. Government Printing Office; 69-81; cited in Robert T. Golembiewski and Jack Rabin (1975). *Public Budgeting and Finance.* Itasca, Ill.: Peacock, p. 6.

Kaldor, N. (1939). "Welfare Propositions of Economists and Interpersonal Comparisons of Utility." *Economic Journal.* (September): pp. 549–552.

Kamlet, Mark S., David C. Mowery, and Tsai-Tsu Su (1987). "Whom Do You Trust? An Analysis of Executive and Congressional Economic Forecasts." *Journal of Policy Analysis and Management.* 6(3): pp. 365–384.

Kaplan, Abraham (1964). *The Conduct of Inquiry.* Scranton, Penn.: Chandler.

Kaufman, George G. (1984). "Measuring and Managing Interest Rate Risk: A Primer." *Federal Reserve Bank of Chicago: Economic Perspectives.* 8(1) (January-February): pp. 16–29.

Kaufman, Herbert (1956). "Emerging Conflicts in the Doctrines of Public Administration." *American Political Science Review.* 50: pp. 1057–1073.

Kaufman, Herbert (1960). *The Forest Ranger: A Study in Administrative Behavior.* Baltimore, Md.: Johns Hopkins University Press.

Kelley, Joseph T. (1984). *Costing Government Services: A Guide for Decision Making.* Washington, D.C.: Government Finance Research Center, Government Finance Officers Association.

Kettl, Donald F. (1986). *Leadership at the Fed.* New Haven, Conn.: Yale University Press.

Key, V. O. (1940). "The Lack of a Budgetary Theory." *American Political Science Review.* 34(6): pp. 1137–1144.

King, John Leslie and Kenneth L. Kraemer (1985). *The Dynamics of Computing.* New York: Columbia University Press.

Kingdon, John W. (1984). *Agendas, Alternatives, and Public Policies.* Boston: Little, Brown.

Klapper, Byron (1980). "Municipal Commercial Paper." *Standard & Poor's Perspective.* (September 17): p. 1.

Klay, William Earle (1983). "Revenue Forecasting: An Administrative Perspective," in Rabin, Jack and Thomas D. Lynch, eds., *Handbook of Public Budgeting and Financial Management.* New York: Marcel Dekker.

Klay, William Earle (1985). "The Organizational Dimension of Budgetary Forecasting: Suggestions from Revenue Forecasting in the States." *International Journal of Public Administration.* 7(3): pp. 241–265.

Klein, Lawrence R. (1978). "The Supply Side." *American Economic Review* (March): pp. 1–7.

Koppenhaver, G. D. (1984). "Trimming the Hedges: Regulators, Banks, and Financial Futures." *Federal Reserve Bank of Chicago: Economic Perspective* 8(6) (November/December): pp. 3–12.

Kraemer, Kenneth L. (1969). "The Evolution of Information Systems for Urban Administration." *Public Administration Review.* 29(4): pp. 389–402.

Kraemer, Kenneth L., Willliam H. Dutton, and Alana Northrop (1981). *The Management of Information Systems.* New York: Columbia University Press.

Kuhn, Thomas S. (1970). *The Structure of Scientific Revolutions,* 2nd ed. Chicago: University of Chicago Press.

Lamb, Robert and Stephen P. Rappaport (1980). *Municipal Bonds: The Comprehensive Review of Tax-Exempt Securities and Public Finance.* New York: McGraw-Hill.

Landau, Martin (1969). "Redundancy, Rationality, and the Problem of Duplication and Overlap." *Public Administration Review.* 29: pp. 346–358.

Lauth, Thomas (1985). "Performance Evaluation in the Georgia Budgetary Process." *Public Budgeting and Finance* 5(Spring): p. 2.

Lauth, Thomas and Glen Abney (1986). *The Politics of Administration.* Albany, N.Y.: State University of New York Press.

Lawler, Edward E. and John Grant Rhode (1976). *Information and Control in Organizations.* Pacific Palisades, Calif.: Goodyear Publishing Co.

Leiserson, Avery and Fritz Morstein-Marx (1959). "The Study of Public Administration," in Morstein-Marx, Fritz, ed., *Elements of Public Administration,* 2nd ed. Englewood Cliffs, N.J.: Prentice-Hall, pp. 23–48.

LeLoup, Lance (1980). *The Fiscal Congress: Legislative Control of the Budget.* Westport, Conn.: Greenwood Press.

LeLoup, Lance T. (1988), "From Microbudgeting to Macrobudgeting: Evolution in Theory and Practice," in Rubin, I., ed., *New Directions in Budget Theory.* Albany: State University of New York.

Levine, Charles H. (1980). *Managing Fiscal Stress.* Chatham, N.J.: Chatham House.

Lewis, Verne (1952). "Toward a Theory of Budgeting." *Public Administration Review.* 12(1): pp. 43–54.

Lindblom, Charles E. (1959). "The Science of Muddling Through," *Public Administration Review.* 19: pp. 79–88.

Lindblom, Charles E. (1965). *The Intelligence of Democracy.* New York: Free Press.

Lineberry, Robert L. and Edmund P. Fowler (1967). "Reformism and Public Policies in American Cities." *American Political Science Review.* 61: pp. 701–716.

Lineberry, Robert L. and Ira Sharkansky (1971). *Urban Politics and Public Policy.* New York: Harper & Row.

Linowes, David F. (1988). *Privatization: Toward More Effective Government.* Urbana, Ill.: University of Illinois Press.

Lintner, John (1964). "The Valuation of Risk Assets and the Selection of Risky Investments in Stock Portfolios and Capital Budgets." *Review of Economics and Statistics.* 47: pp. 13–37.

Long, Norton (1958). "The Local Community as an Ecology of Games." *American Political Science Review.* 64: pp. 251–261.

Lovrich, Nicholas P. (1981). "Professional Ethics and the Public Interest: Sources of Judgment." *Public Personnel Management.* 10(1): pp. 87–92.

Lowenthal, M. (1950). *The Federal Bureau of Investigation.* New York: Shane.

Lyden, Fremont J. and Ernest G. Miller (1978). "Introduction," in Lyden, Fremont J. and Ernest G. Miller, eds., *Public Budgeting.* Chicago: Rand McNally.

MacDonald, T. J. (1988). "A History of Urban Fiscal Politics in America, 1830–1930: What Was Supposed To Be Versus What Was and the Difference It Makes," in Rabin, Jack, W. Bartley Hildreth, and Gerald J. Miller, eds., *Review of Public Budgeting and Financial Management, International Journal of Public Administration.* 11: pp. 679–712.

McCaffery, Jerry (1981). "The Impact of Resource Scarcity on Urban Public Finance: A Special Issue." *Public Administration Review.* 41: pp. 105–202.

McCaffery, Jerry (1983). "Analyzing the Pedagogic Deficit in Budgeting," in Rabin, J. and T. D. Lynch, eds., *Handbook of Public Budgeting and Financial Management*. New York: Marcel Dekker.

McCaffery, Jerry (1987). "The Development of Public Budgeting in the United States," in Chandler, Ralph Clark, ed., *A Centennial History of the American Administrative State*. New York: Free Press.

MacManus, Susan A. (1984). "Budgetary Skills Needs of Different Types of Local Governments: A Market Survey." Unpublished paper prepared for presentation to the National Task Force on Curriculum Reform, College of Urban Affairs, Cleveland State University.

McSwain, Cynthia J. (1987). "A Structuralist Perspective on Organizational Ethos." *Dialogue*. 9(4): pp. 35–58.

Mair, John (1765). *Book-Keeping Methodozied: Or a Methodological Treatise of Merchant-Accounts According to the Italian Form*, 8th ed., Edinburgh: Publisher unknown.

March, James G. (1978). "Bounded Rationality, Ambiguity, and the Engineering of Choice." *The Bell Journal of Economics*. 9: pp. 587–608.

March, James G. (1981). "Decision Making Perspective: Decisions in Organizations and Theories of Choice," in Van De Ven, Andrew H. and William F. Joyce, eds., *Perspectives on Organization Design and Behavior*. New York: John Wiley & Sons.

March, James G. and Johan P. Olsen (1976). *Ambiguity and Choice in Organizations*. Bergen, Norway: Universitetsforlaget.

March, James G. and Johan P. Olsen (1986). "Garbage Can Models of Decision Making in Organizations," in March, James G. and Roger Weissinger-Baylon, eds., *Ambiguity and Command: Organizational Perspectives on Military Decision Making*. Marshfield, Mass.: Pitman.

March, James G. and Johan P. Olsen (1989). *Rediscovering Institutions: The Organizational Basis of Politics*. New York: Basic Books.

March, James G. and Guje Sevon (1984). "Gossip, Information and Decision Making," in Sproull, L. S. and P. D. Larkey, eds., *Advances in Information Processing in Organizations*. Greenwich, Conn.: JAI Press.

March, James G. and Herbert A. Simon (1958). *Organizations*. New York: Wiley.

March, James G. and Roger Weissinger-Baylon (1986). *Ambiguity and Command: Organizational Perspectives on Military Decision Making*. Marshfield, Mass.: Pitman.

Margolis, Julius (1975). "Comments [on William A. Niskanen, 'Bureaucrats and Politicians']. *Journal of Law and Economics*. 18: p. 645–659.

Markowitz, H. M. (1959). *Portfolio Selection: Efficient Diversification of Investment*. Cowles Foundation Monograph 16. New Haven: Yale University Press.

Markowitz, Harry M. (1952). *Portfolio Selection: Efficient Diversification of Investments*. New York: John Wiley.

Maynard-Moody, Steven, Donald D. Stull, and Jerry Mitchell (1986). "Reorganization as Status Drama: Building, Maintaining and Displacing Dominant Subcultures." *Public Administration Review*. 46(4): pp. 301–310.

Maynard-Moody, Stephen and Charles McClintock (1987). "Weeding an Old Garden: Toward a New Understanding of Organization Goals." *Administration and Society*. 19(1): pp. 125–142.

McCloskey, Donald N. (1985). *The Rhetoric of Economics*. Madison: University of Wisconsin Press.

Mead, George Herbert (1934). *Mind, Self and Society*. Chicago: University of Chicago Press.

Meier, Kenneth (1986). "Political Economy and Cost-Benefit Analysis: Problems of Bias," in Stone, Alan and Edward J. Harpham, eds., *Political Economy of Public Policy*. Beverly Hills, Calif.: Sage Publications.

Meltsner, Arnold J. (1971). *The Politics of City Revenue*. Berkeley, University of California Press.

Merton, R. K. (1940). "Bureaucratic Structure and Personality." *Social Forces*. 23: pp. 405–415.

Methe, David, Jerome Baesel, and David Shulman (1983). "Applying Principles of Corporate Finance in the Public Sector," in Perry, James L. and Kenneth L. Kraemer, eds., *Public Management: Public and Private Perspectives*. pp. 243–255. Palo Alto, Calif.: Mayfield Publishing Company.

Meyer, Marshall W. (1971a). "Some Constraints in Analyzing Data on Organizational Structures." *American Sociological Review*. 36: pp. 294–297.

Meyer, Marshall W. (1971b). *Bureaucratic Structure and Authority*. New York: Harper & Row.

Meyer, Marshall W. (1975). "Leadership and Organizational Structure." *American Journal of Sociology*. 81: pp. 514–542.

Meyer, Marshall W. (1985). *The Limits to Bureaucratic Growth*. New York: Walter de Gruyter.

Mieszkowski, Peter M. (1972). "The Property Tax: An Excise Tax or a Profits Tax?" *Journal of Public Economics*. 1: pp. 73–96.

Milgram, Stanley (1964). *Obedience to Authority: An Experimental View*. New York: Harper & Row.

Miller, Merton, H. and Daniel Orr (1966). "Model of the Demand for Money by Firms." *Quarterly Journal of Economics*. 80(August): pp. 413–435.

Miller, Gerald J. (1980). "Overseas Applications of Behavioral Science Technology." *Southern Review of Public Administration*. 4: pp. 229–252.

Miller, Gerald J. (1980–1981). "The Liability of Federal Officials: Administrative Malpractice Policy Before and After *Butz v. Economou*." *The Bureaucrat*. 9(4): pp. 25–32.

Miller, Gerald J. (1983). "Organizational Environments," in Golembiewski, Robert T. and Frank K. Gibson, eds., *Readings in Public Administration: Institutions, Processes, Behavior, Policy*, 4th ed. Boston: Houghton Mifflin.

Miller, Gerald J. (1984a). "Decision Making," in Rabin, J., S. Humes, and B. S. Morgan, eds., *Managing Administration*. pp. 201–232, New York: Marcel Dekker.

Miller, Gerald J. (1984b). "Organizational Budgeting," in Rabin, J., S. Humes, and B. S. Morgan, eds., *Managing Administration*. New York: Marcel Dekker, pp. 233–263.

Miller, Gerald J. (1985). "Coping with Uncertainty," in Rabin, Jack, Gerald J. Miller, and W. Bartley Hildreth, eds., *Annual Review of Public Budgeting and Finance*. New York: Marcel Dekker.

Miller, Gerald J. (1987). "The Timid Manager: A Slow-Moving Target for Civil Suits." *Public Administration Quarterly*. 10(4).

Miller, Gerald J. (1988). "Will Governments Hedge Interest Rate Risks?" *Public Administration Quarterly*. 11(3).

Miller, Gerald J. and Robert Klein (1987). *The County Executive Form of Government in New Jersey: Unique Routines and Problems Related to Spending and Taxing*. Unpublished study. Newark, N.J.: Essex County Charter Study Commission.

Miller, Gerald J. and Kenneth Olson (1983). *Preliminary Assessment of Specific Dimensions of Balanced Base Budgeting, State of Kansas*. Topeka: State of Kansas, Division of the Budget.

Miller, Gerald J., Jack Rabin, and W. Bartley Hildreth (1987). "Strategy, Values, and Productivity." *Public Productivity Review*. 11: pp. 81–96.

Miller, Girard (1982). *A Public Investor's Guide to Money Market Instruments*. Chicago:: Government Finance Officers Association.

Miller, Girard (1982). "The Investment of Public Funds: A Research Agenda." *Public Budgeting and Finance*. 7: pp. 47–56.

Moak, Lennox, L. (1982). *Municipal Bonds: Planning, Sale and Administration*. Chicago, Ill.: Government Finance Officers Association.

Modligliani, Franco and Merton H. Miller (1958). "The Cost of Capital, Corporation Finance and the Theory of Investment." *American Economic Review*. 48: pp. 261–297.

Modigliani, Franco and Merton H. Miller (1967). "Dividend Policy, Growth and the Valuation of Shares." *Journal of Business*. 34: pp. 411–433.

Montgomery, Douglas C. and Lynwood A. Johnson (1976). *Forecasting and Time Series Analysis*. New York: McGraw-Hill.

Morris, Charles William (1946). *Signs, Language, and Behavior*. New York: George Braziller.

Morris, Milton D. (1974). *The A-95 Review Process: Its Implications for Civil Rights*. Washington, D.C.: Joint Center for Political Studies.

Morstein-Marx, Fritz (1957). *The Administrative State*. Chicago: University of Chicago Press.

Moscovici, S. (1976). *Social Influence and Social Change*. New York: Academic Press.

Mosher, Frederick C. (1984). *A Tale of Two Agencies: A Comparative Analysis of the General Accounting Office and the Office of Management and Budget.* Baton Rouge: Louisiana State University Press.

Mosher, Frederick C. (1979). *The GAO: The Quest for Accountability in American Government.* Boulder, Co.: Westview Press.

Moulton, Harold G. (1938). *Financial Organization and the Economic System.* New York: McGraw-Hill.

Mowery, David C., Mark S. Kamlet, and John P. Crecine (1980). "Presidential Management of Budgetary and Fiscal Policy Making." *Political Science Quarterly.* 95: pp. 395–425.

Muchmore, Lynn and Harley Duncan (1982). *The Kansas Budget Process: Concept and Practice.* Topeka, Kan.: Capital Complex Center, University of Kansas.

Murin, William and Judith Pryor (1988). *Delivering Government Services: An Annotated Bibliography.* New York: Garland.

Musgrave, R. A. (1959). *The Theory of Public Finance.* New York: McGraw-Hill.

Myers, Margaret G. (1970). *A Financial History of the United States.* New York: Columbia University Press.

Nash, Gary B. (1979). *The Urban Crucible: Social Change, Political Consciousness, and the Origins of the American Revolution.* Cambridge: Harvard University P ress.

National Service to Regional Councils (1971). "Coordination Eliminates Conflicting Efforts." *Regional Review.* 4(1): pp. 18–22.

National Task Force on Curriculum Reform, Section on Public Budgeting and Financial Management, American Society for Public Administration (1985). *Graduate Curricula in Budgeting and Financial Management: Recommendation for Reform.* Washington, D.C.: American Society for Public Administration.

Nehrbass, Richard G. (1979). "Ideology and the Decline of Management Theory." *Academy of Management Review.* 4: pp. 427–431.

Netzer, Dick (1974). "Stae-Local Finance and Intergovernmental Fiscal Relations," in Blinder, A. S., ed., *The Economics of Public Finance.* Washington, D.C.: Brookings Institution.

Novick, David (1968). "The Origin and History of Program Budgeting," *California Management Review.* 11(1): pp. 7–12.

Oates, Wallace E. (1968). "The Theory of Public Finance in a Federal System." *Canadian Journal of Economics.* 1: pp. 37–54.

Oates, Wallace E. (1972). *Fiscal Federalism.* New York: Harcourt Brace Jovanovich.

Olsen, Johan P. (1970). "Local Budgeting: Decision-Making or a Ritual Act?" *Scandinavian Political Studies.* 5: pp. 85–118.

Olson, Mancur (1969). "The Principle of Fiscal Equivalence: The Division of Responsibilities Among Different Levels of Government." *American Economic Review*. 59: pp. 479–487.

Osborn, Alex (1953). *Applied Imagination: Principles and Procedures of Creative Thinking*. New York: Scribner.

O'Toole, Laurence J., Jr. (1986). "Harry F. Byrd, Sr. and the New York Bureau of Municipal Research: Lessons from an Ironic Alliance." *Public Administration Review*. 46(2): pp. 113–123.

Padgett, John F. (1980). "Managing Garbage Can Hierarchies." *Administrative Science Quarterly*. 25: pp. 583–604.

Pagano, Michael A. (1982). "The Urban Public Sector as Lagging or Leading Sector in Economic Development." *Urban Interest*. 4: pp. 131–140.

Pagano, Michael A. and Richard J. T. Moore (1985). *Cities and Fiscal Choices: A New Model of Urban Public Investment*. Durham, N.C.: Duke University Press.

Parsons, Talcott (1960). *Structure and Process in Modern Societies*. Glencoe, Ill.: Free Press of Glencoe.

Patton, James N. and Hempel, George H. (1975). *Understanding the Market for State and Local Debt*. Washington, D.C.: Advisory Commission on Intergovernmental Relations.

Perrow, Charles (1970). *Organizational Analysis: A Sociological View*. Belmont, Calif.: Wadsworth.

Petersen, John E. (1981). "The Municipal Bond Market: Recent Changes and Future Prospects," in Walzer, Norman and David L. Chicoine, eds., *Financing State and Local Governments in the 1980s*. Cambridge, Mass.: Oelgeschlager, Gunn & Hain, Publishers, pp. 129–141.

Petersen, John E. (1988). "Information Flows in the Municipal Securities Market: A Preliminary Analysis." Unpublished manuscript, Government Finance Research Center. Washington, D.C.: Government Finance Officers Association.

Petersen, John E. and Buckley, Michael P. (1983). *A Guide to Registered Municipal Securities*. Washington, D.C.: Municipal Finance Officers Association.

Petersen, John E., Lisa A. Cole, and Maria L. Petrillo (1977). *Watching and Counting: A Survey of State Assistance to and Supervision of Local Government Debt and Financial Administration*. Chicago: Municipal Finance Officers Association and National Conference of State Legislatures.

Petersen, John E., Pat Watt and Paul Zorn (1986). *Organization and Compensation in Local Government Finance*. Washington, D.C.: Government Finance Research Center, Government Finance Officers Association.

Pfeffer, Jerry (1982). *Organizations and Organization Theory*. Boston: Pitman.

Pfeffer, Jerry (1981). *Power in Organizations*. Marshfield, Mass.: Pitman.

Phillips, A. W. (1958). "The Relation Between Unemployment and the Rate of Change of Money Wage Rates in the United Kingdom, 1861–1957." *Economia*. (November): pp. 283–299.

Phelps, Edmund (1970). *Microeconomic Foundations of Employment and Inflation Theory*. New York: W. W. Norton.

Pilegge, Jr., Joseph C. (1988). "The Line-Item Budget: Ubiquitous and Indestructible." *Discussion Pieces for The Barnard Society, U.S.A.* 2: entire issue.

Pierce, Lawrence D. (1971). *The Politics of Fiscal Policy Formation*. Pacific Palisades, Calif.: Goodyear.

Plott, Charles R. (1976). "Axiomatic Social Choice Theory: An Overview and Interpretation." *American Journal of Political Science*. 22(3): pp. 511–596.

Pomper, Gerald M. (1968). *Elections in America: Control and Influence in Democratic Politics*. New York: Dood, Mead.

Pondy, Louis R. (1978). Leadership Is a Language Game, in McCall, Jr., M. W. and M. M. Lombardo, eds., *Leadership: Where Else Can We Go?* Durham, N.C.: Duke University Press.

Powers, Mark J. and David Vogel (1984). *Inside the Financial Futures Market*, 2nd ed. New York: John Wiley & Sons.

President's Committee on Administrative Management (1937). *Report*. Washington, D.C.: U.S. Government Printing Office.

Price Waterhouse & Co. (1979). *Enhancing Government Accountability*. New York: Price Waterhouse.

Pyhrr, Peter A. (1977). "The Zero-Base Approach to Government Budgeting." *Public Administration Review*. 37 pp. 1–8.

Quade, E. S. (1975). *Analysis for Public Decisions*. New York: Elsevier.

Quint, Michael (1988). "New York Weighs Shift in Setting Bond Rates." *New York Times*. (August 28): p. A48.

Rabin, Jack (1975). "State and Local PPBS," in Golembiewski, Robert T. and Jack Rabin, eds., *Public Budgeting and Finance*, 2nd ed. Itasca, Ill.: F. E. Peacock Publishers.

Rabin, Jack, W. B. Hildreth and Gerald J. Miller (1979). "Suing Federal Executives for Damages," *The Bureaucrat*. 8(1): pp. 54–56.

Rabin, Jack, Gerald J. Miller, and W. B. Hildreth (1980). "The Liability of Public Executives: Implications for Practice in Public Personnel Administration." *Review of Public Personnel Administration*. 1(1): pp. 45–56.

Rabin, Jack, Gerald J. Miller, and W. B. Hildreth (1981). "Administrative Malpractice Suits: Tort Liability of Public Officials." *Public Personnel Manaagement*. 10(1): pp. 119–125.

Rabin, Jack, Gerald J. Miller, and W. B. Hildreth (1989). *Handbook of Strategic Management*. New York: Marcel Dekker.

Reich, Charles (1964). "The New Property." *Yale Law Journal* (April): pp. 120–155.

Reich, Charles (1964). "Individual Rights and Social Welfare: The Emerging Legal Issues." *Yale Law Journal.* (June): pp. 1–55.

Reich, Charles (1966). "The Law of the Planned Society." *Yale Law Journal.* (July): pp. 1255–1280.

Rein, Marlin and Sherry Brown (1982). *The Appropriations Process in the Kansas Legislature.* Topeka: University of Kansas, Capitol Complex Center.

Rifkin, Jeremy (1980). *Entropy.* New York: Viking.

Roberts, Paul Craig (1984). *The Supply-Side Revolution: An Insider's Account of Policy Making in Washington.* Cambridge: Harvard University Press.

Ross, Stephen A. (1976). "The Arbitrage Theory of Capital Asset Pricing." *Journal of Economic Theory.* 13: pp. 341–360.

Rubin, Irene S. (1982). *Running in the Red: The Political Dynamics of Urban Fiscal Press.* Albany: State University of New York Press.

Rubin, Irene S. (1985). *Shrinking the Federal Government: The Effect of Cutbacks on Five Federal Agencies.* New York: Longman.

Rubin, Irene S. (1988). *New Directions in Budget Theory.* Albany: State University of New York Press.

Samuelson, Paul A. (1948). *Income, Employment and Public Policy.* New York: W. W. Norton.

Savage, James D. (1988). *Balanced Budgets and American Politics.* Ithaca, N.Y.: Cornell University Press.

Savas, E. S. (1982). *Privatizing the Public Sector: How to Shrink Government.* Chatham, N.J.: Chatham House Publishers.

Sbragia, Alberta M. (1983). "Politics, Local Government, and the Municipal Bond Market," in Sbragia, Alberta M., ed., *The Municipal Money Chase: The Politics of Local Government Finance.* Boulder, Col.: Westview Press, pp. 67–111.

Schick, Allen (1966). "The Road to PPB: The Stages of Budget Reform." *Public Administration Review.* 26(December): pp. 243–258.

Schick, Allen (1971). *Budget Innovation in the States.* Washington, D.C.: Brookings Institution.

Schick, Allen (1973). "A Death in the Bureaucracy: The Demise of Federal PPB." *Public Administration Review.* 33: pp. 146–156.

Schick, Allen (1980). *Congress and Money: Budgeting, Spending, and Taxing.* Washington, D.C.: Urban Institute Press.

Schick, Allen (1986). "Macrobudgetary Adaptations to Fiscal Stress in Industrialized Democracies." *Public Administration Review.* 46(2): pp. 124–134.

Schick, Allen (1988). "An Inquiry into the Possibility of a Budgetary Theory," in Rubin, I., ed., *New Directions in Budget Theory.* Albany: State University of New York Press.

Schiesl, Martin J. (1977). *The Politics of Efficiency: Municipal Administration and Reform in America, 1800–1920.* Berkeley: University of California Press.

Schlesinger, Arthur (1986). *The Cycles of History*. Boston: Houghton-Mifflin.

Schumpeter, Joseph A. (1942). *Capitalism, Socialism, and Democracy*. New York: Harper & Bros.

Schwartz, Eli (1981). "Inventory, Purchasing and Risk Management," in Aronson, J. Richard and Eli Schwartz, eds., *Management Policies in Local Government Finance*. Washington, D.C.: International City Management Association.

Selznick, Philip (1949). *TVA and the Grass Roots*. Berkeley, Calif.: University of California Press.

Selznick, Philip (1957). *Leadership in Administration*. Evanston, Ill.: Row, Peterson.

Shapiro, Harvey D. (1985). "The Securization of Practically Everything." *Institutional Investor*. 19(5) (May): pp. 197–202.

Sharkansky, Ira (1968). "Agency Requests, Gubernatorial Support and Budget Success in State Legislatures." *American Political Science Review*. 62: p. 1223.

Sharp, Elaine (1986). "The Politics and Economics of New City Debt." *American Political Science Review*. 80: pp. 1271–1288.

Sharpe, W. (1963). "A Simplified Model for Portfolio Analysis." *Management Science*. 9: pp. 277–293.

Sharpe, William F. (1964). "Capital Asset Prices: A Theory of Market Equilibrium Under Conditions of Risk." *Journal of Finance*. 19: pp. 425–442.

Shultz, William J. (1934). *American Public Finance and Taxation*, rev. ed. New York: Prentice-Hall.

Siegel, Sidney (1956). *Nonparametric Statistics for the Social Sciences*. New York: McGraw-Hill.

Simon, Herbert A. (1962). "The Architecture of Complexity." *Proceedings of the American Philosophical Society*. 102(6): pp. 467–482.

Simon, Herbert A. (1976). *Administrative Behavior*. 3rd ed. New York: Free Press.

Simon, Herbert A., George Kozmetsky, Harold Guetzkow, and Gordon Tyndall (1954). *Centralization vs. Decentralization in Organizing the Controller's Department*. New York: Controllership Foundation.

Sinding, Rick (1986). "The Unmaking of a County Executive." *New Jersey Reporter*. 16: pp. 15–21.

Sloane, Leonard (1985). "New Securities Tied to Assets." *New York Times*. (July 20): p. 32.

Smithies, Arthur (1955). *The Budgetary Process in the United States*. Committee for Economic Development. New York: McGraw-Hill.

Snider, H. Wayne (1964). "The Management of Risk," in Dennenberg, Herbert S., Robert D. Eilers, G. Wright Hoffman, Chester A. Kline, Joseph J. Melone and H. Wayne Snider, eds., *Risk and Insurance*. Englewood Cliffs, N.J.: Prentice-Hall.

Solomons, Ann (1983). *Legislators Attitudes toward the Balanced Base Budgeting System after Two Fiscal Years.* Unpublished Masters of Public Administration Policy Paper. Lawrence: University of Kansas.

Starling, Jay D. (1986). *Municipal Coping Strategies.* Beverly Hills, Calif.: Sage.

Stedry, Andrew C. (1960). *Budget Control and Cost Behavior.* Englewood Cliffs, N.J.: Prentice-Hall.

Stigler, George J. (1961). "The Economics of Information." *Journal of Political Economy.* July/August: pp. 706–738.

Stockman, David A. (1986). *The Triumph of Politics: Why the Reagan Revolution Failed.* New York: Harper & Row.

Storing, Herbert J. (1962). "The Science of Administration: Herbert A. Simon," in Storing, Herbert J., ed., *Essays on the Scientific Study of Politics.* New York: Holt, Rinehart & Winston.

Stourm, Rene (1917). *The Budget,* T. Plazinski, trans. New York: Appleton.

Straussman, Jeffrey D. (1988). "Rights-Based Budgeting," in Rubin, I., ed., *New Directions in Budget Theory.* Albany: State University of New York Press.

Sundquist, James L. (1981). *The Decline and Resurgence of Congress.* Washington, D.C.: Brookings Institution.

Taylor, Paul W. (1973). *Normative Discourse.* Westport, Conn.: Greenwood Press.

Thai, Khi V. (1985). "Public Budgeting and Financial Management Curriculum Reform: A Conceptual Framework." Unpublished paper presented at the 79th Government Finance Officers Association annual conference, May.

Thompson, James D. (1967). *Organizations in Action.* New York: McGraw-Hill.

Thompson, James D. and Arthur Tuden (1959). "Strategies, Structures, and Processes of Organizational Decision," in Thompson, James D., Peter B. Hammond, Robert W. Hawkes, Buford H. Junker, and Arthur Tuden, eds., *Comparative Studies in Administration.* Pittsburgh: University of Pittsburgh Press.

Thompson, Joel A. (1987). "Agency Requests, Gubernatorial Support and Budget Success in State Legislatures Revisited." *Journal of Politics.* 49: pp. 756–779.

Thurow, Lester (1975). *Generating Inequality.* New York: Basic Books.

Tichy, Noel M., Michael L. Tushman, and Charles Fombrun (1979). "Social Network Analysis for Organizations." *Academy of Management Review.* 4: pp. 507–519.

Tierney, John T. (1988). *The U.S. Postal Service: State and Prospects of a Public Enterprise.* Dover, Mass.: Auburn House.

Tinkum, Marsha Williams (1982). *Legislators' Attitudes about the Balanced Base Budget System of the State of Kansas.* Unpublished Masters of Public Administration Policy Paper. Lawrence: University of Kansas.

Tobin, James (1956). "The Interest-Elasticity of the Transaction Demand for Cash." *Review of Economics and Statistics.* (September): pp. 241–247.

Trice, Harrison M., James Belasco, and Joseph A. Alutto (1969). "The Role of Ceremonials in Organization Behavior." *Industrial and Labor Relations Review*. 23: pp. 40–51.

Tufte, Edward R. (1978). *Political Control of the Economy*. Princeton: Princeton University Press.

U. S. Bureau of the Census (1989). *Governmental Finances in 1986–1987*. Superintendent of Documents. Washington, D.C.: U. S. Government Printing Office.

U. S. Bureau of the Census (1982). *Governmental Finances in 1981–1982*. Superintendent of Documents. Washington, D.C.: U. S. Government Printing Office.

U. S. Bureau of the Census (1980). *Number of Inhabitants*, PC80-1-A, Chapter A, Superintendent of Documents. Washington, D.C.: U. S. Government Printing Office.

U. S. Department of Housing and Urban Development (1973). *Local Government Participation in A-95, Project Notification and Review System*, Community Development Evaluation Series No. 11. Washington, D.C.: Superintendent of Documents.

U. S. Department of Housing and Urban Development (1974). *The Chief Executive Review and Comment (CERC) Procedure and Other Local Coordinating Mechanisms: A Reconnaissance Evaluation in Two Cities*. (January 2), department mimeograph.

U. S. General Accounting Office (1975). *Improved Cooperation and Coordination Need Among All Levels of Government—Office of Management and Budget Circular A-95*. (GGD-75-52), February 11. Washington, D.C.: Superintendent of Documents.

U. S. General Accounting Office (1983). *Trends and Changes in the Municipal Bond Market as They Relate to Financing State and Local Public Infrastructure*. Report to the Chairman, Subcommittee on Economic Stabilization, Committee on Banking, Finance and Urban Affairs, House of Representatives, GAO/PAD-83-46, September 12. Washington, D.C.: U. S. Government Printing Office.

U. S. General Accounting Office (1985). *Managing the Cost of Government: Building an Effective Financial Management Structure*, GAO/AFMD-85-35, February. Washington, D.C.: U. S. Government Printing Office.

U. S. House of Representatives, Subcommittee on Intergovernmental Relations (1974). *Hearings* 93d Congress, 2d Session, January–February. Washington, D.C.: U. S. Government Printing Office.

U. S. Senate Committee Investigating Executive Agencies, 75th Congress, 1st Session (1937). Senate Report No. 1275. Washington, D.C.: U. S. Government Printing Office.

Van Horne, James C. (1981). "Cash Management," in Aronson, J. Richard and Eli Schwartz, eds., *Management Policies in Local Government Finance*. Washington, D.C.: International City Management Association.

252 *References*

Van Horne, James C. (1986). *Financial Management and Policy*. Englewood Cliffs, N.J.: Prentice-Hall.

Vartan, Vartanig, G. (1985). "Tax-Exempt Trusts Flourish." *New York Times*. (August 22): p. 31.

Vogt, A. John and Lisa A. Cole (1983). *A Guide to Municipal Leasing*. Washington, D.C.: Municipal Finance Officers Association.

von Neumann, John and Oskar Morgenstern (1955). *Theory of Games and Economic Behavior*, rev. ed. Princeton, Princeton Universitiy Press.

Waldo, Dwight (1948). *The Administrative State: A Study of the Political Theory of American Public Administration*. New York: Ronald Press.

Walker, Wallace Earl (1986). *Changing Organizational Culture: Strategy, Structure, and Professionalism in the U. S. General Accounting Office*. Knoxville: University of Tennessee Press.

Wall Street Journal (1982). "Cities Getting Part of Profits for Giving Aid to Developers." *Wall Street Journal*. (September 29): p. 27.

Wanat, John (1973). "Budget Format and Budget Behavior." *Experimental Study of Politics*. 2(October): 58–69.

Wanat, John (1974). "Bases of Budgetary Incrementalism." *American Political Science Review*. 68(September): pp. 1221–1228.

Wanat, John (1978). "Personnel Measures of Budgetary Interaction." *Western Political Quarterly*. 29(June): pp. 295–297.

Waterman, R. H. (1987). "In Search of Renaissance." *New York Times*, March 31: p. D2.

Webber, Carolyn and Aaron Wildavsky (1986). *A History of Taxation and Expenditure in the Western World*. New York: Simon & Schuster.

Weber, Max (1946). *From Max Weber: Essays in Sociology*, trans. H. H. Gerth and C. Wright Mills. New York: Oxford.

Weick, Karl E. (1969). *Social Psychology of Organizing*. Reading, Mass.: Addison-Wesley.

Weick, Karl E. (1976). "Educational Organizations as Loosely-Coupled Systems." *Administrative Science Quarterly*. 21: pp. 1–19.

Weick, Karl E. (1979). "Cognitive Processes in Organizations," in Staw, B. M., ed., *Research in Organizational Behavior*, vol. 1. Greenwich, Conn.: JAI Press, pp. 41–74.

Weick, Karl (1980). "The Management of Eloquence." *Executive*. 6(Summer): pp. 18–21.

Weick, Karl E. (1985). "The Significance of Corporate Culture," in Frost, P. J., L. F. Moore, M. R. Louis, C. C. Lundberg, and J. Martin, eds., *Organizational Culture*. Beverly Hills, Calif.: Sage.

Weiner, Norbert (1948). *Cybernetics*. New York: Wiley.

Wetzler, J. W., and J. E. Petersen (1985). "The Finance Officer as Public Strategist." *Government Finance Review*. April: 7.

White, Leonard D. (1933). *Trends in Public Administration*. New York: McGraw-Hill.

White, Leonard D. (1955). *Introduction to the Study of Public Administration*, 4th ed. New York: Macmillan Co.

White, Orion F. Jr., and Cynthia J. McSwain (1983). "Transformational Theory and Organizational Analysis," in Morgan, Gareth, ed., *Beyond Method: Strategies for Social Research*. Newbury Park, Calif.: Sage.

Wildavsky, Aaron (1961). "Political Implications of Budgetary Reform." *Public Administration Review*. 21: pp. 183–190.

Wildavsky, Aaron (1964). *The Politics of the Budgetary Process*. Boston: Little, Brown.

Wildavsky, Aaaron (1966). "The Political Economy of Efficiency: Cost-Benefit Analysis, Systems Analysis, and Program Budgeting." *Public Administration Review*. 26: pp. 292–310.

Wildavsky, Aaron (1975). *Budgeting: A Comparative Theory*. Boston: Little, Brown.

Wildavsky, Aaron (1978). "A Budget for All Seasons? Why the Traditional Budget Lasts." *Public Administration Review*. 38: pp. 501–509.

Wildavsky, Aaron (1986). *Budgeting: A Comparative Theory of Budgetary Processes* 2nd rev. ed. Piscataway, N.J.: Transaction Books.

Wildavsky, Aaron (1987). *Speaking Truth to Power: The Art and Craft of Policy Analysis*. Piscataway, N.J.: Transaction Books.

Wildavsky, A. (1988). *The New Politics of the Budgetary Process*. Boston: Little, Brown.

Wildavsky, Aaron and Arthur Hammond (1965). "Comprehensive Versus Incremental Budgeting in the Department of Agriculture." *Administrative Science Quarterly*. 10(3): pp. 321–346.

Williams, John Burr (1964). *The Theory of Investment Value*. Amsterdam: North-Holland.

Wilson, Leonard U. and L. V. Watkins (1975). *State Planning*. Lexington, Ky.: Council of State Governments.

Wolf, Jr. Charles (1988). *Markets or Governments: Choosing between Imperfect Alternatives*. Cambridge: MIT Press.

Wright, Deil (1989). "The Origins, Emergence and Maturity of Federalism and Intergovernmental Relations: Two Centuries of Territory and Power," in J. Rabin, W. B. Hildreth, and G. J. Miller, eds., *Handbook of Public Administration*. New York: Marcel Dekker, pp. 331–386.

Wright, George and Peter Ayton (1987). *Judgmental Forecasting*. Chichester, England: Wiley.

Yacik, George (1985). "A New Use for an Old Bond." *Bond Buyer*. 272(27139) (May 28): p. 10.

Yearley, C. K. (1970). *The Money Machines: The Breakdown and Reform of Governmental and Party Finance in the North, 1860–1920*. Albany, N.Y.: State University of New York Press.

Index